EARTHWORKS
AND BEYOND

EARTHWORKS

ABBEVILLE PRESS PUBLISHERS   NEW YORK   LONDON   PARIS

AND BEYOND

CONTEMPORARY ART IN THE LANDSCAPE
THIRD EDITION

JOHN BEARDSLEY

Editor: Nancy Grubb
Designers: Robin Fox, Ada Rodriguez, and Celia Fuller
Picture researchers: Amelia Jones, Massoumeh Farman-
    Farmaian, and Elizabeth Boyle
Production managers: Dana Cole and Lou Bilka

Front cover: Andy Goldsworthy. *Yellow Elm Leaves Laid
    over a Rock, Low Water,* October 15, 1991. See plate 51.
Back cover: Martha Schwartz. *Untitled,* 1996. Federal
    Plaza, New York. Commissioned by the General
    Services Administration (GSA).
Title page: Charles Jencks. *Snake Mound,* in *Landscape of
    Waves,* 1992–94. Earth and turf, length of mound:
    900 ft. Scotland.
Endpapers: Walter De Maria. *The Lightning Field,*
    1974–77. See plate 60.

Marginal numbers in the text refer to works illustrated in
this volume.

Library of Congress Cataloging-in-Publication Data
Beardsley, John.
    Earthworks and beyond / John Beardsley. — 3rd ed.
        p.   cm. — (Abbeville modern art movements)
    Includes bibliographical references and index.
    ISBN 0-7892-0296-4
    1. Earthworks (Art)   2. Avant-garde (Aesthetics)—
History—20th century.   I. Title.   II. Series.
    N6494.E27B4   1998
    709'.04'076—dc21   96-46936

Third edition, 1998
10 9 8 7 6 5 4 3 2 1

Acknowledgments

Portions of chapter 3 were first published in the fall 1982
issue of *Art Journal,* "Earthworks: Past and Present." I am
grateful to Rose Weil, managing editor, for permission to
draw from that source. Reuben Rainey, professor in the
Division of Landscape Architecture in the School of Architecture at the University of Virginia, was my guide in a
study of the monuments in landscape design of the past.
Such mastery as I can display of this historical material is
largely to his credit. Pam Lawson, who has assisted me on
so many projects before, was there to help this time as well.
Nancy Grubb, my editor at Abbeville Press, helped shape
my thoughts to a more coherent and articulate whole. Amy
Jones, Massoumeh Farman-Farmaian, and Elizabeth Boyle
managed the unwieldy task of researching photographs. I am
grateful to all of them. This text touches upon many artists,
though perhaps none in sufficient depth to please any but
the most agreeable of them. Yet without exception, the artists I have had occasion to speak with have answered my
queries with good cheer. Their cooperation is much appreciated. In the solitude of writing, friends assume even more
than their usual measure of importance. Stephanie Ridder
and Jane Livingston both provided needed reassurance at
critical moments. Be it as it may an insufficient gesture of
thanks, it is to them that this book is dedicated.   J.B.

CONTENTS

1. Stonehenge is a megalithic monument
(c. 2000 B.C.) on the Salisbury Plain in Wiltshire,
England. Although its precise purpose remains
a mystery, it is presumed by many to have
served both religious and astronomical
functions.

INTRODUCTION

In the early 1980s, when the first edition of this book was written, it was clear that landscape was reappearing as one of the most consequential subjects in art—a position it had not enjoyed since the mid-nineteenth century. It was also evident that landscape was emerging in a different guise. While some artists continued to represent its image in painting and photography, others — starting especially in the late 1960s — chose to enter the landscape itself, to use its materials and work with its salient features. They were not depicting the landscape, but engaging it; their art was not simply *of* the landscape, but *in* it as well.

The first works of this kind — by Michael Heizer, Robert Smithson, Walter De Maria, and Robert Morris — have come to be known as "earthworks" or "land art." Their physical presence in the landscape itself distinguishes them from other, more portable forms of sculpture. But the involvement with landscape goes deeper than that: most of these works are inextricably bound to their sites and take as a large part of their content a relationship with the specific characteristics of their particular surroundings. Although most of them could have been made in any one of a number of similar locations, these are not discrete objects, intended for isolated appraisal, but fully engaged elements of their environments, intended to provide an inimitable experience of a certain place.

What was less clear at the time of the first edition was how dramatically the forms of this new art would proliferate and how significant they would come to seem. Adapting the scale and ambition of earthworks to the challenges of the urban space, some civic-minded sculptors are now shaping a new kind of public landscape, strong both in sculptural form and in symbolic allusions. Questioning the environmental impact of earthworks, other artists have favored a lighter touch, opting for ephemeral projects with a meditative, ritualistic character. Elaborating on the inchoate environmental aspirations of some of the first earth artists, still others have become ecological activists and social critics, pressing for the remediation of cultural practices that have inhibited ethical stewardship of the earth. What began as a relatively isolated episode in the great deserts of the American West has expanded into a wide-ranging phenomenon — now more commonly known as "environmental art" — with ambitions to articulate, even to shape, the contemporary relationship to nature.

What was also less apparent in the early 1980s was how dramatically the basic concept of nature was being rethought. What was once assumed to be vast and inexhaustible has come to seem fragile and imperiled; what was once thought to be independent from culture — an inviolate other — has now come to be recognized as a cultural creation. Inhabited landscapes are clearly shaped by human action, but the survival of wilderness has also come to be seen as the consequence of deliberate choice. Even the larger health of the planet seems to hinge on cultural attitudes, as examined in books like *The End of Nature* (1989), Bill McKibben's gloomy assessment of the impact of fossil-fuel consumption on global warming. Artists have played their part in transforming the perception of nature, signaled initially and perhaps most forcefully by Robert Smithson in his 1967 essay, "A Tour of the Monuments of Passaic, New Jersey." Armed with a Kodak Instamatic and a mordant wit, Smithson recorded a landscape of belching pipes, pumping derricks, used-car lots, and unfinished highway construction. He saw the city as a place of "monumental vacancies that define, without trying, the memory traces of an abandoned set of futures."[1]

Bearing marks of erosion and sedimentation along with signs of seemingly random human interventions, the landscape was perceived by Smithson as a place in constant

2. Arnaldo Pomodoro (b. 1926). *Drawing of Graveyard,* 1973. Colored pencil on paper; 19¹¹/₁₆ x 27⅛ in. Collection of the artist.

metamorphosis, revealing entropy — the law of thermodynamics that measures the gradual, steady disintegration in a system. Smithson presented a particularly contemporary vision of the environment, one in which nature is altered and often debased by human action. Although he did not speak for all the artists of his generation, he articulated ideas that would become increasingly important in the late twentieth century. He recognized that we are physically and culturally bound to the earth and that the classic metaphor of nature as a primordial garden was obsolete for a landscape that bore so many scars of disruption. Implicit in Smithson's writing and in his sculpture was a challenge to develop a more realistic and empathic relationship with transmuted nature. Revealing how other artists have responded to this challenge is the main business of this book.

My approach here is in equal parts reportorial and interpretive; as befits a contemporary subject, my observations are intended more to advance than to conclude critical debate on the subject. From a discussion of the American avant-garde, which confirmed the widespread reengagement with landscape in the late 1960s, the commentary moves out to the contemporary English response, back to traditions and twentieth-century antecedents, and forward to sited sculpture and the application of landscape art to the improvement of public spaces. A final chapter looks at the role of artists in the larger debate about environmental practices. For the most part, I focus on American and British artists, a parochialism that may be excused by the fact that I am most familiar with Anglo-American cultural history. But this leaves out as much as it includes: the park projects by the French sculptor Jean-Pierre Raynaud; the photographic manipulations of landscape by the Dutch artist Jan Dibbets; and the plaza and cemetery designs 2* by the Italian Arnaldo Pomodoro, for example.

Behind this text are several basic presumptions. The first is that a people's relationship to landscape is one of the most significant expressions of culture, in many respects equal in importance to the relationship to the sacred. Indeed, the two are not so dissimilar: Ralph Waldo Emerson spoke for many in his own generation and ours when he wrote that "the noblest ministry of nature is to stand as the apparition of God."[2] The grandest achievements of nineteenth-century American landscape painting — by Frederic Church, Thomas Cole, and Albert Bierstadt, among others — spring from this philosophical ground. Witness, too, the William H. Jackson photograph 4 and the Thomas Moran painting of the Mountain of the Holy Cross, a peak in Colorado with deep, snow-filled crevices in the shape of a cross near its summit. These are reverential depictions of the symbol of the Passion made manifest in nature, according with the notion that the landscape itself has sacred qualities and reveals the Divinity.

The landscape is rich with man-made forms that have been offered in tribute. Prehistoric

*Marginal numbers refer to works illustrated in this volume.

3. Like the more famous Great Serpent Mound at Chillicothe, this vast geometrical earthwork at Newark, Ohio, is associated with the Hopewell Indian culture, which flourished in Ohio from about 1000 B.C. to A.D. 700. Photograph by James Pierce.

4. William H. Jackson (1843–1942). *Mountain of the Holy Cross,* 1873. Photograph mounted on cardboard, 9¾ x 13¼ in. Ewell Sale Stuart Library, Academy of Natural Sciences, Philadelphia.

3

4

remains are merely the best known: Stonehenge, for example, whose purpose we imagine to be a pagan decoding of terrestrial and astronomical mysteries. In seventeenth-century France, the imposition of Cartesian geometry on the landscape — as at Vaux-le-Vicomte or Versailles — expressed all the bravura of an age that believed that in simple geometric shapes lay the key to the intelligible order of the universe. And in eighteenth-century England came that most remarkable episode in British intellectual history, when many of the nation's greatest thinkers — from prime ministers to poets — were engaged in the formation of gardens and vast landscaped parks that conformed to an arcadian ideal. The landscapes at Stowe, Stourhead, and Castle Howard are only three among the almost innumerable creations of that era.

The efforts of our own time must seem mundane by comparison, as they are seen without the romanticizing haze of temporal distance. Yet the human imagination is no less vivid or powerful than before. The contemporary works derive a great poignance from a purpose similar to that of their antecedents: to reveal the world to us anew, to combine symbolic form with the landscape in the creation of differentiated and evocative places. Some of the most remarkable of these works are arguably sacred or at least transcendent in intention, in that they assert a nonanthropocentric view of the world: they are attempts to reconcile humans with the natural environment and its implicitly sacrosanct character. At their best, they are carefully construed physical environments for the sensuous apprehension of form, while at the same time they seek to reveal the extraordinary in both the landscape and the human spirit. These are consecrated spaces for a willfully secular era.

My second presumption is a corollary of the first. It is that the entire history of form building in the landscape is the foundation for this contemporary work. Indian mounds

and cliff dwellings in this country, temple gardens in Japan, Roman and Renaissance villas in Italy, as well as the creations referred to above, compose a vocabulary of forms and attitudes that is unavoidably influential. The last century in this country has witnessed a considerable enlargement of this repertory, from picturesque public parks, suburbs, golf courses, and cemeteries to the utilitarian landscape of highways, telephone poles, and roadside advertising. While few of the contemporary projects are direct counterparts of these antecedents, echoes do reverberate across the years: historical references are nearly universal, and this is all for the best. A certain allusiveness cannot help but enrich the content and effect of a contemporary work, while it remains unmistakably of our own time.

A third underlying presumption is that in the last several decades the distinctions between sculpture and other forms of artistic activity have blurred. This is particularly pronounced

5

6

5, 6. The Pebble Beach Golf Course, overlooking the Pacific Ocean near Monterey, California, occupies one of the most dramatic natural settings of any course in the world. Designed by California State Amateur Champion Jack Neville with the assistance of Douglas Grant, it opened for play in 1919.

in the case of art in the landscape, which only sometimes has the formally distinct character of conventional sculpture. At other times it has the impalpability of empty space or the evanescence of performance. With the even more recent appearance of artist-designed parks and collaborations between artists and architects has come a still more pronounced merging of intentions, so much so that in the final chapter, I take up the impact of sculpture on the contemporary practice of landscape architecture.

The last of my presumptions merits a text all its own, for it concerns a signal feature of our culture. Americans are afflicted with a profound ambivalence toward nature, manifest

in a seemingly irresolvable conflict between the impulse to exploit the landscape with ever more sophisticated tools and the urge to nurture and protect such little as is left of the natural world, not only for its beauty, but also for its morally and spiritually uplifting effects. As long ago as the early 1780s, Thomas Jefferson complained that rapacious farming practices were destroying the quality of the soil. Even then, repeated cultivation of tobacco without crop rotation was depleting the soil of essential nutrients, resulting in ever greater exertion on the part of its producers and ever dwindling returns. Poverty and malnourishment were its rewards. Tobacco growing, Jefferson asserted, "is a culture productive of infinite wretchedness."[3] There is some irony in this observation, for Jefferson was one of the most ardent promoters of the agrarian ideal, with all its links to contemporaneous British ideas of creating a rural Elysium. "Those who labor in the earth are the chosen people of God," he wrote, "if ever He had a chosen people; whose breasts He has made His peculiar deposit for substantial and genuine virtue."[4]

Jefferson's ideal agrarian world was not composed of solitary individuals; it was a society of small landholders whose political and social interactions were facilitated, even perfected, by their rural residence. His attitude was distinctly antiurban, but still modestly gregarious.[5] Henry David Thoreau, on the other hand, revered nature as an escape from society altogether — urban and rural alike. "I wish to speak a word for nature, for absolute freedom and wildness, as contrasted with a freedom and culture merely civil — to regard man as an inhabitant, or a part and parcel of nature, rather than a member of society."[6] As artists began their headlong rush into the landscape in the late 1960s, it was perhaps Thoreau who was their most obvious guide, in his apparent extremism and his rejection of the world "merely civil."

Yet as this art has developed, it has moved

7. The Long Meadow at Prospect Park in Brooklyn, like Central Park in Manhattan, is one of the triumphs of the nineteenth-century landscape architects Frederick Law Olmsted and Calvert Vaux.

7

away from the romantic and rejectionist postures of Thoreau toward the more pragmatic, socially engaged attitudes of Jefferson. The latter's early recognition that the landscape was in need of protection and restoration has been followed by several overlapping episodes of vigorous conservation. One of these, in the latter half of the nineteenth century, gave rise to the National Park System, which, together with the phenomenal spread of the urban and wholly public park, might be considered America's most distinguished contribution to the history of landscape design. Another episode occurred in the 1930s with the establishment of the Civilian Conservation Corps and the consequent growth of the state park system. A third, still more vigorous and controversial, began in the 1960s and continues even now. The preservation of wilderness areas, the passage of the Strip Mine Reclamation Act, and the Alaska Lands Bill are among its major accomplishments, although recent efforts to weaken the Clean Air, Clean Water, and Endangered Species acts, along with the burgeoning resistance to environmental regulation in the form of the deceptively named "wise use" movement, all threaten to roll back these gains. Some degree of environmental concern, however, seems finally to have won a place in contemporary culture. This conservationist impulse finds a parallel in the efforts of artists who use their work as a means of restoring environmental devastation in both the city and the country.

If contemporary artists draw on an impulse that is rooted in a rich and diverse tradition, they find in Frederick Law Olmsted and Calvert Vaux, designers of Central Park in Manhattan and Prospect Park in Brooklyn, their most eloquent forebears. By the mid-nineteenth century, these men had recognized the social benefit of improved environmental design and outdoor recreational spaces in urban and rural areas. There is hardly an aspect of the beneficent environment in America — from single urban parks and metropolitan and national park systems to planned communities and college campuses — that does not owe its success, at least in part, to Olmsted in particular.[7] His work reflects a more widespread shift among his contemporaries away from the antiurban pronouncements of Jefferson and Thoreau to an engagement with the ever more pressing and distinctly urban problems that accompanied industrialization. To the extent that contemporary artists seek to improve the environment through land reclamation or the creation of parks, they are the inheritors of the reformist spirit of the mid-nineteenth century.

Yet the fundamental ambivalence that characterizes our national attitude toward nature is never far from any of the works I will discuss here. Indeed, some combine the reverential desire to reveal all the grandeur and mystery of the earth with the inevitable desire to use and abuse it. This is just one of the complexities of recent art in the landscape. Some works appear to be willfully modern, in the sense of employing a reductive and frankly nonallusive vocabulary, yet they speak with an ancient voice. Conversely, some are deliberately historicist, but look entirely contemporary. Some are vast and very palpable, but seldom seen except in photographs. Some are so discreet in form or utilitarian in function that they remain unrecognized as art. Originally thought to be radical and anti-urban in character, many of these works are now celebrated for their socially constructive and distinctly pro-urban motives. And while thus emphatically of this world, they frequently aspire to the quality of a revelation. Such is the character of recent art in the landscape that it resounds with paradox.

8. Michael Heizer (b. 1944). *Displaced-Replaced Mass*, detail, 1969. Three granite masses in concrete-lined depressions; overall: 900 x 400 x 13 ft. Silver Springs, Nevada (dismantled). Commissioned by Robert Scull.

1. MONUMENT AND ENVIRONMENT: THE AVANT-GARDE, 1966–1976

Michael Heizer, born in Berkeley in 1944, had by the late 1960s a high sense of mission for his sculpture. "Art had to be radical," he asserted recently. "It had to become American."[8] Much is implied in his terse statement. A Californian, he felt that sculpture needed to express the character and scale of the great Western landscapes. In an era of space exploration, and of social unrest caused by an unpopular war and racial antagonisms, he felt that art needed to look new, nonconformist, and not at all complacent. Further, it had to shake its dependence on European models, those refined objects in the tradition of Rodin and Brancusi that seemed then to be exhaling their last gasp in the form of Minimalist sculpture. Heizer's antidote was to throw off nearly all the conventions of recent three-dimensional art in favor of environmental projects.

Heizer shared in a then widespread notion that the art world was afflicted with a too grand preciosity, that artworks were valued only as commodities, and that they were limited by their preoccupation with strictly formal concerns. In 1969 Heizer decried what he perceived to be a surfeit of objects of this kind, and their seemingly inescapable associations with the marketplace: "The position of art as malleable barter-exchange item falters as the cumulative economic structure gluts. The museums and collections are stuffed, the floors are sagging, but the real space exists."[9] In the Western deserts, Heizer said that he found "that kind of unraped, peaceful, religious space artists have always tried to put in their work."[10] And he provided a blunt explanation of the differences between those works of the urban marketplace that he censured and a work in the landscape. "The intrusive, opaque object refers to itself. It has little exterior reference. It is rigid and blocks space. It is a target. An incorporative work is aerated, part of the material of its place and refers beyond itself."[11]

These ideas formed a part of the currency of artistic discourse by the late '60s. A shared enthusiasm for environmental work provided the basis of a friendship between Heizer and Walter De Maria; Heizer was also friendly with the many artists who gathered at the bar at Max's Kansas City in New York, including Robert Smithson, Nancy Holt, and Carl Andre. By the time Heizer was introduced to Smithson in 1968, he had already executed some ten temporary works in the Western deserts — trenches, motorcycle drawings, and dispersals of soil from moving vehicles and pigments into the wind. His landscape works had begun in 1967, when he sank an open cube into the ground in the Sierra Nevada, the first element in a projected four-part sculpture to be called *NESW* after the four cardinal directions. Heizer and De Maria drove across the country together inspecting potential work sites, and Heizer was on hand to help when De Maria produced his first Western work in April of 1968: two parallel lines a mile long laid down in chalk on the Mojave Desert in California. That summer, Smithson and Holt joined Heizer in Nevada, where he was working on a series of works called the *Nine Nevada Depressions*. A photograph taken by Holt shows Smithson helping to dig a trench for *Isolated Mass/ Circumflex*, giving him an early experience of working in the Western landscape.[12] Heizer's family boasted several geologists who had been active throughout the West, and there is no doubt that he was a fount of information about where to work and how to secure land by lease. But beyond that, these artists were united by a common assault on sculptural conventions. "It was a beautiful moment," Heizer recalled. "There was a lot of potential."

Heizer executed the first of his works entirely on his own initiative, without any sponsorship. By 1968, however, he had enlisted the financial aid of collector Robert Scull, who commissioned both the *Nine Nevada Depressions* and three works called *Displaced-*

9

8

13

9

10

9. Michael Heizer. *Isolated Mass/Circumflex,* no. 9 of the *Nine Nevada Depressions,* 1968. Excavation: 120 x 12 x 1 ft. Massacre Dry Lake, Nevada (deteriorated). Commissioned by Robert Scull.

10. Michael Heizer. *Double Negative,* 1969–70. 1,500 x 50 x 30 ft. Near Overton, Nevada. Museum of Contemporary Art, Los Angeles; Gift of Virginia Dwan.

11. Michael Heizer *Complex One/City,* 1972–76. Concrete, granite, and earth; 110 x 140 x 23½ ft. Collection of Virginia Dwan and the artist.

11

Replaced Mass (all 1969). For the latter, huge slabs of granite from the High Sierra were brought down to the Nevada desert and set in concrete-lined depressions in the ground. At the same time, dealer Virginia Dwan was taking an interest in Heizer's work. He had shown her a portfolio of photographs of his Western works in 1968, and she had included him, along with Smithson and Robert Morris, in her *Earthworks* exhibition that fall. Next she offered him a solo exhibition. He agreed, on the understanding that the exhibition would not be limited to the gallery. With her backing, he returned to Nevada, secured a site on the Mormon Mesa, hired contractors and earthmoving equipment, and began work on a piece he was to title *Double Negative*: two cuts in the mesa surface facing each

other across a deep indentation in the escarpment. Heizer had excavated the thirty-foot-wide cuts to a depth of forty-two feet when he ran short of cash. He called Dwan for additional help; she came to Nevada to see the piece and gave him the authorization to finish the work. It was deepened to 50 feet, and expanded to a total length of 1,500.

Double Negative took the art world by surprise. Its debut in a Dwan Gallery exhibition in early 1970 was hardly placid. One critic subsequently wrote that "it proceeds by marring the very land, which is what we have just learned to stop doing."[13] Referring to Heizer's work several years later, another asserted that "earth art, with very few exceptions, not only doesn't improve upon its natural environment, it destroys it."[14] If these criticisms are justified, they are also incomplete. The aggressiveness of Heizer's intervention in the landscape of the Mormon Mesa must be seen in the context of the entirely new syntax he was proposing for sculpture. Rather than being a form that occupies space, with a surface delineating the limits of an internal volume, *Double Negative* is composed of space itself: it is a void. Although massive in scale, it is barely palpable. The two sunken enclosures call to each other across the great chasm of the escarpment, providing an experience of vastness conveyed through the arrangement of space that is compellingly distinct from the intrusive, space-occupying character of traditional monuments. One is *inside* this piece. And while that is typical of architecture and landscape design, it is certainly distinct from most previous sculpture.

Some years later, Heizer sought to clarify his intentions, which many found disturbingly radical: both antiart and antiestablishment. He was realistic enough to acknowledge that the economics of the art world represented an unassailable bulwark. By then it was also clear that earthworks relied on fairly conventional forms of patronage. He recognized that the importance of his work lay not in what it rejected, but in what it offered instead. "I was never out to destroy the gallery system or the aesthetic object," he explained. "I wasn't trying to make impermanent works—I was just doing the best I could with the tools I could afford. I'm not a radical. In fact, I'm going backward. I like to attach myself to the past."[15] That past is frankly archaeological. Heizer's father was a noted archaeologist and provided his son with an early introduction to the monuments of the past, particularly those of pre-Columbian America. The three *Displaced-Replaced Mass* sculptures allude to the moving of the great monoliths that form the Colossi of Memnon in the Valley of the Kings in Egypt, which Heizer's father had studied, as well as to the giant "wandering rocks" that were hauled

hundreds of miles around the desert in pre-Inca Bolivia.

Heizer's next major Western work after *Double Negative* was likewise a deft blending of archaeological references with his spare, geometric idiom. Located in south-central Nevada, *Complex One* (1972–76) is a long mound of earth with sloping sides and trapezoidal ends; it is some 140 feet long and nearly 24 feet high. The western face — the front — includes a group of concrete "framing elements," which read as a continuous band when viewed directly from the front of the piece, but break up as one moves to the sides. Some of them are attached to the mound itself, while others are set a good distance from it; some lie flat while others are cantilevered. The central unit at the top, for example, is thirty feet long and hangs thirty feet out from the front, producing constantly changing shadows across the face of the mound. Heizer has identified the snake bands lining the ball court at Chichen Itza in the Yucatán as a source for these framing elements, while the mound itself relates to Egyptian mastabas, ancient tombs that predate the pyramids.[16]

Complex One is just the first of a group of massive works planned for the site. Heizer has excavated the area directly in front of *Complex One*, creating an enormous depression around which the other works will be placed. One of them, a long sloping mound with an austerely geometric façade, is presently under construction. *Complex One* will thus eventually be one side of a square, forming an enclosed precinct rather like the one in front of the Pyramid of the Moon at Teotihuacán near Mexico City, or the great plazas at Monte Alban in the Mexican state of Oaxaca, or Tikal in Guatemala. Doubtless the ceremonial associations of these pre-Columbian works will be felt, lending Heizer's complex an air not only of history, but of incompletely understood ritual as well.

When finally completed, Heizer's precinct

13. Walter De Maria (b. 1935). *Las Vegas Piece*,
1969. Overall length: three miles. Tula Desert,
Nevada.

will exclude all views of the surrounding landscape. The works will completely enclose the viewer, who will stand well below ground level. Part of the motivation for this, Heizer explains, is to clear up any remaining confusion about the intent of his work. "It's about art, not about landscape," he insists. Some association with the landscape is unavoidable: the works are, after all, situated in a flat basin whose distant mountain ranges echo the long, ground-hugging, rough character of Heizer's mounds. But the point is well taken, reminding us that the purpose of these works is to create art, not simply to make a statement about the landscape. Indeed, when he first began work on these additional elements, Heizer had some cause for wanting to exclude the adjacent landscape: it was then being studied as a possible site for an MX missile base.

One imagines that Heizer's quadrangle will have more of the character of conventional monuments than his *Double Negative*. The elements will be massive and occupy space emphatically. Yet though the parts may be large in size, they can never be truly large in relation to the scale of the surrounding basins and ranges. And the excavation between them will be a part of, if not the principal element of, the work. The parts will define an environment for which we, the viewers, are the center, rather than occupying the center themselves as conventional monuments do. Heizer will thus have remained true to his original intentions for his art in the landscape: to offer in place of the rarefied and self-referential barter-object an art that is richly allusive in content and environmental in character.

In 1969, the year after he drew his chalk lines in the company of Heizer, De Maria was 13 back in the West to execute his *Las Vegas Piece*, four shallow cuts made by the six-foot blade of a bulldozer in the central Nevada desert. These cuts form a square with half-mile sides, with two of the sides extending

another half a mile at opposite corners. All are oriented north to south or east to west. This is a piece that yields its charms slowly. While one eventually comes to learn its configuration, it is never entirely visible. Instead, it presents itself as a series of options, invitations to move along a horizontal plane in the four cardinal directions. De Maria's lines are compelling: one feels that one's progress along them is somehow involuntary. Yet with this comes a feeling of relief that there is a delineated path on which to progress, in a landscape where one might otherwise wander aimlessly. As one walks the piece, its monotony is at first soothing and finally invigorating as one realizes the completeness with which one has experienced both the work and its surrounding landscape. This creation of dimensional, directional space with an understated, almost immaterial means reappeared in De Maria's later *Lightning Field* 59,60 (discussed in chapter 3).

For his part, Smithson took advantage of his Western visit with Heizer in 1968 to collect for his "Nonsites": sculptures composed of materials gathered outdoors, set in geometric containers, and frequently exhibited with maps or photographs of the sites from which they were taken. Smithson devoted much of that year to these sculptures, amassing sand from the New Jersey Pine Barrens in the winter, for example, limestone from Franklin, New Jersey, in the spring, and pumice and cinders from Mono Lake, California, in the summer. The resulting works were indoor evocations of outdoor locations, establishing what Smithson termed a dialectic between site — the outdoor source of the earth materials — and nonsite — the sculpture in its dissociated setting, functioning as a signifier of the absent site. Smithson produced a variation on these the following year, a group of rock salt and mirror pieces for the *Earth Art* exhibition at Cornell University in Ithaca, New York.[17] Like the subsequent *Rocks and Mirror Square* (1969), these used reflection to

phur, contrasting the viscous with the solid, the black with the yellow. But it was in 1970 that Smithson made his major mark on the landscape. Like Heizer, he enlisted the sponsorship of Virginia Dwan, went West, and produced his *Spiral Jetty*: 1,500 linear feet of   15–17 black basalt and limestone rocks and earth that curls into the Great Salt Lake, Utah, at a site Smithson leased on its northeastern shore.

"A sense of place" has become the dominant cliché in describing the effect of recent works in the landscape. It alludes, however unconsciously, to the celebrated admonition of the eighteenth-century English poet Alexander Pope, who advised that one "Consult the Genius of the Place in all."[18] In other words, one should design in conformity with nature, drawing out the best characteristics of the site, and thereby enhance the work created upon it. *Spiral Jetty*, as revealed in Smithson's own writings, provides a particularly lucid example of this correspondence between art work and site. Smithson was a prolific if occasionally confused writer;[19] indeed, it was as much through his numerous essays as through his sculptures that he was largely responsible for engaging the attentions of a large and influential art-world audience — including curators, critics, and magazine editors — for the landscape activities of the avant-garde.

Two years after the completion of the *Spiral Jetty*, Smithson published an essay about the work.[20] In it he detailed finding the site, his reactions to it, and how they resulted in this particular piece. It is an illuminating account and worth quoting at length. He described driving down a wide valley toward the Salt Lake, "which resembled an impassive faint violet sheet held captive in a stoney matrix, upon which the sun poured down its crushing light." He reached the lake at a place called Rozel Point, where industrial wreckage and abandoned vehicles bore witness to recent unsuccessful efforts to extract oil from

simulate the scale of the out-of-doors.

The same year — 1969 — Smithson began producing his works in the landscape itself. He composed a sequence of temporary mirror pieces on the beach and in the jungle of the Yucatán, and poured asphalt down the side of a quarry outside of Rome, simulating a lava flow. One of Smithson's many draw-
14 ings, *Texas Overflow*, subsequently proposed another, potentially more intriguing poured work. Into the center of a circular mount, ringed with brilliant yellow sulphur rocks, hot asphalt would have been poured and allowed to run down between the sul-

tar deposits. "A great pleasure arose from seeing all those incoherent structures. This site gave evidence of a succession of man-made systems mired in abandoned hopes." This infatuation with decay and industrial ruin had a great influence on Smithson (though it was more particularly manifest in the reclamation projects that postdated the *Spiral Jetty*). He continued:

About one mile north of the oil seeps I selected my site. Irregular beds of limestone dip gently eastward, massive deposits of black basalt are broken over the peninsula, giving the region a shattered appearance. It is one of the few places on the lake where the water comes right up to the mainland. Under shallow pinkish water is a network of mud cracks supporting the jig-saw puzzle that composes the salt flats. As I looked at the site, it reverberated out to the horizons only to suggest an immobile cyclone while flickering light made the entire landscape appear to quake. A dormant earthquake spread into the fluttering stillness, into a spinning sensation without movement. This site was a rotary that enclosed itself in an immense roundness. From that gyrating space emerged the possibility of the Spiral Jetty.

If the spiral form of Smithson's jetty was derived from a reading of the local topography, it had additional relevance to the site. The salt crystals that coat the rocks on the water's edge form in the shape of a spiral. "Each cubic salt crystal echoes the Spiral Jetty in terms of the crystal's molecular lattice. . . . The Spiral Jetty could be considered one layer within the spiraling crystal lattice, magnified trillions of times." In addition, while visiting the region Smithson had learned of a legend that the Great Salt Lake was connected to the ocean by an underground channel, which revealed itself in the middle of the lake as an enormous whirlpool. The spiral was thus a key not only to the mac-

roscopic world, but the microscopic and mythological as well.

Smithson was drawn to the Great Salt Lake by the knowledge that it contained a microorganism that colored the water pink. He had read of similar lakes in South America and was eager to see this phenomenon for himself. One knows from his writings that he was invigorated by the kind of desolation encountered at this site: "A bleached and fractured world surrounds the artist. To organize this mess of corrosion into patterns, grids and subdivisions is an aesthetic process that has scarcely been touched."[21] Smithson's vocabulary — *shattered, fractured, corrosion* — reveals his preoccupation with entropy as a measure of disorder. The spiral — open, irreversible, "coming from nowhere, going nowhere," as Smithson put it[22] — accords with this preoccupation. At the *Spiral Jetty*, the gyre is not widening, but falling inward: it is "matter collapsing into the lake mirrored in the shape of a spiral."[23]

After the *Spiral Jetty*, Smithson's work took a different turn. In 1971 he was invited to the Netherlands to participate in an international exhibition called *Sonsbeek 71*. Feeling that the Dutch landscape was already very cultivated and that a work of art upon it would be superfluous, he asked to work at a disrupted site instead. A virtually exhausted sand quarry that was destined to be converted into a recreation area was found for him in Emmen, in northeastern Holland. It became the location of his first effort to reclaim an industrially devastated landscape through art.

Smithson's sand quarry was composed of white and yellow sand, red and brown loam, and a blue-green pond. At one edge of the water, Smithson had a slope graded flat, a curving channel cut into it, and an arced jetty built out into the water, forming the *Broken Circle* (about 140 feet in diameter). On the slope above, *Spiral Hill* was made of overburden and a covering layer of topsoil, with a counterclockwise path of white sand that 18 wound to the top. While the latter work is not particularly distinguished for either the deftness of its execution or the originality of its form, *Broken Circle* is intriguing for its symmetry of opposites: semicircles of water and soil, canal and jetty. It is also given an enchanted quality by the huge glacial boulder that was discovered while grading the site. The boulder apparently plagued Smithson, who felt that it added an undesirable focal point to the work, but it proved too large to be moved. In the end, Smithson grew to appreciate this boulder for its associations with prehistoric burial markers found in the area.[24]

The significance of the *Broken Circle* and *Spiral Hill* lay in the incentive they gave to Smithson to pursue his pairing of art with land reclamation. "Across the country," he wrote in the aftermath of these works, "there are many mining areas, disused quarries, and polluted lakes and rivers. One practical solution for the utilization of such devasted places would be land and water re-cycling in terms of 'Earth Art.' "[25] Smithson did not entirely detest industrial activities, recognizing them as a necessary corollary of the life we have developed for ourselves. He viewed human interventions in the landscape as no more unnatural than earthquakes and typhoons. What he did take exception to, however, was the lack of sensitivity he perceived among industrialists to the visual values of the landscape, which he rightly realized were "traditionally the domain of those concerned with the arts."[26] He wrote to a host of mining companies offering his services to enhance the visual qualities of their reclamation activities. "Art can become a physical resource that mediates between the ecologist and the industrialist," he claimed, facilitating the aims of both.[27]

In two cases, Smithson's ideas received considerable elaboration, though both failed to reach fruition. In 1972 he entered into negotiations with the Hanna Coal Company, which was beginning the reclamation of a thousand-acre site in the Egypt Valley in southeastern Ohio. Smithson proposed incorporating his earthworks not as a substitute for but an addition to the company's standard efforts, in order to add visual focus to the site and draw attention to the surrounding reclamation work. In October of that year he sent the company two drawings for a specific piece. It would have been morphologically related to *Broken Circle*, with a curved jetty embracing a semicircular cove on the shore of a lake. Paths along the shoreline would have been covered with crushed limestone, and portions of the piece would have been planted with crown vetch, a legume that aids in preventing soil erosion and restoring fertility.

Early the next year, Smithson began discussions with the Minerals Engineering Company of Denver concerning the disposition of tailings at their mine in Creede, Colorado. Tailings are the waste material that remains after the desired ore is extracted from mined rock. Because they often contain residue of valuable minerals, they are set aside in the event that future recovery becomes practicable. Smithson proposed utilizing these tailings to build a group of earthworks. Some of the waste was being flushed into basins; he suggested building a series of concentric dams down the slope of a hill, creating ponds that would gradually fill to become terraces as they received the tailings. One drawing indicated the scale at which he hoped to work: it was for a semicircular pond that would be 2,000 feet in diameter, and contain nine million tons of material deposited over twenty-five years. Two other drawings propose a *Garden of Tailings* — curved berms radiating from a common center — and a *Meandering Ring* — random piles with bulldozed pathways between them, the whole forming a circle with an open center.

It is significant that in neither of these proposals did Smithson suggest disguising entirely the postindustrial character of his site

16
17

16, 17. Robert Smithson, *Spiral Jetty*. See plate 15.

18. Robert Smithson. *Broken Circle* and, on the slope above, *Spiral Hill*, 1971. Diameter of circle: 140 ft.; of hill: 75 ft. Emmen, the Netherlands.

19. Robert Smithson. *Amarillo Ramp*, 1973. Diameter: 150 ft. Amarillo, Texas. Collection of Stanley Marsh, Amarillo.

18

19

and materials. He felt it was inappropriate to attempt to recreate a perfect landscape and endeavored instead to evolve an artistically enriched and distinctly man-made landscape that acknowledged technological use. Smithson's proposals thus have a brutally realistic character, and something of a commemorative function. His projects for tailings would have stood as memorials to industrial disruption of the landscape, and as provocations to contemplate the efficacy and necessity of our resource development policies.

Frustrated by the slow pace of negotiations with these mining companies, Smithson accepted the opportunity to work on a ranch in west Texas. He selected a site on the shore of an irrigation lake and staked out the shape of an ascending ramp forming an open circle 150 feet in diameter. While he was making a routine inspection of the planned piece from the air, the plane crashed, killing Smithson, the pilot, and a photographer. The *Amarillo Ramp* was subsequently completed by Nancy Holt and Smithson's friends Tony Shafrazi and Richard Serra. Smithson's early death effectively foreclosed further consideration of his reclamation proposals. They remain, however, his richest legacy, a source of inspiration for a host of subsequent artists.

Like Smithson, Robert Morris was invited to participate in *Sonsbeek 71;* he too had been developing his ideas for art in the landscape for several years. Among the first had been a *Project in Earth and Sod* (1966), a large grassy ring proposed for the Dallas–Fort Worth Regional Airport. Over the next several years Morris produced numerous other proposals—for serpentine mounds, spiral hills, and the like—but his invitation to Holland in 1971 was his first opportunity to see any of these works realized. The result was his *Observatory,* originally built near the Dutch coastal town of Velsen. It was razed at the conclusion of the exhibition but, largely through the efforts of its original sponsors and with considerable Dutch governmental support, it was rebuilt in a slightly enlarged form on new land created from the vast IJsselmeer or Zuider Zee. This new land, or polder, is formed by erecting long, thick dikes and pumping out the seawater. Once the bottom of a shallow inland sea, this land is unwaveringly flat and consequently ideal for the purposes Morris had in mind.

As reconstructed in 1977, *Observatory* consists of two concentric rings of earth with an outer diameter of nearly 300 feet. The inner ring—nine feet high and seventy-nine feet in diameter—is formed of earth piled up against a circular wooden stockade. The outer circumference consists of three embankments and two canals. Entrance to the piece is gained via a triangular passage cut through the embankment to the west; a path leads from there through a break in the central enclosure. Once inside the stockade, three other openings are visible. The first looks due east along two parallel channels, each of which terminates in a ten-foot-square steel plate propped on a diagonal. The interval between these plates, as seen from within the central enclosure, marks the position of the sunrise on the equinoxes. Two other openings look thirty-seven degrees northeast and southeast, through notches on the outer embankment lined with granite boulders and marking the points of the sunrise on the summer and winter solstices, respectively.

Morris's deployment of archaic references—solar sight lines and large granite blocks—parallels Heizer's strategy at *Complex One:* to blend an empathetic historicism with a contemporary idiom. Morris was likewise disaffected from much recent art. "It seems a truism at this point," he wrote in 1971, "that the static, portable indoor art object can do no more than carry a decorative load that becomes increasingly uninteresting."[28] What interested Morris instead was not simply revealing the world to the observer, but also the conditions of perception. With an apparent

nod in the direction of the phenomenology of the French philosopher Maurice Merleau-Ponty, Morris aimed at creating "a place in which the perceiving self might take measure of certain aspects of its own physical existence."[29] By creating — as at his *Observatory* — an art work that was too large or too complex to be viewed in an instant, that required the viewer to walk through and around it, Morris provided an "experience of an interaction between the perceiving body and the world which fully admits that the terms of this interaction are temporal as well as spatial, that existence is process, that the art itself is a form of behavior. . . ."[30]

In the case of the *Observatory*, this behavior leads to an awareness of how information is absorbed by the senses and combined to produce a coherent mental image of something that is impossible to comprehend instantaneously. It also leads to an awareness of the different measures of time. There is the viewer's time — the amount required to move around and comprehend the piece. Contrasted with this are times of two vastly different sorts: the far longer time of human history, implicit in the reference to neolithic monuments, and the virtually imponderable measure of astronomical time revealed

through the use of solar sight lines. The use of archaic references and the solar orientation are thus not only historicist. They also require us to acknowledge the subjectivity of our own sense of time by juxtaposing it with two more awesome and enduring measures.

Morris's emphasis on the importance of the viewer's participation in coming to know an art work is crucial to understanding his *Grand Rapids Project* as well. This work came about in the aftermath of an outdoor sculpture exhibition organized by the Women's Committee of the Grand Rapids Art Museum in 1973. Entitled *Sculpture off the Pedestal*, the exhibition was intended to explore the use of a wide variety of sculptural types in different public situations. When Morris was invited to participate, he recognized this as an opportunity to focus public attention on the notion of art in the landscape. On a visit to Grand Rapids, he found a badly eroded hillside in one of the city's recreation areas. He later described this site as "in tune with my concerns for outside works — works which cooperate and do not become applied 'objects'. . . stuck onto the landscape."[31] He proposed recontouring the slope and linking the top and bottom of the hill with a pair of intersecting pathways in the shape of an X. This proposal

22

21. Robert Morris, *Observatory*. See plate 20.

22. Robert Morris. *Grand Rapids Project*, 1973–74. Length of ramps: 478 ft. Belknap Park, Grand Rapids, Michigan. Collection of the City of Grand Rapids.

21

was reviewed by the City Parks and Recreation Department to insure, among other things, adequate plant cover and proper drainage. The piece was then constructed in the summer and fall of 1974, with funds from the National Endowment for the Arts, the Michigan Council for the Arts, the Women's Committee of the Museum, and with "in-kind" contributions from the city.

Although the configuration of this work seems quite obvious at first glance, there are in fact subtle shifts in the grade of the slope and the length of the paths that become obvious only when experiencing the piece. Like the *Observatory*, it becomes a place for the enactment of various sorts of behavior: "runnings, walkings, viewings, crossings, waitings, meetings, coolings, heatings," among the many others that Morris mentioned in a catalog published about the project.[32]

Morris's *Grand Rapids Project* was to prove enormously significant to the future of art in the landscape in the United States. While Smithson's *Broken Circle* and *Spiral Hill* and Morris's *Observatory* came into being with government support in Holland, the *Grand Rapids Project* marked the first time that public funds had been involved in effecting a large-scale environmental work in America. From this date, the National Endowment for the Arts, the General Services Administration, and numerous state, county, and municipal organizations displayed increasing receptiveness to this sort of art. This coincided with a growing commitment among artists to the evolving public purposes of art in the landscape. Smithson's notion that artists have not only the capacity but also the social obliga-

22

23

tion to make a beneficial contribution to the use and restoration of the landscape was to win ever-wider approval as the years passed. And while projects continued to come into being entirely through private sponsorship, more and more public patrons were to accept both the aesthetic and utilitarian aims of recent art in the landscape. It is ironic that this public support began with what is certainly among the most inscrutable and, in visual terms, the least captivating works of this genre.

23 Nineteen seventy-four also saw the completion of Richard Fleischner's *Sod Maze* in Newport, Rhode Island. This too was the result of an outdoor sculpture exhibition, called *Monumenta*, which came about with partial public sponsorship. While most of the forty-one artists showed preexisting works, Fleischner created one especially for the exhibition. He selected the grounds of Château-sur-Mer, a mansion belonging to the Preservation Society of Newport County, from

among the sites made available to him. There he constructed a mounded turf maze some 142 feet in diameter and a scant 18 inches high. It has only a single path to the center, which is visible in any case because of the low relief; it therefore does not function like the deliberately puzzling topiary mazes that are the best known of the labyrinth types. Instead it relates to more ancient maze forms: those cut in the stone floors of medieval cathedrals, as at Chartres, and functioning as allegories of penance and purification (often quite literally, as penitents traversed them on their knees); and those cut in the ground — dug and low mounded — in medieval England, based perhaps on Roman models, and having an ornamental purpose. It is this sort of maze that appears in *A Midsummer Night's Dream*: "The nine men's morris is filled up with mud; / and the quaint mazes in the wanton green, / for lack of tread, are undistinguishable."

Meanwhile, the Western landscape con-

23. Richard Fleischner (b. 1944). *Sod Maze*, 1974. Sod and earth; height: 18 in., diameter: 142 ft. Newport, Rhode Island. Collection of the Preservation Society of Newport County.

24. Ant Farm (Chip Lord, Hudson Marquez, Doug Michels). *Cadillac Ranch*, 1974. 10 Cadillacs. Amarillo, Texas. Commissioned by Stanley Marsh, Amarillo.

24

tinued to blossom with art works, albeit of a very different sort. A San Francisco collective called Ant Farm—including Chip Lord, Hudson Marquez, and Doug Michels—upended 24 ten Cadillacs along Route 66 near Amarillo, Texas, in 1974. Ranging in vintage from 1948 to 1962, the cars were buried to their midsections in what can only be described as a requiem for the golden age of the American automobile. The flamboyance of this gesture has been equaled only by the work of the Bulgarian-born artist Christo. In 1971 he made his first attempt at hanging the *Valley Curtain*, a glistening orange nylon drape spanning the more than 1,300-foot width of Rifle Gap in Colorado. A gust of wind damaged the fabric, however, and final installation was delayed until the summer of 1972. Even then, a vicious windstorm shredded the *Curtain* a mere twenty-eight hours after it was unfurled from the suspension cables and anchored to the ground.

25, 26   In 1976 came Christo's *Running Fence*, by far the most publicized of the recent works in the landscape. It ran twenty-four and a half miles across the hills of Sonoma and Marin counties, leaping roads and crossing cattle pastures before plunging into the Pacific. It was composed of 2,050 panels of a white nylon fabric, each 18 feet high and 68 feet wide, held aloft by cables and hooks strung between steel poles. It graced the rolling landscape of Northern California for a brief two weeks in the middle of September, at a cost of some three million dollars raised privately through the sale of Christo's drawings and collages.

There is something undeniably captivating in the images of Christo's *Fence* snaking its way through the landscape, revealing the contours as it goes. Yet Christo was emphatic that this was not the sole content of his work. "I didn't just want a nice fence and a beautiful landscape," he said. Instead, encouraged by his knowledge of the activities of the post-Revolutionary avant-garde in Russia (acquired

25, 26. Christo (b. 1935). *Running Fence*,
1972–76. Steel poles, steel cables, and 2½
million square ft. of woven nylon; height:
18 ft., overall length: 24½ miles. Sonoma and
Marin counties, California (dismantled).

26

while an art student in Bulgaria), Christo sought a closer interaction between his art and its broader cultural context. "Just as religion was important to the Quattrocento artist," he explained, "so are economics, social problems and politics today . . . the greatest drama. Knowledge of these areas should be an important part of one's work."[33] Forty-two months were required to realize the *Running Fence*. Permission was negotiated to cross fifty-nine ranches. Eighteen public hearings were held; three sessions in the Superior Courts of California were devoted to the project; and 450 pages of environmental impact statements were prepared. These are the cultural structures that help determine the visible form of human interventions in the landscape; revealing them was at least as important a part of the *Fence* to Christo as its physical configuration. They were elaborately documented in the book and film that were produced about the project.

Despite all the public preparation, still the *Fence* ended in controversy. It had many enthusiastic partisans, but it was scorned by some for having so extravagant a price tag and no apparent purpose. Others objected to the fact that it was to cross the strip of land along the coast protected by the California Coastal Zone Commission. The commission's regulations require that at certain designated places nothing be constructed without their approval in a 1,000-foot-wide strip beginning at the tide line. Christo sought and received a permit, but the commission's decision was appealed. His permit was thus under review at the time he completed the *Fence*, bringing it the full distance into the ocean. To some, Christo's cavalier disregard of this regulation undermined the premise of his project, which was avowedly to reveal and not to circumvent the economic, social, and political structures governing the landscape.[34]

Christo's was a new form of art in the landscape: temporary, theatrical, and involving large numbers of people. When Nancy Holt

completed her first major work in 1976 she continued the tradition of remote, large-scale, and durable works initiated by Heizer and Smithson. Constructed in the desert of northwestern Utah, her *Sun Tunnels* consists of four concrete pipes, each eighteen feet long and slightly over nine feet in diameter, placed in an open X configuration about fifty feet apart. They are aligned to the rising and setting of the sun on the summer and winter solstices — roughly thirty-two degrees north and south of true east and west. At sunrise and sunset on the summer and winter solstices and for about ten days before and after, the sun is visible through the pairs of pipes. Additional visual incident is brought to the piece by holes that are cut in the upper surfaces of the pipes in the shape of different constellations: Draco, Perseus, Columba, and Capricorn. These holes are variously seven to ten inches in diameter, with the size relative to the magnitude of the star to which the hole corresponds. During the day and by moonlight, spots of light move across the inside of the tunnels in the configurations of these constellations. As Holt herself has nicely explicated, "Day is turned into night, and an inversion of the sky takes place: Stars are cast down to earth, spots of warmth in cool tunnels."[35]

A surprising lyricism is achieved by Holt's rough pipes, which barely disguise their industrial origin. They provide welcome shelter, cool solace from the desert sun. Likewise, they offer a reassuring indication of direction in a trackless landscape and frame vistas within the disconcerting vastness. Holt compares the site with a passage from T. S. Eliot's *Four Quartets* (1943): "Dawn points, and another day / Prepares for heat and silence." Her *Sun Tunnels* are a dignified yet humanly scaled setting in which to experience the grand awfulness of the natural surroundings.

Two other still-unfinished works for the Western deserts were also given birth in the middle years of the 1970s. In 1974 Charles

27–29

29. Nancy Holt, *Sun Tunnels*, sunset on the summer solstice.

30. James Turrell (b. 1943). *Amba*, 1982. A temporary light installation at the Center on Contemporary Art, Seattle, Washington.

31. Roden Crater, near Flagstaff, Arizona.

30

31

32. Charles Ross (b. 1937). *Star Axis,* begun 1971. Earth, stone, and steel; height: 11 stories; width: ¹/₁₀ mile. The Star Tunnel will be placed in the central channel. New Mexico.

32

Ross found a site in the semiarid mesa country east of Albuquerque for a work to be called
32 *Star Axis.* When completed, it will consist of a vastly elongated steel cylinder—200 feet long and 7 feet in diameter—rising diagonally up the escarpment of the mesa and some 50 feet into the air beyond. It will be oriented to astronomical north: the infinite extension of the earth's axis into space. Because of a wobble in the earth's rotation, the point we perceive as north changes, with a cycle of 26,000 years. At certain times in this wobble, the axis aligns quite closely with a particular star. When the Great Pyramid was built over 4,500 years ago, it was oriented to what was then

the North Star, Thuban in the constellation Draco. In our own time, the earth's axis has rotated into a near alignment with Polaris. By the middle of the next century, this alignment will be almost perfect.

Star Axis is planned to demonstrate the relationship between Polaris and the earth's axis. At the time of their closest alignment, Polaris will describe a one-degree circle around the astronomical pole each day. Standing at the bottom of Ross's cylinder, one will look up at a one-degree circle of sky; Polaris will be seen to rotate around the rim of the opening each day. Climbing up the cylinder, one will see ever larger circles of sky, each describing the circumpolar orbit of Polaris as the earth's axis moves away from it. And from the top, one will see evidence of an entirely different phenomenon. A bow-shaped field, larger at either end than in the middle, will describe the limits of the area in which the shadow of the cylinder's tip will fall during the year. This shadow field will give evidence of the earth's seasonally varying relationship to the sun. Ross has investigated this in another form already, in a series of works called *Sunlight Convergence/Solar Burns: The Year Shape.* Using a lens set up on the roof of his New York studio to focus sunlight, Ross allowed the sun to burn an image of its daily course onto a piece of wood. When these boards are set end to end at the conclusion of the year, they form a spiral that reverses midway. This reversing curve will be apparent in the shadow field at *Star Axis.*

It is still anyone's guess what will be the precise effect of Ross's piece. The accomplishments of James Turrell that have led up to his *Roden Crater Project,* however, give this proposed work fair promise of magic. For the past two decades, Turrell has created ethereal environments in which light is perceived almost as a palpable, physical presence. Initially accomplished through the use of projected or fluorescent light cast around, through, or onto carefully arranged constructions, these pieces demonstrated how manipulated light could control or alter the perceived character of a space. The means by which Turrell accomplished this transformation were

confounding, but the effects were transfixing. Room shapes were altered by light; perceived walls turned out to be voids.

Turrell has also worked with natural light, an enthusiasm that will reach an apogee with his *Roden Crater Project.* In and around the red and black cinder cone of a long-extinct volcano near Flagstaff, Arizona, Turrell will fashion seven spaces in which to experience the changing qualities of sun and moonlight. Five will be on the outside slope of the cone, in a side vent. From there, a long tunnel will lead into a chamber at the bottom of the caldera, and finally into the bowl of the cinder cone itself. The rim of the cone will be somewhat recontoured, as will the bowl, to enhance the reception of light. Looking out from these spaces, one will be able to observe at periodic intervals what Turrell describes as "imaged events": a moonrise here, a solstice sunset there. These will work in concert with daily fluctuations of sun and moonlight to create ever-changing perceptual environments.

Monumental in scale, yet exceedingly subtle in form, Turrell's project is like many others of the recent avant-garde. Like them, it exploits the characteristics of the surrounding landscape—its contours and materials, its ambient light—no less than its symbolic and emotional qualities. Turrell's high ambition is to reveal to us anew the extraordinary properties—physical, symbolic, and psychic—of light, one of the commonplaces of our lives. Like many other recent artists in the landscape, he aims to create an environment of rapture.

2. THE RAMBLE

In England, circumstances similar to those in the United States prevailed in the latter half of the 1960s. A group of younger artists, dissatisfied with the current forms of painting and sculpture, opted for alternatives to the precious object in environmental and performance art. Two sculptors, Richard Long and Hamish Fulton — both of whom matriculated in the mid-1960s at St. Martin's School of Art in London, then the testing ground for advanced art in Britain — led the way forward, and back, into the English landscape. But what they did when they got there displayed a sensibility quite unlike that of their American contemporaries. They barely intruded upon the landscape at all. Indeed, Fulton made no mark other than footprints and took nothing but photographs. Long also made photographs, and while he sometimes reorganized landscape elements — rocks and sticks — he did so in ways that were hardly discernible. Walking was the principal form of artistic activity for both these men.

Theirs was a sensibility no less romantic in its reveries than the American, but decidedly less heroic in its means.[36] Nourished by the long tradition of landscape veneration in Britain — in painting, literature, and garden design — the contemporary English sensibility may well find its clearest antecedent in the life and work of William Wordsworth, with his physical ramblings through the landscape of the Lake District and his poetic musings on the same. The antiheroism of the recent work is no doubt a reflection of the present-day character of the English countryside. A land more densely populated than America and without its vast open spaces, England presents fewer opportunities for grand gestures than the United States. While Smithson could assert that the organization of the American landscape represented "an aesthetic process that has scarcely been touched," this is decidedly less true for England, where the landscape has been subject to continuous and ef-

fective organization at least since Enclosure (the redistribution of grazing and crop land and the creation of private estates from communal holdings) reached its peak in the seventeenth and eighteenth centuries. Even now, England is far more subject than the United States to rigorous zoning, which regulates every aspect of land use. In addition, it is a nation fairly groaning under the burden of industrial development. In such a land, there is less occasion and less tolerance for the large-scale interventions of an art sometimes wilfully unbeautiful.

While still a student in 1967 Long had made ephemeral sculptures in the landscape: concentric circles of paper laid on the ground or paths trodden in the grass. On a rocky Somerset beach in 1968 he arranged a group of stones in the barely perceptible outline of a square. And in 1969 he made walking itself

34

33. Richard Long (b. 1945). *Walking a Line in Peru*, 1972. Photograph by the artist.

34. Richard Long. *A Line in Bolivia*, 1981. Photograph by the artist.

into a sculpture: from the twelfth to the fifteenth of October, for example, Long walked the figures of four concentric squares in the Wiltshire countryside. Each square was walked as accurately as possible, the time noted and the square drawn on a map. The activity constituted the artwork; the map provided its visual record.

"A walk is on the ground, passing by, moving through life. A sculpture is still; a stopping place."[37] Thus Long in 1981 described the distinction between his two forms of art making. A photographic work from 1973 serves as an emblem of this distinction. It consists of ten black and white images of irregular but roughly circular groupings of stones in the landscape. As Long walked, he paused at intervals to rearrange the stones he encountered along the way, and then photographed them. The group of photographs he entitled *A Rolling Stone. Resting Places along a Journey, 1973*. He used stones as his medium. ("Stones are the material of the Earth. I pray the Earth still has a future.") Long himself can be seen as the rolling stone; the sculptures are the discreet signs of his resting places.

By now it seems that Long has walked nearly everywhere: in the Himalayas and the Andes, on Dartmoor and in Africa. Sometimes he simply walks, and records his journeys on a map. At other times, he has continued to make his unobtrusive marks in the landscape: not just with stones, but with driftwood and seaweed and bits of shrubbery as well. His preference is for the more remote and uninhabited, even exotic landscapes; there is a melancholy absence of any human trace except his own in his photographs. The configuration of his walks and the form of his marks have remained unwaveringly simple: circles and squares, spirals and straight lines. These are simple shapes with multiple references. "A circle is shared, common knowledge. It belongs equally to the past, the present and the future." The circle, the line, and the spiral are employed precisely because of these associations; Long appropriates them to render his privately ritualistic work more universal. Sometimes these appropriations are quite literal. *Walking a Line in Peru, 1972* 33 took place on one of the extraordinary ground markings made over two thousand years ago by the Nazca Indians on the coastal deserts of Peru. In 1975 Long walked every road, lane, and double track within a six-mile radius of the Cerne Abbas Giant, an ithyphallic chalk drawing on a hillside in Dorset. His lines have also traced the course of recent history. *Power Line Walk: From a Water Wheel to a Nuclear Power Station* in 1980 emphasized the relentless and potentially cataclysmic development of technology. "A walk is just one more layer, a mark," Long explains, "laid upon the thousands of other layers of human and geographic history on the surface of the land."[38]

As Smithson did with his Nonsites, Long sometimes brings his sculptures indoors to galleries or museums. No doubt he feels a measure of frustration in this, for these works can never match the layered, richly referential quality of the works in the landscape. Yet they too are signifiers of Long's resolute involvement with earth and its materials. Some of these sculptures are simple circles or rectangles of indigenous materials; others recreate the distance of outdoor walks. For the Whitechapel Art Gallery in London in 1971, Long compressed a line the length of a straight walk from the bottom to the top of Silbury Hill — a large, man-made mound in Wiltshire — into a spiral that fit within the walls of the gallery. The indoor line itself was made by walking: Long coated his feet with clay and imprinted the piece on the floor.

Long expresses through his work only an implied comment on the more interventionist projects of his American contemporaries. Hamish Fulton is more explicit. Asked in a recent interview how he regarded

35

36

37. Richard Long. *California Wood Circle*, 1976. Wood; diameter: 18 ft. Musée National d'Art Moderne, Centre Georges Pompidou, Paris.

38. Hamish Fulton (b. 1946). *Standing Coyote*, 1981. Photograph by the artist.

39. Hamish Fulton. *Ringdom Gompa*, 1978. Photograph by the artist.

37

Smithson, Heizer, and De Maria, Fulton replied that he believed artists ought to support each other, but went on to say, "I feel the three artists you mention use the landscape without . . . any sense of respect for it. . . . I see their art as a continuation of 'Manifest Destiny'. . . the so-called 'heroic conquering' of nature."[39] Acknowledging that they generally work outside the city, he said that he nevertheless found the content of their work to be "inescapably urban." To the extent that rapture before nature has always been felt most strongly by those most alienated from it—i.e., inhabitants of a large city—Fulton is certainly correct. But his work is equally reactionist; in this sense it too is urban generated. "My art is a passive protest against urban societies that alienate people from the world of nature."[40]

The walk is also Fulton's principal form of activity. But, unlike Long, the walk itself is not his artwork. "The walk is the walk and the artwork is the framed photograph and text,"

he explained. Somewhere along the way, he makes a photograph that evokes either the landscape he has passed through or his state of mind. Fulton also differs from Long in that he never makes a mark of any sort — other than footprints — in the landscape. He is the most emphatically reverential of these artists. "The natural environment was not built by man and for this reason it is to me deeply mysterious and religious."[41] Consequently, he does not alter it, and he prefers to select landscapes with little or no evidence of human activity. "The photographs show the land the way it should remain." People generally do not appear in Fulton's work, except, for example, in a few photographs taken in the Himalayas or the rural areas of Bolivia, where he feels people live in greater harmony with the natural environment.

David Nash has entwined his art-making and his existence even more resolutely. If Long and Fulton demonstrate how personal behavior or ritual can become art, then Nash

STANDING COYOTE

A SEVEN DAY WALK IN NORTHEASTERN CALIFORNIA

ENDING ON THE NIGHT OF THE OCTOBER FULL MOON 1981

RINGDOM GOMPA

NORTHERN INDIA   JULY 1978

A 14½ DAY WALKING JOURNEY OF APPROXIMATELY 200 MILES TRAVELLING BY WAY OF

RINGDOM GOMPA   THE PEN ZI PASS   THE ZANSKAR RIVER   ATING GOMPA

HUTTRA   THE MUNI GLACIER   MACHAIL AND THE CHANDER BHAGA RIVER

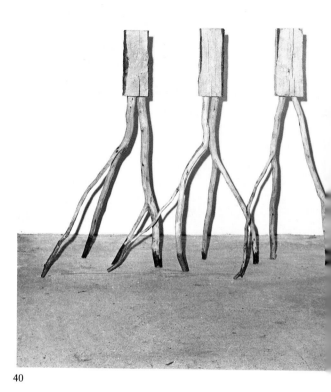

40. David Nash (b. 1945). *Chorus Line (Three Dandy Scuttlers)*, 1976. Oak and beech: height: 63 in. Private collection.

reveals how the practice of art can become a way of life. After he completed art college in London in 1967, Nash removed himself to one of Britain's wettest mountain fastnesses, the slate-quarrying village of Blaenau Ffestiniog in North Wales. One can hardly imagine a less picturesque place: Nash described it as "a small derelict quarrying town, just above the tree line."[42] It is surrounded by slag tips that rival the mountains in height; on the many rainy days, sky and slag coalesce in a somber and monochrome gray. Nash maintains that it was pragmatism, at least in part, that led him to Blaenau. Life is far less expensive there than in London; he was able to acquire a large chapel in which to work, with living quarters behind it. But Nash was also motivated by dissatisfaction with the stranglehold of the urban centers on contemporary art, an attitude that was shared by many in England and America at the time. A single encounter with Blaenau was enough to convince me that Nash was obviously not in search of an arcadian alternative. He selected an unbeautiful village, where he lives in close proximity to his neighbors in an emphatically Welsh community that the more fainthearted might find alarmingly parochial.

It was here that Nash began to work with wood. At first, it was milled lumber, but soon it was wood from trees that he cut himself. "Three valleys fall away from this damp grey ledge toward the sea. In the valleys are trees." Green wood and dead; ash, oak, and beech: they were axed and sawed into balls, roped together into tripods and arches, or fashioned into tables with stacks of rough circles and blocks upon them. These were deliberately coarse pieces, without the finished look of fine carpentry. The green wood cracked as it seasoned; the surfaces were irregular, and pegs protruded from the joins.

In 1977 Nash added planted pieces to his sculptural repertory. Twenty-two ash trees were planted in a thirty-foot circle on land

40

he owns near Blaenau. Over a period of thirty years, they will be thrice fletched—cut part way through and bent over—and thereby coaxed to grow into an *Ash Dome*, which Nash expects to resemble "a volcano of growing energy." This was an idea locally inspired; hedgerows used for fencing are often made by such fletching. It also has considerable artistic precedent: elaborate topiary chambers were a feature in medieval gardens, while Alexander Pope apparently considered —and may have implemented—a scheme for planting at his celebrated garden at Twickenham a stand of trees that would grow to resemble a Gothic cathedral.[43] Two other pieces were planted by Nash in 1978 in Grizedale Forest, near the Lake District in Cumbria. One was a ring of larch trees, planted on the diagonal to

44

41. David Nash. *Wooden Waterway, Kakehi*, 1982. Mizunara (water oak), stone, and water; length: 100 ft. Collection of the Tochigi Prefectural Museum of Fine Arts, Japan.

42. David Nash. *Wooden Waterway*, 1978. Oak, ash, sycamore, birch, stone, and water; length: 150 ft. Grizedale Forest, Cumbria, England.

give them the appearance of sweeping down a slope. The other was a *Willow Ladder*, for which two young willow trees were cut down and inverted in the soil. Willows will root quite willingly from any point on the trunk or branches: these upside-down trees will sprout from their trunk tops shoots that will be entwined to form a structure like a ladder.

At the same time, Nash has continued with his cut pieces. He gouged troughs in fallen tree trunks and laid them end to end, beginning in a small spring and running down a hill, forming a wooden waterway with forks and falls. He quartered a tree trunk, each part of which had a branch, and pegged the parts

43 together to form a *Running Table*: a great lumbering beast in the forest. Nash plants and cuts; he works with living wood and dead. He has come to identify with wood as a metaphor for his own life. "I want a simple approach to living and doing. I want a life and work that reflects the balance and continuity of nature. Identifying with the time and energy of the tree and with its mortality, I find myself drawn deeper into the joys and blows of nature. Worn down and regenerated; broken off and reunited; a dormant faith revived in the new growth on old wood."[44]

If there is something self-conscious in Nash's close identification of his art and his life, it is amply excused by the quality of his work, which has become more simple and more deft as he matures. He allows the wood to retain its own character, while not being reluctant to coax from it biomorphic forms. In this, he is in the tradition of Henry Moore and Barbara Hepworth, the great British practitioners of an abstracted but still organically suggestive naturalism. At the same time, he is not afraid of a certain amount of whimsical surrealism and the touch of modesty that it brings to his sculpture. The bestial character of the Grizedale *Running Table* has already been noted; it is also evident in the amusing

40 *Chorus Line (Three Dandy Scuttlers)*.

41

42

43. David Nash. *Running Table*, 1978. Oak; height: 60 in. Grizedale Forest, Cumbria, England.

44. David Nash. *Fletched Over Ash Dome*, 1977. Pencil, charcoal, and watercolor on paper; 29¼ x 41¼ in. Private collection.

45. David Nash. *Wooden Fish*, 1982. Mizunara (water oak). Collection of the Tochigi Prefectural Museum of Fine Arts, Japan.

43

Fletched over Ash Dome

Planted March 1977 at Cae'n-y-Coed, Maentwrog, North Wales.

22 young ash trees planted in a circle (March 1977)

Planted on a promontory on a h. U side.
By tending, grafting and fletching the trees
will be persuaded into a 30ft Dome.

Three 'fletches' at ten year intervals.

Once the Dome is formed there will be no
further pruning or tending.

The Ash Dome
A silver linear structure in winter,
a green mass in summer,
a Volcano of growing energy.

David Nash

44

45

As Nash's reputation has grown, he has been invited to work farther and farther away from Blaenau: in the United States, Holland, and Japan. While this distance from his home base might be expected to weaken his work, it has not. In Japan, in particular, Nash and his hosts felt what can only be described as a remarkable sense of mutual self-recognition. For the exhibition *Aspects of British Art Today*, which opened in Tokyo and toured Japan in 1982, arrangements were made for Nash to go to Japan and work in a rural, mountainous area above Nikko, where an aged mizunara, or water oak tree, was found for him. He spent twenty days there, fashioning from the tree some ten pieces, including *Wooden Fish, Cracking Box*, an arch, a wood stove, a wooden waterway (later permanently installed at the Tochigi Prefectural Museum of Fine Arts), and *River Tunnel*, a hollow log that was set adrift with a fire burning inside it. Nash's sensitivity to the biomorphically suggestive forms inherent in wood—what might be termed a reverence for the spirit of the material—drew comment from the Japanese for its relationship to Shinto, the pre-Buddhist veneration of nature spirits. To Nash, different trees have distinctive characters, "an oak being defined as brutal and full of compact energy, while a birch is seen as delicate, ethereal and passive."[45] *Wooden Fish* certainly exploited both the form and spirit inherent in the wood; it had the additional appeal of an oblique reference to the architecture of Japanese temples with their multiple, upturned, and overhanging cornices.

Nash's natural gregariousness has made him something of a patron of recent landscape art in Britain. Students come to live and work with him, and he encourages younger artists with whom he feels a kinship. One such is Andy Goldsworthy, who lives in Cumbria. Goldsworthy has spent some time in Blaenau, making while there a large slate arch that resembled the bridges spanning the creeks on the upland moors. But Goldsworthy is a wanderer in the spirit of Long and Fulton, and creates his subtle and mysterious works as he goes. He gathers sticks and weaves them into spheres. In a patch of leaves on the ground he cuts an opening through the green leaves on top, exposing the rotted ones below and creating a dark circle of decay. He gathers heron or crow feathers, splitting them open to make a jagged line drawing on the earth. He combines these feathers with autumnal leaves to make brilliantly colored collages that are dispersed by the first wind. Goldsworthy preserves these private oblations in exquisite photographs. He is one of the very few of the recent artists in the landscape to make a virtue of fine photography. While most others feel that photographic refinement obscures the true, nonphotographic content of their work, Goldsworthy rightly finds it necessary for conveying the immaculacy of his efforts.

Although the ramble seems a particularly British approach to the landscape, it is an American who has developed wandering into a true epic. That the work of Charles Simonds should be described as epic might come as a surprise, given its diminuitive scale. But each piece he makes is an episode in an extended narrative, told in a consistent voice and celebrating the sweeping history of an imaginary civilization of little people. That Simonds figures in a discussion of contemporary art and landscape might also seem odd given the frequently urban and sometimes indoor settings of his work. Yet implicit in his art is a constant and almost mystical sense of earth as the giver of all life. The little people demonstrate an indissoluble bond with the physical and spiritual constituents of their environment. Simonds is their chronicler and their cultural geographer, telling their history and revealing how they live in different landscapes (and, by implication, how we live in ours). If Sim-

46. Andy Goldsworthy (b. 1956). *Arch*, 1982.
Stone. Blaenau Ffestiniog, Wales. Photograph
by the artist.

47. Andy Goldsworthy. *Cracked/Broken Pebbles*, 1978. Lancashire, England. Photograph by the artist.

48. Andy Goldsworthy. *Elder Patch*, 1983. Brough, Cumbria, England. Photograph by the artist.

49. Andy Goldsworthy. *Heron Feathers*, March 1982. Photograph by the artist.

50. Andy Goldsworthy. *Stacked Sticks*, June 1980. Photograph by the artist.

47

48

49

50

51. Andy Goldsworthy. *Yellow Elm Leaves Laid
over a Rock, Low Water,* October 15, 1991.
Scaur Water, Dumfriesshire, Scotland.
Photograph by the artist; courtesy of Galerie
Lelong, New York.

51

52. Charles Simonds (b. 1945). *Dwelling,
P.S. 1, Long Island City, New York*, 1975. Clay
and wood; length of bricks: ½ in. Temporary
installation. Collection of the artist.

onds's presence is not often seen in the physical landscape, it is still to be felt in the landscape of fantasy and the intellect.

Simonds gave symbolic birth to himself and
to the little people in a New Jersey clay pit in
1970, where he had himself filmed emerging naked from the muck. Like Adam, he
was clay made animate; he was simultaneously exploiting the sexual and sacred associations of earth. Later, covered again with
clay, he lay down, making himself into a
landscape. On the hillside of his hip, he
constructed the dwellings of the little people. This ritual, called *Landscape ↔ Body ↔
Dwelling*, asserted his own sense of identity
with the earth and the link between the architectural forms of the little people and the
physical character of their environment. The
earth, architecture, and the body were anal-
ogized as different forms of dwellings.

Since the enactment of the birth ritual,
Simonds and his miniature civilization have
been all around the world: to Paris, Genoa,
Berlin, even Shanghai. He began by building
their dwellings on abandoned buildings and
in vacant lots on the Lower East Side of New
York. He was all the time elaborating the fantasy of their migrations, appropriate to that
decaying quarter of New York that has been
home to successive waves of immigrants. He
worked by spreading clay on a ledge or in a
niche, then building with tiny clay bricks the
shelters and ritual places of his little people.
Dwellings were clustered on slopes or made
to surround domed kivas; altars were built on
breast and genital shapes that occurred in the
landscape. Labyrinths, tombs, observatories,
and arenas of justice were formed to allude
to the work habits and beliefs of this civilization. As the art world began to take notice,
museums and private collectors throughout
the United States and Europe commissioned
his works. The little people were presented
for themselves, but also as a tool for examin-
ing our own architecture and social struc-

tures. Each piece offered a comparison: between the technologically naive little people
—whose architecture conformed to the contours of the landscape and whose earth-
centered rituals were everywhere in evidence
—and the technologically sophisticated constructions of our urban environments, imposed upon if not hostile to the landscape.

The history of the little people is told
primarily through Simonds's sculptures. He
has provided them with one eloquent written
account, however, which reveals that they
wander as freely as their creator. Entitled
Three Peoples, this small book tells of three
branches of the miniature civilization: the
linear, circular, and spiral peoples.[46] The linear
people inched along through the landscape,
building new homes adjacent to their last
ones, leaving all their possessions behind
when they moved as a museum of personal
artifacts. "Their dwellings make a pattern on
the earth as of a great tree laid flat, branching
and forking according to their loves and
hates, forming an ancestral record of life lived
as an odyssey, its roots in a dark and distant
past. . . ." The circular people bridged the
past and the future. They were careful histo-
rians, marking time and recording the past,
but their life's energies were concentrated on
a yearly ritual of procreation that "reenacted
original creation in a dizzying celebration of
sexual possibility." The circular people lived
within a closed system, moving always within
the same circle. They built their new
dwellings on the remains of the old, advancing one unit each year away from the recent
past and into the distant past. At the center of
the circle was the underground kiva, the
"dome-womb" that was the site of the orgias-
tic dance on the winter solstice.

The spiral people yearned only for an ec-
static death. They built their dwellings in an
ascending ring that tightened upon itself,
"with the past, constantly buried, serving as a
building material for the future." They cared

52

little for their surroundings or their relationship to the natural environment. They built their dwellings higher and higher, throwing their artifacts and, as the living space was reduced, even themselves into the center of the spiral to support its climb. Their sacrifice was volitional: "They believed resolutely that they were contributing to the most ambitious monument ever conceived by man." Their goal "was to achieve both the greatest possible height and to predict the very moment of collapse, the moment when the last of their resources would be consumed and their death inevitable. They lived for that moment alone." There is more than a coincidental similarity between the spiral people and ourselves. They are Simonds's evocation of twentieth-century man.

As the omniscient chronicler of the little people's history, Simonds bears an intriguing resemblance to characterizations of the Wandering Jew, that eternal traveler who has lived the entire history of his people since the Crucifixion. Condemned to wander endlessly for his denial of Christ on the road to Calvary, the Wandering Jew achieves in many versions of the story — particularly that of Guillaume Apollinaire[47] — an almost godly knowledge of life. He is a tireless observer of events who has been everywhere and seen everything. He is set apart by his profound knowledge. As Simonds's little people are a race of wanderers, so is he their Wandering Jew, their historian and cultural geographer. A sense of his own peregrinations informs the work: an

early exposure to the cliff dwellings and kivas of the Southwestern American Indians provided him with a basic vocabulary of forms, which was elaborated by subsequent study of other prehistoric civilizations as well as animal architecture and botanical shapes. His wanderings have also led to an awareness of and a commentary on present-day social and environmental conditions. Using the forms and myths of the little people, he has participated in the development of inner-city parks and playlots; proposed the creation of hanging gardens in abandoned tenements; and constructed a human-scaled circular dwelling 57 of earth and seeds that was converted from shelter to food as the plants matured.

Simonds and his British contemporaries share a kind of preindustrial innocence. Combined with their modesty in scale is a freedom from the tools and techniques required by the more grandiose projects of the Americans. Like latter-day Luddites — those British working men who, at the turn of the nineteenth century, smashed the newly created textile machinery that threatened their employment — these artists recoil from the perceived malevolence of many modern developments. Not all are as explicit as Long, with his earnest plea, "I pray the Earth still has a future." But taken together these artists express a conscious and articulate reaction to our alarming capacity to lay waste to our landscapes and dwellings through a technological capability that seems to exceed the limits of our wisdom and sanity.

53

54

55

56

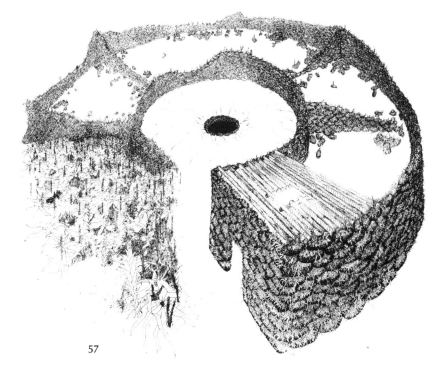

53. Charles Simonds. *Landscape ↔ Body ↔ Dwelling,* 1973. Clay; length of bricks: ¹/₂ in. Collection of the artist.

54. Charles Simonds. *Dwelling, Chicago,* 1981, detail. Clay and wood; overall length: 44 ft. Formerly installed at the Museum of Contemporary Art, Chicago.

55. Charles Simonds. *Age,* 1982–83, detail. Clay, wood, and plaster; height: 10 ft., diameter: 30 ft. Temporary installation at the Solomon R. Guggenheim Museum, New York. Private collection.

56. Charles Simonds. *Head,* 1993. Clay and plaster, 26¹/₂ x 35³/₈ x 29¹/₂ in. Private collection.

57. Charles Simonds. *Growth House,* 1975. Ink on paper; 25 x 29¹/₂ in. Collection of the artist. This is a seasonably renewable dwelling. As the seeds sprout, growth transforms the built structure; the dwelling is transformed from shelter to food and harvested and eaten.

57

58. This is a general view of the Garden of
History at Pratt Farm, near Clinton, Maine,
which was begun by James Pierce in 1970. The
Turf Maze and its *Observatory* can be seen
in the foreground; *Earthwoman* appears in
the distance.

3. TRADITION AND ANTECEDENT

Art in the landscape encompasses multiple allusions, some of which have been touched upon already. The technological innocence shared by Simonds and some of his British and American contemporaries, together with an earnest longing for the kind of close accord with the natural world we assume to be characteristic of earlier peoples, provide a link to the culture of prehistory. This link is also asserted through the use of archaisms (as discussed in chapter 1): the solstitial alignments of both Holt's *Sun Tunnels* and Morris's *Observatory*, for example, or the mastaba shape of Heizer's *Complex One*. The significance of this correspondence with prehistoric art lies in its implied refutation of mainstream contemporary culture, with its emphasis on consumption and conformity to fashion. By reviving an anonymous tradition of earthworking as a form of artistic activity and by removing themselves to distant locations land artists hoped, however quixotically, to free themselves from these unpleasant associations. They were continuing a tendency in modern art identified by Robert Goldwater in 1938 as "Romantic Primitivism": the use of models from outside the tradition of Western European art, such as African or Oceanic sculpture, to reinvigorate the forms and purposes of the prevailing art.[48]

Goldwater also identified a concern for the purity of abstract form as an expression of "Intellectual Primitivism." Freed from realism's limitations of representation and narration, abstract works were felt by many in this century to be more capable of conveying to the viewer universal, basic, and eternal sensations. This was certainly true of several of the Abstract Expressionist painters. "Abstraction enables man to break the finite barrier and enter into the actuality of infinity," Arshile Gorky wrote.[49] And Barnett Newman asserted that Theodoros Stamos "reveals an attitude toward nature that is closer to true communion. . . . He redefines the pastoral experience

as one of participation with the inner life of the natural phenomenon. . . . In this Stamos is on the same fundamental ground as the primitive artist who never portrayed the phenomenon as an object of romance and sentiment, but always as an expression of the original noumenistic mystery in which rock and man are equal."[50] The abstract image — whether in primitive or modern art—was felt to present reality as known in the mind rather than merely perceived by the senses. It became a visible icon for the metaphysical. Adolph Gottlieb and Mark Rothko asserted that "the subject is crucial and only that subject matter is valid which is tragic and timeless. That is why we profess kinship with primitive and archaic art."[51] Their tragic and timeless subjects were also abstract.

In their use of reductive forms to convey metaphysical content, several of the land artists—Heizer and De Maria chief among them — share in this intellectual primitivism. But their work can also be interpreted as a contemporary expression of the sublime. Indeed, the evocations of this eighteenth-century aesthetic and philosophical attitude toward the landscape are no less pervasive than the allusions to prehistory; they are merely less frequently discussed. The sublime has figured in considerations of Abstract Expressionist painting,[52] but its applicability to land art is equally intriguing. The eighteenth century also produced an answer to the sublime in the theories of the picturesque, which were applied to painting and landscape design long before they were given extended written exposition. As suggested in the introduction, the picturesque literally transformed the British landscape and was conveyed to the United States most eloquently through the work of Olmsted and Vaux. It, too, continues to have a significant impact today.

Edmund Burke's *Philosophical Enquiry into the Origin of Our Ideas of the Sublime and Beautiful*, published in England in 1757, dif-

59

59, 60. Walter De Maria (b. 1935). *The Lightning Field*, 1974–77. Stainless steel poles; average height of poles: 20 ft. 7½ in.; overall dimensions: 5,280 x 3,300 ft. Near Quemado, New Mexico. Collection of the Dia Art Foundation.

ferentiated between two principal classes of objects and, by implication, of landscapes and vistas. Those that were smooth, gentle, and pleasing stimulated the instinct of self-propagation and were thus perceived as beautiful. Those that induced terror by a suggestion of solitude, vastness, or power touched the instinct of self-preservation and were perceived as sublime. Writing in 1927, the art historian Christopher Hussey attributed seven characteristics to the sublime, based on his reading of Burke: *obscurity*, both physical and intellectual; *power*; *privations*, such as darkness, solitude, and silence; *vastness*, either vertical or horizontal, both of which diminish the relative scale of the human observer; *infinity*, which could either be literal or induced by two final characteristics of the sublime: *succession* and *uniformity*, both of which suggest limitless progression.[53]

Hussey's seven attributes of the sublime provide a virtual prescription for Walter De Maria's *Lightning Field*, completed in 1977 near Quemado, New Mexico. De Maria's piece is composed of 400 stainless steel poles 2 inches in diameter, standing at an average height of 20 feet, 7½ inches, in such a way that all the tops are level. They are arranged in a grid with 16 rows of 25 poles stretching east to west and 25 rows of 16 poles stretching north to south. The poles are 225 feet apart, 311 on the diagonal, with the total east-west dimension of the piece running exactly one mile, the north-south distance just over a kilometer.

The Lightning Field stands in a flat, semi-arid basin in west-central New Mexico; the site is ringed by distant mountains. This is an area of seemingly limitless vistas and a numerically negligible human population. It is also a region with a relatively high incidence of lightning. For all these reasons, it was a location that particularly appealed to De Maria. He planned his work scrupulously to attract the lightning and thereby to celebrate its power and visual splendor. He wanted a place where one could be alone with a trackless earth and an overarching sky to witness their potent interchange through apparently wanton electrical discharge. The work is neither of the earth nor of the sky but is of both; it is the means to an epiphany for those viewers susceptible to an awesome natural phenomenon. Few leave *The Lightning Field* untouched by the splendid desolation of its setting and the majesty of its purpose.

But few are lucky enough actually to witness lightning discharging itself on De Maria's rods. For all other visitors, *The Lightning Field* has more subtle charms. It is a fugitive work, disappearing in the bright midday sun and becoming visible only at dawn and dusk when the entire length of each pole glows with reflected light. At all times the piece is an experience in the demarcation of space, referring through the use of the mile and the kilometer to the manner in which much of the earth has been divided and brought under human sovereignty. The grid form and the mile dimension in particular bring to mind the endless mile-square sections that form a checkerboard across the Midwest and West, which resulted from Jefferson's National Survey of 1785. Like De Maria's *Las Vegas Piece*, *The Lightning Field* is also an experience of the relatively insignificant physical scale of humans and their creations when contrasted to the vast basins and ranges that compose the geography of the American Southwest.

It is probable that De Maria intended to evoke the sublime; yet it seems unlikely that he was aware of how exactly he employed its attributes as defined by Hussey. His *Lightning Field* is *obscure*, both in the sense of being difficult to perceive — especially at midday — and in being remote and troublesome to reach. Its central image is *power* — the sometimes lethal power of lightning.

The *privations* of solitude and silence are integral to the experience of the work; it is *vast*, both in its own dimension and in the setting it employs. And everywhere is the inference of *infinity*. The poles stand in stately *succession*, *uniform* in height and in the distance between them. As they diminish in the distance, they create the illusion — like telephone poles or railroad tracks — of endless progression. This is reinforced by a tidy and clever mathematical sequence: the number of poles on the kilometer side is equivalent to four-squared; on the mile side five-squared; the total number of poles is twenty-squared. One can extrapolate an endless grid from this numerical formula. The infinite is also in evidence, if not in the horizontal spread of the earth, then in the extraterrestrial dominions to which the work emphatically points.

Other works compare to De Maria's in effect. The grand scale and emptiness of the Western landscape perhaps make an association with the sublime unavoidable for any art work created there. But the selection of sites often remote and uninhabited emphasizes its characteristics, as does the use of simple, commanding forms. By excavating a space for his *Double Negative*, Heizer literally wraps one in solitude. By focusing one's view through her *Sun Tunnels*, Holt emphasizes the discomfiture produced by a sense of great distance. And the projected works of Turrell and Ross both may have the result of underscoring the puniness and mortality of humanity in comparison with the infinite scale and duration of the heavens.

In his *Essay on the Picturesque* (1794), the Englishman Uvedale Price added a third category of objects—and landscapes—to Burke's beautiful and sublime ones. Price felt that the sublime and the beautiful failed to account for those things that were crude, rustic, and irregular, but visually engaging nevertheless. These he described as *picturesque*; literally, like a picture, especially those of Jan

van Goyen, Jacob van Ruisdael, Salvator Rosa, and Claude Lorrain. To Price, the landscape paintings of these men, with their sudden and extreme contrasts of light and dark, their intricate and irregular compositions and oftentimes rustic or humble subjects, represented just those qualities that were neither sublime nor beautiful, but found expression in the picturesque.

Another English essayist, Richard Payne Knight, simultaneously offered a competing view of the picturesque in *The Landscape: A Didactic Poem*, 1794; and *Analytical Inquiry into the Principles of Taste*, 1805. Although Knight agreed with Price that it was largely aesthetic or objective qualities that produced a picturesque effect, he suggested that there were nonaesthetic elements that contributed as well. These elements functioned psychologically, arousing multiple ideas and associations. This principle of association had its relevance to painting and landscape design alike. The appearance of a Gothic ruin, a Chinese temple, a Druidical stone circle, or even a hermit's cottage enhanced a picturesque effect by evoking the ancient, the unfamiliar, or the exotic.

While the principles of the picturesque were not codified until late in the eighteenth century, they had begun to find expression some eighty years before in early Georgian garden design. The visual values of complexity, irregularity, and concealment began to be favored over geometrical plans; while some formality remained, variety and a sensitivity to the vagaries of natural terrain became the mode of the day. Charles Bridgeman and William Kent were the most prominent practitioners of this new aesthetic in the first half of the century. Horace Walpole, Joseph Addison, and Alexander Pope were among those who provided the written foundations for the landscape attitudes that were later modified and elaborated into the picturesque by William Gilpin, Price, and Knight.[54]

61. Begun in the mid-eighteenth century by Henry Hoare, Stourhead is one of the best preserved of the picturesque landscape parks in Britain.

Bridgeman and Kent both worked at Stowe in Buckinghamshire, perhaps the most widely known of the early eighteenth-century landscaped parks; Pope created his own celebrated but long since destroyed garden at Twickenham.

But it was a banker and amateur gardener, Henry Hoare, who gave us what is one of the best preserved of the landscapes arranged in the picturesque manner. Begun at mid-century, 61 Stourhead includes both open meadows and dense groupings of trees, an irregularly shaped artificial lake, hills, fine prospects, and shadowed vales that obscure all views. A pathway meanders through the landscape, around the lake, past streams and cascades. Stourhead also incorporates associative elements, sometimes known as follies. These diverse structures — a stone grotto with statues of a river god and a nymph, Temples of Apollo and Flora, a rustic cottage and convent, a Pantheon, an obelisk — add to the visual variety of the park, and enhance the picturesque effect by evoking unfamiliar cultures or ancient civilizations.

The visual and psychological complexity thus achieved is underscored by a rich and apparently autobiographical iconographic program.[55] Over the entrance to the grotto is an inscription from Book I of the *Aeneid;* another from Book II is in the Temple of Flora. The circuit walk around the lake may have been intended as an allegory of Aeneas's travels, with particular reference to his descent into the underworld to see his father, which began at Lake Avernus. Hoare's only son had died in 1751, so he may have felt especially inspired to evoke this story of the reunion of father and son, above and beyond the then customary appreciation for classical literature.

The picturesque finds its strongest contemporary expression in the work of James Pierce at Pratt Farm on the Kennebec River in central Maine. Pierce combines the visual values of the picturesque with its associative or evocative elements. Over a period of a dozen years, on seventeen acres of meadow and woodland, he created a work he describes as a "garden of history," that is, a landscaped park containing numerous individual but interdependent elements rich with historical associations. He began in the summer of 1970 with the excavation of a still unfinished *Kiva*, based on the Indian ceremonial structures also evoked by Simonds. The next summer and every summer through 1982, Pierce added to his garden of history. First came a pair of forts and a burial mound. The *Triangular* and *Circular Redoubts* are made of 62 mounded turf and are similar to crude fortifications used in North America by the British and French in the eighteenth century; indeed, Pierce sometimes calls these the *British* and *French Redoubts* in observance of the fact that for a time the Kennebec marked the boundary between the colonial settlements of these two nations. The *Burial Mound,* like the *Kiva,* is modeled on Indian prototypes and is intended eventually to hold the remains of its creator.

Between 1972 and 1974, Pierce executed an unusual triangular *Turf Maze* some 120 58 feet on a side. Although based on the plan of a topiary maze published in the seventeenth century, it is formed of earth in the manner of late medieval models, like Richard Fleischner's contemporaneous *Sod Maze*. But unlike Fleischner's work, it is cut into the ground with raised pathways between the cuts, and the path to the center is not continuous, but confounding, marked by choices and dead ends. A small *Observatory* provides an overlook for the *Maze*. On a hill above it, Pierce built in 1975 a spiral hill, or *Motte,* eight feet high and twenty feet in diameter. Like the *Redoubts,* it brings to mind defensive structures, in this case the mounts that sometimes form the central keep in medieval castles.

62. James Pierce (b. 1930). *Triangular Redoubt*, 1971. Earth; height: 5 ft., length of each side: 65 ft. Pratt Farm.

63. James Pierce. *Stone Ship*, 1975. 40 ft. x 12 ft. *Burial Mound*, 1971. Earth; height: 4 ft., diameter: 4 ft. Pratt Farm.

64. James Pierce. *Altar*, 1977. Wood and rock; 7½ ft. x 23 in. x 12 in. Pratt Farm.

62
63

Several more burial monuments were added to Pratt Farm in the mid-1970s. Near the *Burial Mound*, Pierce arrayed a group of glacial boulders to suggest the partially disrupted outlines of a boat, which rises in profile toward the bow and stern. This *Stone Ship* alludes to Viking burial practices: the deceased were sometimes interred in their boats. At forty feet long and twelve feet wide, it is approximately the size of the precariously small Viking vessels that explored the northeast coast of North America a millennium ago. It is oriented to Polaris, in reference to both navigation and the voyage to the afterlife.

In a nearby grove of pine and birch trees, Pierce built another type of Scandinavian bronze-age tomb. This is the *Tree Burial*: a log large enough to contain a corpse that rests on a bed of glacial boulders. In an authentic burial, the log would have been hollowed out to contain the corpse. Near it is the *Shaman's Tomb*, a wooden coffin raised on four posts. It alludes to the belief among certain Siberian peoples that the soul of the deceased shaman was a bird that would return to the same family only if the body were left unburied.

Another piece of Central Asian inspiration stands in the woods near the *Tree Burial* and the *Shaman's Tomb*. This is a cruciform *Altar*, a single post and a crosspiece that supports two granite boulders. The iconography here is clearly Christian and amusingly sexual (as Pierce tells it, granite is igneous, a "hot rock"). But the altar also makes reference to the worship of stones among a Central Asian people, the Buriats, who, for the sake of agricultural fruitfulness, elevated on platforms certain stones that they believed had fallen from the sky.

The shift inaugurated by the *Altar* from mortuary to suggestively procreative works was continued in a group created between 1976 and 1978 in the central area of the gar-

64

den. Under a large white pine that Pierce has designated the Tree of Life, he set a wooden ithyphallic *Monk's Post*. Near it is the recumbent *Earthwoman*, inspired by the dorsal view of the prehistoric Venus of Willendorf in Vienna. Some thirty feet long, half as wide, and five feet high, she lies face down, spread-eagled. She is oriented to the sunrise on the summer solstice, in such a way that the sun rises through the cleft in her buttocks in a symbolic fertilization. On the opposite side of the *Monk's Post* from her lies, face up, the similarly spread-eagled *Suntreeman*. Like the Cerne Abbas Giant in Dorset, he has an erect phallus. His arms suggest tree branches, and his round head, which doubles as a fire pit, alludes to the sun.

In 1979 Pierce coiled a *Stone Serpent* some eighty feet in length along the edge of the woods near the *Earthwoman*. At the same time, he continued with a number of earthen pieces. One was cut into the ground like the *Maze*: a schematic representation of a boat called the *Quebec Expedition*, commemorating Benedict Arnold's arduous passage in the autumn of 1775 up the Kennebec, past the site of Pratt Farm, on the way to his unsuccessful siege of British-held Quebec City. Another, the *Erechwagon*, was mounded like the *Sun-*

63

64

65–67

68

69

65

66

65. James Pierce. *Earthwoman*, 1976–77. Earth; 5 x 30 x 15 ft. View with a long grass coat. Pratt Farm.

66. James Pierce. *Earthwoman*, view at sunset.

67. James Pierce. *Earthwoman*, sunrise on the summer solstice.

67

68. James Pierce. *Suntreeman,* 1978. Earth
and rock; 2 x 50 x 45 ft. Pratt Farm.

69. James Pierce. *Stone Serpent,* 1979. rock;
1 x 80 x 55 ft. Pratt Farm.

treeman and is based on the first known representation of a wheeled vehicle, found on a tablet about 5,500 years old at Erech, in present-day Iraq. The third is a four-faced Janus figure, a pyramidal mound with a profiled nose at each corner and eyes formed of ceramic pipes. Through one of the eyes of this *Janus*, symbol of ending and beginning, is visible the *Kiva*, the first work in Pierce's garden of history and the source of the earth for the *Janus*.

In no instance is any of these various works a direct copy of its prototype. Some, like the *Shaman's Tomb* or the *Stone Ship*, are free adaptations from a specific source. In others, the *Suntreeman* for example, there is no clear precedent at all but an inventive use of historically suggestive forms instead. These are not reproductions but evocations, consistent with the eighteenth-century picturesque use of associative elements. Like the Temple of Apollo or the grotto at Stourhead, Pierce's works are allusions to exotic cultures, prehistoric monuments, or partially forgotten episodes in the history of our own nation. They have a rich visual and psychological character, summoning recall of the indistinctly known past.

Pierce's historical forms are arrayed in a landscape that is itself picturesque. Open meadows contrast with dense stands of evergreen and birch, which meet the meadows in a serpentine line. At the bottom of a slope, the Kennebec pursues its meandering

68

69

course; the view of the opposite bank is dominated by a chapel spire. A series of alignments draws the works together, as between the *Kiva* and the *Janus*; the *Motte*, the *Observatory*, and the apex of the *Earthwoman* form an alignment with the chapel across the Kennebec. Picturesque vistas are also employed: breaks in the trees frame certain of the works, while paths through the woods grant telescopic views of others.

The kind of programmatic unity that has been detected at Stourhead is also evident at Pratt Farm. Pierce's work began with a series of forts and burial monuments, making his garden a mock necropolis. In the midst of these came the *Turf Maze*, representative of passage and choice and psychologically a more neutral work. The more recent pieces are dominated by images of fertility and procreation and, with the *Janus* figure, of ending and beginning anew. Pierce's garden of history is thus also a garden of life, death, and regeneration.

Other thematic interpretations are possible. Pierce works only with materials found at the site: soil, glacial boulders, deposits of sand and clay, and driftwood from the Kennebec. His is thus also a garden of natural history. And with his deliberate evocation of previous landscaped parks, it is even a garden of the

history of gardens of history. Individual works carry multiple meanings as well. The *Turf Maze* is an allegory of choice; in one's journey into and out from it, it is also an allegory of insemination and birth. The *Altar* is a cross; it is an erect phallus. The *Suntreeman* combines images of male potency with botanical growth; it can also be seen as a male Daphne transforming himself into a tree to elude the ravishments of some female Apollo. The white pine that dominates the center of the garden is the tree of life in the procreative group that includes the *Suntreeman* and the *Earthwoman*; it becomes the tree of knowledge when the same works are interpreted as Adam and Eve with the *Stone Serpent*.

"Modern sculpture is *wilfully* ignorant," the Scotsman Ian Hamilton Finlay has declared.[56] One suspects that few of the artists in this volume would escape his opprobrium, with the possible exception of Pierce. For Pierce is Finlay's only rival in a deliberately wide-ranging deployment of historical references in the full knowledge of their aesthetic, moral, and political implications. If Pierce is distinguished as a sculptor, landscapist, and historian, then Finlay is all of these and aesthetic philosopher and botanist as well. Beside his ecumenical knowledge, most other artists must seem myopic at the least.

70

71

72

70. Ian Hamilton Finlay (b. 1925). *The Great Piece of Turf*, at Stonypath, begun 1967. Stone: 5 x 5 in., overall dimensions: 5 x 2 ft. Lanarks, Scotland.

71. Ian Hamilton Finlay. The main path in the front garden, Stonypath.

72. Ian Hamilton Finlay. *Wood Wind Song*. Slate stele in a grove of pines. Stonypath.

73. Ian Hamilton Finlay (with John Andrew). *Nuclear Sail*, c. 1973. Slate; height: 5 ft. Stonypath.

73

Even the most cursory exposure to Finlay's garden, Stonypath, in Lanarkshire in the southern regions of Scotland, suggests a veneration of the picturesque. Into a mere few acres is condensed a rich array of botanical specimens, sculpture, and poetic inscriptions. Finlay's garden is visually complex, incorporating ponds and streams and contrasting dense plantings with open grassy areas, the cultivated with the wild. Yet he does not aim for the appearance of nature untouched, which was the highest goal of the best known of the eighteenth-century landscape designers, Capability Brown. Instead, he aspires to an image of nature improved upon by the intellect. He writes that his garden "suggests the Neoplatonic idea of improved or Ideal Nature, as opposed to the modern view, which is of 'nature' itself as being the ideal (and more ideal the more it is untouched by the human intellect)."[57] In this he reveals a closer link to Nicolas Poussin, who organized his landscapes with precision and clarity to present nature as if it were perfect. Indeed, Finlay titled one of the exhibitions of his garden work *Nature Over Again After Poussin*,[58] an obvious play on Cézanne's avowal to do "Poussin over again after nature," but also and more importantly an exposition of the intellectual foundations for his work.

Finlay professes a kinship as well with the Neoclassicism of Jacques Louis David (himself a neo-Poussinist), with its deft combination of aesthetic and political content, and with the revolutionary ideology of David's contemporaries. As Neoclassicism was an assault on the corrupt and outmoded values of an absolutist regime, so is it Finlay's inspiration for his emphatic critique of the intellectual bankruptcy of contemporary culture. And as it was a recall of a presumably more learned age, so is it Finlay's means of entreaty for a more multidimensional world, for an end to what one of Finlay's principal en-

thusiasts has called "the vulgar disjunction of traditional culture and contemporary art."[59] "Tradition is not dead," Finlay writes, "it has never been heard of." Finlay quotes one of his heroes, the French revolutionary Louis Antoine Léon de Saint-Just: "the world has been empty since the Romans." One suspects that to Finlay, the world has likewise been empty since the philosopher-statesmen of the French Revolution dominated the politics and culture of their brief era. Finlay links Saint-Just with the notions of Jean Jacques Rousseau (another of his heroes) on the moral superiority of "natural man," describing Saint-Just's political philosophy as a "pastoral of politics (a vision of politics as a kind of neoclassical pastoral, with Rousseau as its Virgil)." And Finlay thinks of his garden, like David's paintings of Socrates and Marat, as being an act or deed, an assertion of moral and political principle.

If Neoclassicism provides the major part of Finlay's philosophical program, it is not the only source of his references. In his single-minded effort to keep alive as much as any one person can of the rich history of landscape painting and design, he draws on Claude Lorrain as much as Poussin; on Italian Renaissance and Roman villas; on Albrecht Dürer and Jean Baptiste Corot; on William Shenstone's garden, the Leasowes, and the Marquis de Girardin's garden at Ermenonville, which for a time was home to the beleaguered Rousseau and also for a time the place of his entombment. In so doing, Finlay has created not simply a landscape, but a tribute to art. He is reluctant, however, to have his garden identified as his only or even his principal activity. He wrote metrical poetry, short stories, and plays in the 1950s; in the 1960s he became involved with the concrete poetry movement which, with an extreme economy of language, substituted for metrical sequences of words the virtually solitary word as emblem and graphic image, replacing rhythm

74. Ian Hamilton Finlay (with John Andrew), *See Poussin/Hear Lorrain.* Stone. Stonypath.

74

with stasis. (This influence remains important in Finlay's garden work to this day.) Since his move to Stonypath in the winter of 1966–67, he has continued to publish books, prints, and pamphlets, as well as having his sculptural works realized elsewhere, chiefly at the Kröller-Müller Museum in the Netherlands and the Max Planck Institute in Stuttgart.

Finlay's work at Stonypath was realized with the collaboration of his wife, Sue. When they began in 1967, Stonypath was little more than a collection of rough domestic and agricultural buildings surrounded by about four acres of moorland. Piece by piece and without a complete overall scheme, the Finlays began re-forming the site: transplanting trees and shrubs, damming and diverting streams to form ponds, moving earth and laying stones, and adding a variety of botanical specimens. This all transpired rather slowly, due as much to the Finlays' limited financial resources as to the pace of gardening activities. By now, the garden has matured considerably and contains several distinct sections: a front garden before the cottage; a courtyard garden with a small pond behind it in a space bordered by the old farm buildings (one of which has been converted into a garden temple); and a less intensively cultivated area beyond, with two more small ponds (upper and middle) and a larger one (Lochan Eck) leading into the moorland.[60]

Throughout this richly developed landscape, Finlay has arrayed his sculptural and poetic objects. Often made with the collaboration of various craftsmen, these have both a visual function, unifying the various parts of the garden, and a psychological one (like Pierce's works), arousing a variety of associations. The objects provide both visual and thematic unity. "Modern all-plant gardens are wholly lacking in harmony," Finlay asserts; "the entire Notion — in Hegel's word — is absent." Finlay's inscribed works are Neoplatonic emblems that can be "a) looked at, b) read, c) ignored, d) read and meditated upon. Each, as one pleases, on the day." Thus something that can be used to provoke associations can also be appreciated solely for its visual character. Finlay underscores these multiple functions by saying, "All these works are works in themselves, as well as references, and (importantly) elements in larger compositions which include the plants."

Only a few of these works can be described here. In the front garden, a path formed of 71 diamond-shaped concrete slabs leads between borders of flowers and shrubs. On these slabs are engraved the names of different types of vessels — brig, keel, schooner, ketch — in one of Finlay's many references to the sea. Also in the front garden is a slate stele, *Wood Wind Song,* bearing three 72 different sequences of these three words. It stands in a grove of pines "which do indeed 'sing' with the wind which so often blows

75

here." Nearby, a large tree bears a plaque that reads *Mare Nostrum*, the Roman name for the Mediterranean and a tribute to this tree that is a source of sea sounds in Finlay's inland garden.

In one corner is an area that Finlay calls the *Roman Garden*: separated by cypresses from the rest of the front garden, it contains an homage to the Villa d'Este in the stone form of a modern warship, which alludes to the use of carved galleys as decoration in Roman gardens and to their subsequent reappearance in the Renaissance, as at the Villa d'Este at Tivoli. In the courtyard garden this analogy is continued with an aircraft-carrier fountain: a bronze warship spouts water, like the stone ships that are used to the same purpose on the terrace of the One Hundred Fountains at the Villa d'Este. In the courtyard pond is a miniature landscape of marsh grasses and flowers, "signed" with a stone bearing Dürer's monogram and having the title *The Great Piece of Turf*. This is a living evocation of Dürer's watercolor of the same name (*Das Grosse Rasenstuck*), and a remark-

able composition in its own right.

This tribute — elegy, even — to Dürer has numerous parallels elsewhere in the garden. By the upper pond, overlooking a landscape of water and grasses and undulating hills, lies a stone bearing the inscription "See Poussin/ Hear Lorrain." This is an invitation to meditate upon the landscape as it might have been depicted in the clearly ordered compositions of the former, or the more atmospheric, lyrical ones of the latter. Elsewhere, Finlay has placed a column base bearing the name of Rousseau at the bottom of a tree. The tree thereby becomes a living column, the whole a classicist tribute. A similar conceit lies behind the piece *Five Columns for the Kröller-Müller*. There, a narrow path leads into a "secret garden" in a grove enclosed by rhododendrons, where five such column bases are placed against the trees. Each base is inscribed with a name: Corot, Lycurgus, Michelet, Robespierre, and Rousseau. The elegiac character of these works is reminiscent of elements in the now largely lost garden of the poet Shenstone. Along the winding walk that circled his ornamented farm, Shenstone placed urns and seats dedicated to his friends, living and dead. He inscribed other seats with lines from Virgil and built a roothouse dedicated to a neighbor. There was a grove of trees also named for Virgil, and a grotto with a Latin inscription that evoked the Nereids. Even Shenstone's *Unconnected Thoughts on Gardening* (1764) finds an echo in Finlay's *Unconnected Sentences on Gardening* (see page 133), though Shenstone was different in stressing the supremacy of nature over art.

Fewer of Finlay's works are found by Lochan Eck, which lies the greatest distance from the house. On its shore, however, stands the unsettling *Nuclear Sail*. As Finlay explains this title, "Sailors call submarine conning towers 'sails,' and nuclear-powered subs 'Nuclear Sails.' " While Finlay's various aircraft-carrier sculptures utilize military imagery, this has a far more realistic scale and something of a malevolent character. In evoking terror and thereby triggering the instinct of self-preservation, this work adds an element of the sublime to the garden. It also provides an ironic comparison to the organic abstractions of Henry Moore, which are likewise often seen in the landscape.

"Certain gardens are described as retreats when they are really attacks,"[61] Finlay has written. Recently, his war on contemporary culture has taken a more literal turn. In 1978 the Strathclyde Regional Council withdrew discretionary rates relief on his garden temple. They claimed that only nonprofit art "galleries" are eligible for tax exemption; they insisted they had no category for art "temples" and his was thus subject to taxation. Finlay has refused to pay the rates, asserting that, like the garden, the temple has both artistic and spiritual purposes, despite the fact that its description confounds the Council. The temple is dedicated to Apollo and contains three chambers: one displays Finlay's

73

76

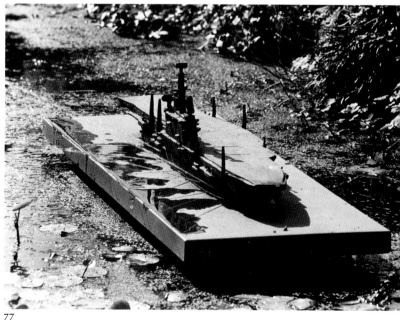

77

sculptural objects and publications; a second, a kind of indoor "sacred grove," permits a view out into the garden; and a third, inner chamber, lit only by candles, is a meditative space that suggests a cella.

To enforce their rates assessment, the Council sent a sheriff's officer to seize works of art for a warrant sale. On his first visit, the officer's car was barricaded in a "tank trap," and he retreated over the moors on foot. When he returned later in the day with the police to retrieve his vehicle, an imitation Panzer Mk IV erupted in a ball of fire and black smoke. He finally gained access to the garden temple, only to discover that the art works intended for seizure had been removed and hidden by Finlay's "Saint-Just Vigilantes." Video and still cameras recorded the action, while Scottish radio ran a live commentary on what Finlay now calls "The First Battle of Little Sparta (4 February 1983)."

Finlay's forces were less successful a month later when the sheriff's officer returned to take sculpture valued at 5,000 pounds, which was consigned to Christie's for sale. While Finlay and his supporters displayed considerable resourcefulness and not a little humor in these proceedings, one wonders how long he can hold out, physically and financially, in the face of bureaucratic hostility. The continued existence of environmental art works such as Finlay's is always a matter of great uncertainty. As a shrine to the intellect and the imagination, his garden seems particularly worthy of official sufferance, if not support.

It is a signal feature of recent art works in the landscape that their content is inclusive rather than exclusive, that they evoke history and memory as well as stimulating the eye. One might argue that Pierce and Finlay are no different from other land artists in this respect, and that their utilization of historically suggestive forms is no different from the archaisms of Holt or Morris or Heizer. But prehistory is only one small part of our past:

Pierce and Finlay are more far-reaching and even literate in their references. The use of history as an inspiration for contemporary art is more fashionable now than it was when Pierce and Finlay began their work in the late 1960s and early '70s. Yet prescience is the least compelling of their accomplishments. More than most other artists in the landscape, they demonstrate a complete grasp of the importance of appropriating and renewing the full richness of our cultural inheritance

If there are numerous historic and prehistoric sources for contemporary art in the landscape, there are also several distinguished twentieth-century antecedents. One of these is the remarkable sculptural environment created by Constantin Brancusi in the Romanian town of Tîrgu-Jiu, about 150 miles northwest of Bucharest. Brancusi (1876–1957) had lived in the town for a short time as a youth and was called back to create a memorial to local resistance to the Germans in the First World War. Brancusi accepted the commission in February of 1935 and made several visits to Tîrgu-Jiu from his home in Paris before his work was dedicated in 1938.

Brancusi's memorial consists of three major works and some lesser ones organized along an east-west axis running about three-quarters of a mile through the town. It begins in a park along the Jiu river with the *Table of Silence*, a circular stone slab about seven feet in diameter and thirty-one inches high, surrounded by twelve stools, each of which has a round top and the shape of an hourglass. From there, a walk leads past square stools and benches, also designed by Brancusi, to the *Gate of the Kiss*. This is an architectural elaboration of one of Brancusi's principal themes, which reaches back to 1908; it takes the form of a triumphal arch over seventeen feet high and twenty-one feet wide. It was carved in local travertine marble by an assistant under Brancusi's supervision. The lintel is inscribed with pairs of intertwined lovers, sixteen pairs on the front and back and four on each side, in a graphic shorthand variation on Brancusi's sculptural versions of the embrace. Each side of the supporting columns is divided vertically and carries near the top a large circular image that is an abstracted representation of the merged eyes of the lovers, but also an image of cell division as well as of male and female genitalia in sexual congress. Brancusi's triumphal arch thus suggests a dedication to the redemptive and procreative powers of love.[62]

From the *Gate of the Kiss,* a street was opened across town to the *Endless Column.* Named the Way of the Heroes, this street is bisected by the Church of the Holy Apostles and terminates at an open rectangle in which is centered the *Endless Column.* This is likewise a monumental adaptation of an earlier theme. It soars to over ninety-six feet in height and was made of iron cast from a wooden module, with the parts threaded over an internal steel post. Like an obelisk, it is at once an expression of aspiration and achievement; with its undulating surface, it draws the eye resolutely upward, like the spiraling frieze on Trajan's Column.

Research on Brancusi published in Romania confirms that he worked on the settings for all three of these sculptures.[63] He organized pathways and vistas, and arranged the seating. He specified the plantings of poplar and alder along the river near the *Table of Silence.* He dictated the length of the Way of the Heroes, seeing it as a metaphor for struggle: "The way of the heroes is always hard and long," he remarked.[64] A photograph of the site for the *Endless Column* reveals Brancusi's original thoughts for this work: on the photograph Brancusi has drawn his column surrounded by radiating pathways and groups of trees. "A monument depends on the precise place you choose for it, on the way the sun rises and sets upon it, on its surroundings," he wrote.[65]

Brancusi's project in Tirgu-Jiu must surely be the most enigmatic of his works. In the West, it is undoubtedly the least known and discussed of the accomplishments of this widely celebrated artist. This is in some measure a reflection of Tirgu-Jiu's remoteness from most observers. Yet it seems also an expression of the project's paradoxical relationship to the rest of Brancusi's œuvre: these are late works drawn from early themes; environmental works from an artist whose other sculptures appear so self-contained and unitary. Yet to Brancusi, the project represented a summing up. When he accepted the commission, he wrote, "Now all things begun long ago come to a close, and I feel like an apprentice on the eve of getting his working papers. So the proposal could not come at a better time."[66] Certainly the *Gate of the Kiss* and the *Endless Column* represent a kind of climax in Brancusi's work on these particular themes. But the quasi-functional and environmental character of the works at Tirgu-Jiu are likewise the fulfillment of previous ideas.

Brancusi's studio had long contained architectural works: beams and archways, capitals and columns. As early as 1916 Brancusi executed a column bearing a version of the kiss motif. The Japanese-American sculptor Isamu Noguchi, who worked as Brancusi's studio assistant in 1927 while in Paris on a Guggenheim Fellowship, recalled seeing many of these works at the time and has testified to Brancusi's enthusiasm and talent for architectural sculpture. "What a pity," Noguchi remarked, "that he who had the greatest gift for architecture could not have found outlets other than the beautiful memorial in Romania."[67] Brancusi had likewise created sculpture based on functional forms. His wooden cups in particular seem a precedent for the utilitarian character of the *Table of Silence* and its surrounding stools. In addition, the careful creation of bases for his sculptures reveals that, to Brancusi, these objects were

80

intended to be seen as part of larger ensembles, in which all the parts were interdependent. Indeed, Brancusi created a whole environment of sculpture in his studio, which was preserved after his death and is now at the Musée National d'Art Moderne in Paris. From this environment of sculpture to the sculptural environment of Tirgu-Jiu is perhaps not such a large step.

Given that Brancusi's work in Romania is not directly known to many contemporary artists, it is difficult to assess precisely its influence on recent landscape art. However, certain of Brancusi's sympathies were transmitted to the United States through Noguchi. He recalled Brancusi's emphasis on the perfection of form and surface, and on the appropriate use of tools. He also found in Brancusi's attitude toward nature something that was comparable to the Japanese: "Brancusi, like the Japanese, would take the quintessence of nature and distill it."[68] To Noguchi, Brancusi's work was never far from its cultural roots. When Brancusi came to Paris, Noguchi remarked: "He brought with him something more than learning: the memory of childhood, of things observed not taught, of closeness to the earth, of wet stones and grass, of stone buildings and wood churches, handhewn logs and tools, stone markers, walls, and gravestones. This is the inheritance he was able to call upon when the notion came to him that his art, sculpture, could not go forward to be born without first going back to beginnings."[69] These observations on Brancusi's sensitivity to his home environment, its landscape and vernacular traditions, are useful in any attempt to appreciate the success of his work at Tirgu-Jiu; they serve equally as a reflection of Noguchi's own aesthetic philosophy.

Noguchi first saw Brancusi's work at an exhibition in New York in 1926, and he continued to visit periodically with the elder sculptor until Brancusi died in 1957. But while Brancusi provides a distinguished precedent for Noguchi's ideas on sculpture and its environmental applications, he was not Noguchi's sole or even primary source. "I am a student of the use of sculpture in the past," Noguchi said. "Most of it is related to the use of architecture, from Michelangelo to the Greeks and the Egyptians. This was nothing special to Brancusi. It was just that he was aware of it, while perhaps some contemporary sculptors are not." Even before his time with Brancusi, Noguchi was demonstrating an independent view of sculpture, in which nature was paramount. He wrote in his Guggenheim application in 1926, "It is my desire to view nature through nature's eyes, and to ignore man as an object for special veneration. There must be unthought of heights of beauty to which sculpture may be raised by this reversal of attitude."[70] He sought, as he later told it, "a larger, more fundamentally sculptural purpose for sculpture, a more direct expression of Man's relation to the earth and to his environment."[71]

These convictions were strengthened by several experiences. Born in Los Angeles in 1904, Noguchi had lived in Japan from age two to thirteen. In 1931 he returned there for the first time since his youth. He discovered on that visit the inexpressibly beautiful temple gardens, with their compositions of rock and sand, moss and shrubbery, water and trees. These were to continue to have a profound influence on him. Noguchi made a more extensive world tour nearly twenty years later on a grant from the Bollingen Foundation, which he received in 1949 for the purpose of studying sculpture — primarily ancient — in its relation to its setting. In a two-year period, he visited Neolithic sites in Brittany; Greece; Egypt; and the Observatories of the Maharajah Sawai Jai Singh II, the great sculptural toys built during the early eighteenth century in Jaipur.

Noguchi began making proposals for envi-

78. Constantin Brancusi (1876–1957). *Gate of the Kiss*. Travertine; height: 17¼ ft., width: 21½ ft. Part of the monumental ensemble of sculpture at Tîrgu-Jiu, Romania, executed between 1935 and 1938.

79. Constantin Brancusi. *Table of Silence*. Travertine; height: 31½ in., diameter: 7 ft. Tîrgu-Jiu.

80. Constantin Brancusi. *Endless Column*. Cast iron; height: 96¼ ft. Tîrgu-Jiu.

78

79

80

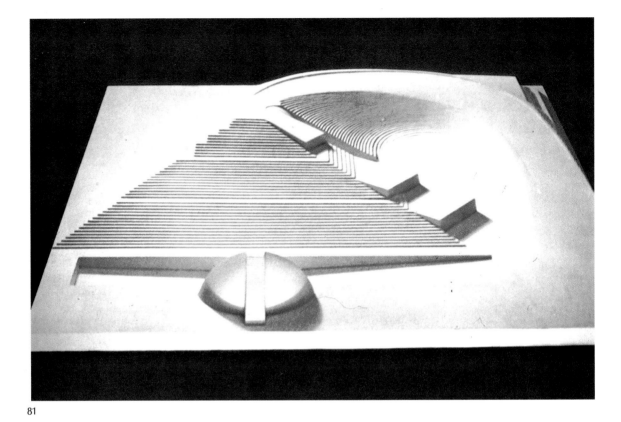

81

ronmental works as early as 1933. A model
81 from that year represents a *Play Mountain,*
conceived as a park and playground. The
same year he proposed a *Monument to the
Plough,* a vast earthen pyramid a mile on each
side, designed for a site in the Great Plains.
It was to be composed of furrowed earth
and surmounted with an enormous stainless
steel plow. "The model indicated my wish to
belong to America, to its vast horizons of
earth," Noguchi explained.[72] It was his tribute
to the vast spaces and pioneer spirit of the
West. Though echoes of the past are evident
in these works, one cannot discount a certain amount of social motivation. They were
offered in the midst of the Depression, when
the social promise of modernist architecture
was likewise most pronounced. Noguchi
continued to press unsuccessfully for parks
and playgrounds, particularly for New York
City, well into the 1960s, continuing his efforts at the artistic amelioration of the urban
environment.

It was in the 1950s, outside of America,
that Noguchi finally saw some of his proposals realized. He was commissioned to design
two bridges for Hiroshima in 1951 as part of
the reconstruction of that devastated city. Between 1956 and 1958 came his remarkable
82 garden for the UNESCO building in Paris,

which was designed by Marcel Breuer. Noguchi's garden is in two parts: an upper stone
terrace with square seats and carved boulders, and a lower area with mounded plantings, pools, paved and grassy areas. There are
distinctly Japanese elements in this garden:
natural stones set in raked gravel, for example, or stepping stones placed in the water.
Some of the rocks, in fact, were brought from
Japan. In consequence, some writers have
compared this composition to the temple gardens at Roanji, in Kyoto, Japan.[73]

This analogy, however, better fits a sunken
garden executed on the Chase Manhattan   83
Bank Plaza in New York City between 1961
and 1964. The landscape at Roanji is best
known for an enclosed "dry stone" garden
built in the late fifteenth century. Fifteen stones
in five unequal groups are arranged asymmet-
rically in a bed of raked gravel. No plants are
included in this walled garden except a little
moss that grows around the base of the rocks.
This is a meditative space, in which the simple stones are emblems of the larger world of
nature and the spirit, an idea that finds its
Western equivalent in William Blake's *Auguries
of Innocence:* "To see a world in a grain of
sand/And heaven in a wild flower/Hold infinity in the palm of your hand/And eternity
in an hour."

81. Isamu Noguchi (1904–1988). *Model for
"Play Mountain,"* 1933. Plaster, 4 $\frac{1}{2}$ x 29 $\frac{1}{4}$ x
25 $\frac{1}{4}$ in. Location unknown.

82. Isamu Noguchi. UNESCO gardens,
1956–58. Granite, grass, and foliage.
UNESCO Building, Paris.

83

83. Isamu Noguchi. *Chase Manhattan Bank Plaza Garden*, 1961–64. Black river stone, granite paving. New York.

84. Isamu Noguchi. *Marble Garden*, 1960–64. Marble. Beinecke Rare Book and Manuscript Library, Yale University, New Haven, Connecticut.

84

85. Herbert Bayer (b. 1900). *Earth Mound*, 1955. Earth; diameter: 40 ft. Aspen Institute for Humanistic Studies, Aspen, Colorado.

Noguchi's garden for the Chase Manhattan Plaza is likewise extremely economical in its forms. A few wildly eroded boulders scattered in a seemingly random pattern serve, as at Roanji, as the principal component of the composition. Concentric circles of granite paving stones replace the raked gravel of the earlier Japanese garden as the setting for the stones; these circles are interrupted by serpentine lines that add a suggestion of waves to the composition. This reference is strengthened in the summer months when the garden is flooded with a shallow layer of water, which spouts from two concentric rings of low jets. The boulders, brought from Japan, likewise carry a reference to water: their contorted shapes are the result of river erosion.

This garden was but one among many of Noguchi's projects that came to fruition in the middle years of the 1960s. Having waited so long to see more than the very occasional execution of his proposals for large-scale environmental works, Noguchi now began a period of enormous productivity. For the Beinecke Library at Yale University — a simple cube with a skin of translucent white marble designed by Gordon Bunshaft of Skidmore, Owings and Merrill — he created a beautifully consonant sunken plaza of white marble with a simple pyramid, a carved ring, and a cube perched on one point, all rising from the flat paving stones. For the IBM Corporation in Armonk, New York, Noguchi designed two gardens: one, representing the past, is a design of rough boulders among trees and grass; the other, representing the future, contains a pyramid of Brazilian granite, a black concrete dome inscribed with notations pertaining to nuclear physics and astronomy, an adjacent concavity of red concrete that serves as a fountain, and a bronze sculpture based loosely on the double helix form of the DNA molecule. And for the Israel Museum in Jerusalem, Noguchi designed a sculpture garden that includes both great undulating plazas contained by curved and sloping walls of stone rubble, and more intimate spaces for smaller sculptures framed by rectangular and circular concrete walls. Noguchi continued this remarkable level of productivity until his death and entered unreservedly into the discourse on the public purposes of art in the landscape, which will receive discussion in the following chapter.

Another artist of Noguchi's generation, Herbert Bayer, also executed environmental works that anticipate the recent effusion. The Austrian-born Bayer, who taught at the Bauhaus for several years in the late 1920s, emigrated from Berlin to New York in 1938, and moved to Aspen in 1946. There he worked as an architect and designer for the Aspen Development Corporation, participating in the planning for the Aspen Institute for Humanistic Studies. In 1955, on the grounds of Aspen Meadows, where guest housing for the Institute is located, Bayer created two environmental works. One is a *Marble Garden*, a composition of rough-hewn geometric elements freely placed around a square pool and fountain. The other, to contrast with it, is an *Earth Mound*. The *Marble Garden* takes the form of a predominantly vertical monument, while the *Earth Mound*, horizontal, forms a kind of enclosed precinct. The latter is forty feet in diameter and surrounds a low mound, a shallow conical depression, and a solitary standing stone. The references to Japanese gardens are apparent here, although particularly American forms such as corrals and Indian mounds have also been noted as sources.[74] That this work in turn provided some encouragement for younger artists is suggested by the fact that in 1968 its photograph was included along with the work of Heizer and Smithson in the Dwan Gallery *Earthworks* exhibition. Like Noguchi, Bayer was to continue to be of considerable significance in the development of the artistically improved public landscape.

86. Harvey Fite (1903–1976). *Opus 40*, 1939–76
(unfinished). Bluestone; 6.5 acres. Saugerties,
New York.

4. BEYOND EARTHWORKS: THE PUBLIC LANDSCAPE

Smithson was quick to recognize the limitations of the picturesque, at least in its more arcadian manifestations. He wrote in 1968: "The 'pastoral,' it seems, is outmoded. The gardens of history are being replaced by sites of time. Memory traces of tranquil gardens as 'ideal nature' — jejune Edens that suggest an idea of banal 'quality' — persist in popular magazines. . . . Could one say that art degenerates as it approaches gardening?" Continuing in a footnote, he asserted: "The abysmal problem of gardens somehow involves a fall from somewhere or something. The certainty of the absolute garden will never be regained."[75] Implicit here is Smithson's preference for landscapes that reveal the passage of time through successive episodes of human and natural upheavals, over those that conform to a preconceived notion of perfection. To Smithson, his preference was at once more appropriate and realistic. We have fallen from grace with the landscape, he implied. We have disrupted and degraded it. It is without the large unsullied vistas on which the picturesque depends. In such a time and such a landscape, Smithson asserted, the creation of artificial Edens is at best problematic, at worst a sham.

The picturesque encompasses far more than the pastoral; one of its many variants, most closely associated with the paintings of Salvator Rosa, shares in Smithson's infatuation with change, disorder, and decay. Yet in its most commonly understood form, the picturesque was no longer valid for Smithson. His aesthetic might instead be termed post-industrial: he accepted human disruption of the landscape and celebrated its renewal through reclamation works such as his own. Although one might quarrel with his complete repudiation of the picturesque — indeed, this survey provides ample evidence of its continued vitality — one must applaud his willingness to confront, even embrace, the problems of the contemporary landscape. In his own way, Smithson provided a parallel to Noguchi's persistent efforts to bring additional parks and playgrounds to New York and other cities. The work of both artists affirms the socially beneficial aspects of landscape art, revealing an ever growing conviction that artists should be involved in the aesthetic decisions that are routinely made as a part of land use and urban planning, as well as land reclamation. This conviction has dominated much recent art in the landscape, inspiring numerous projects to reclaim industrial sites and renew urban spaces. Many of these efforts have been accomplished with partial government sponsorship, as was the case with Morris's *Grand Rapids Project*.

It would be misleading to say that the notion of art as land reclamation was solely the invention of Smithson and other avant-garde artists of his generation. Three decades before, a sculptor named Harvey Fite had unintentionally embarked on a project of a similar nature. In the late 1930s, Fite bought a deserted bluestone quarry in the Catskill Mountains of southern New York. It had been used as a source of building material and curbstones for New York City until it was abandoned at the turn of the century. Fite originally intended to utilize the quarry as a source of material for his representational carvings and as a place to exhibit them when complete. He began his work by building a stone ramp into the quarry, providing himself with access. Piles of unmarketable stone left behind by the nineteenth-century quarrymen were leveled, curving ramps and terraces were added until finally Fite's ambition for the quarry outgrew his original functional intentions.

Unlike Smithson or Morris, Fite worked virtually alone on his project, and used no heavy equipment — only the conventional stonemason's tools. As a consequence, his labor was prolonged. He cut each stone into a rectangular shape and placed stone upon stone

86, 87

89

87

with the short side forming the face of the walls. No mortar was used to secure them. Various natural features of the site were incorporated into the work: exposed bedrock was left uncovered, existing trees were kept in place, and groundwater that seeped through the rock was used to form pools at the lowest levels of the quarry. In the mid-1960s, a bluestone monolith was raised over the accretion of dry stone forms, giving a focal point to the serpentine forms. But even then, the work was not finished. Fite had worked some thirty-seven years on the 6.5 acre project by the time of his death in 1976 and had christened it *Opus 40*, anticipating that it would take four decades to complete.

Fite was without peers at the outset of his effort. His exemplars seem to have been the massive stone structures of the ancients, especially the Mayans, the Incas, and the Aztecs; he spent a year in Honduras restoring Mayan stone work in 1938, and in 1956 he went to Cambodia on a study grant from the Asia Foundation. But in the years since Smithson, Morris, and Fite first explored the utilization of art in land reclamation, the idea has attracted considerable support. The efforts of many individuals, artists and community leaders alike, coalesced in the summer of 1979 in a remarkable project in and around

Seattle, Washington, which went under the title *Earthworks: Land Reclamation as Sculpture*. Organized by the King County Arts Commission, the project was multifaceted. Seven artists were invited to propose art works for disused or abused sites in the Seattle-King County area.[76] The sites included a landfill, an eroded creek bed, three gravel pits, an abandoned naval air station, and a noise-control free zone surrounding the Seattle-Tacoma airport. The designs for all these proposals were exhibited for six weeks from August 17, 1979, at the Modern Art Pavilion of the Seattle Art Museum; during the same time, the Arts Commission hosted a symposium to discuss in detail the implications of the project.

As a practical demonstration, Robert Morris was selected to implement a proposal for a 3.7-acre abandoned gravel pit in southern King County. Morris presented a plan for the site in April of 1979, which was reviewed and subsequently approved by the King County Arts Commission and the County Department of Public Works. Construction was funded in part by the Art in Public Places program at the National Endowment for the Arts, the Department of Public Works, and the County Arts Commission; it began in August and was completed in November. The piece

86

88, 89

90

87. Harvey Fite. *Opus 40*, aerial view. See plate 86.

88. Robert Morris (b. 1931). Untitled reclamation project, 1979. 3.7 acres. King County, Washington. A photograph taken shortly after construction.

89. Robert Morris. Untitled reclamation
project, after seeding. See plate 88.

90, 91. Herbert Bayer (1900–1987). *Mill Creek
Canyon Earthworks*, 1979–82. 2.5 acres. Kent,
Washington. General view; dedication.

89

90

91

consists of concentric terraces and slopes forming an amphitheater in the center of the site, with a hill rising on the lower section. From within this amphitheater, only the sky is visible; from without, one looks over the largely rural Kent Valley to the distant Cascade Mountains. At the top of the slope, a few scattered tree stumps remain as emblems of resource utilization. In addition to demonstrating the artist's ideas on the aesthetics of art-as-reclamation, Morris's piece suggests the economic viability of this kind of art. County figures reveal that the Morris project cost little more than the lowest estimates for conventional reclamation of the site.[77]

Morris used the occasion of the symposium to express the hope, however, that reclamation works would not be promoted solely on the basis of their economics or their utility, but would be valued as art works as well. He also warned of the moral dilemmas that artists would face in undertaking these projects: that their work might be used to aid or disguise questionable resource development policies. "Will it be a little easier in the future," he wondered, "to rip up the landscape for one last shovelful of a non-renewable energy source if an artist can be found (cheap, mind you) to transform the devastation into an inspiring and modern work of art?" Recalling the commemorative function that was detected in Smithson's reclamation proposals, he observed that artists might not opt for disguise: "It would perhaps be a misguided assumption to suppose that artists hired to work in industrially blasted landscapes would necessarily and invariably choose to convert such sites into idyllic and reassuring places, thereby socially redeeming those who wasted the landscape in the first place." But he left the door open a crack. "There may be more choices available than either a cooperative or critical stance for those who participate."[78] Some degree of resource use is essential for life; the point is

that artists can help determine the wisest possible course. Standing apart from this effort and allowing sites to go unreclaimed is certainly no more moral than restoring a site developed under questionable motives or needs.

The King County Earthworks project had a significant spin-off in a scheme by Herbert Bayer that was realized in 1982 in the city of Kent, a Seattle suburb. Bayer, one of the seven artists selected for the project, designed a park containing a group of earthworks and a stormwater retention basin for a badly eroded canyon above the city. Development of land along the creek had resulted in an excessive flow of water during periods of heavy rain, and the city needed a way of containing it and allowing it to recede slowly through the town. Bayer's design provided them with a high berm that stops the water. Upstream is a group of earth forms that are inundated during times of flood and provide an inviting, 2.5-acre grassy park during dry periods. 90–93

The stream itself meanders through the site and has been lined with stone to discourage erosion. As it enters the park, it comes first to a mounded ring one hundred feet in diameter and five feet high, which it breaks with its passage. It then passes under a bridge that is poised between a berm and a conical mound. Another earthen ring is next, this one seemingly suspended in a circular pool of water eighty-five feet in diameter. This pond contains water part of the year, and drains at other times to reveal the full contours of the grass ring. Then comes the high berm, topped with another cone; below it is a final oval mound. Aware of the disruptive character of ordinary dams, Bayer sought instead to create one that would harmonize with its setting. "A dam in the ordinary sense constitutes a radical interference with the natural configuration of the land," he explained. "My intent was, therefore, to give the dams a

92

93

94

95

94. Michael Heizer (b. 1944). *Frog Effigy* of the *Effigy Tumuli Sculptures,* 1983–85. Compacted earth; 170 x 340 x 17½ ft. Buffalo Rock, Illinois. Courtesy of Knoedler and Co., New York.

95. Michael Heizer. *Water Strider* of the *Effigy Tumuli Sculptures,* 1983–85. Compacted earth; 685 x 80 x 14 ft. Buffalo Rock, Illinois.

natural appearance conforming to the landscape (surroundings) and to become integral parts of the landscape being created."[79]

90, 91 Bayer's *Mill Creek Canyon Earthworks* are the focal point of a one hundred-acre park that also includes a play area and a canyon trail. Their existence is a tribute to the enthusiasm and persistence of many in the Kent community. The total project cost came to $572,000, with $450,000 provided by the City Engineering Department to pay for the retention basin. The balance of $122,000 paid for the design and construction of the earthworks. This money came from a wide variety of sources, including the Kent Parks Department and Arts Commission, the King County Arts Commission, the Washington State Arts Commission, the National Endowment for the Arts, a Housing and Community Development Block Grant, and over 150 private donations of varying amounts from individuals and corporations. The city is understandably proud of the project, calling it "a landmark in park design, and a revolutionary concept in solving the problem of how to control surface water."[80] A concert by the Seattle Symphony was held in the park to celebrate the completion of the earthworks and the city has pledged to maintain them as part of the overall upkeep of the park area.

The small town of Hanna, Wyoming, displayed similar resourcefulness in commissioning sculptor Stan Dolega to participate in the reclamation of an abandoned surface coal mine. The site, some 120 acres in all, had been deserted since 1958; it was marred by piles of overburden, stagnant water, and an unauthorized dump. Hanna received a grant for reclamation from the Rural Abandoned Mines Program of the Soil Conservation Service, and a supplemental grant from the Art in Public Places program at the National Endowment for the Arts to incorporate earthworks designed by Dolega. He concentrated his sculptural forms, completed in 1981,

on a twenty-acre parcel of the abandoned mine owned by the state. Working with the existing spoils piles, he recontoured them into a sequence of geometric terraces that link two areas of different elevations. He describes these forms as being "inspired by the flattened buttes typical of the high plains."[81] "The Soil Conservation Service will try to revegetate the sculpture," Dolega added, "but the soil has been severely damaged." An authorized landfill was established on the site: Dolega planned its contours so that they would merge with those of his earthwork after its expected twenty-five-year period of use. Recreational facilities, including a shooting range and a dirt-bike course, were also incorporated into the reclamation scheme.

By far the most ambitious and compelling instance to date of the use of art in land reclamation is Michael Heizer's *Effigy Tumuli Sculptures* near Ottawa, Illinois. Five enormous earth mounds—configured in the abstracted shapes of a frog, a water strider, a 94, 95 catfish, a turtle, and a snake—were built over the site of an abandoned surface coal mine on a bluff overlooking the Illinois River, adjacent to the Buffalo Rock State Park. The 200-acre site had been stripped in the 1930s—before reclamation was required—to extract a narrow seam of coal at a depth of about twenty-five feet. The highly toxic overburden was left in piles, still unvegetated after forty years, and acidified rainwater draining from the site was polluting the river and a nearby lake.

Because of the site's high visibility and toxicity, the state had identified it as a top priority for reclamation. Since the passage of the federal Surface Mining Control and Reclamation Act in 1977—which requires complete restoration of all new strip mines—money has been generated from a surcharge on current coal operations to help states pay for the reclamation of earlier, unregulated sites. The funds are collected by the Department of the

Interior's Office of Surface Mining and distributed to state Abandoned Mined Lands Reclamation Councils. The Buffalo Rock site was owned by the Ottawa Silica Company, whose chairman, Edmund Thornton, sat on the AMLR Council in Illinois. Upon learning that the site was slated for reclamation, he suggested that some form of art be incorporated into the project and volunteered, through the Ottawa Silica Company Foundation, to help make it possible. The foundation selected the artist and paid his fee, supplemented by a grant from the National Endowment for the Arts. The company donated the land to the state—to be administered and maintained by the Department of Conservation as part of the Buffalo Rock State Park—and the AMLR Council provided close to one million dollars for construction.

Three of the effigies were placed on the broad, open plateau that is the main feature of the site. Entering from the park, one comes first to the water strider, whose body rises to 14 feet and whose jointed legs sprawl to over 685 feet. Next to it are the more compact frog and the mammoth catfish: the former is 17½ feet high by 340 feet long; the latter, 18 feet high by 770 feet long. Beyond are the turtle and the snake, both of which bear an intriguing relation to the topography. The back legs and tail of the turtle are up on the plateau, while the front legs and head are discovered at the bottom of the bluff near the water— as if the animal were launching itself into the river. The snake makes an even more tortuous configuration, from its head on a small delta in the river, up a sheer rock escarpment, across the plateau, and back down to its tail—some 2,070 feet in all.

This project marks something of a departure for Heizer from his earlier work, especially in its use of allusive, only semiabstract animal shapes and in its role in reclamation. In his typically recalcitrant way, Heizer insists that looking to biological models was "just another way into geometry," which has always been his chief concern. Moreover, he discounts the importance of the reclamation aspect of this project. He told a reporter for *Smithsonian*, "I'm not for hire to patch up mining sites. The strip-mine aspect of it is of no interest to me. I don't support reclamation-art sculpture projects. This is strictly art."[82]

In procedural terms, there is indeed a distinction between the reclamation scheme and Heizer's work. The site was recontoured, the acid water treated and discharged, and the soil neutralized with limestone. The sculptures were an addition to this reclamation effort. But Heizer studied the existing spoils piles in positioning his pieces to minimize earth-moving expenses. And the use of animal shapes suggests the fundamentally ecological and distinctly poetic nature of his conception: Heizer chose to represent the water strider, the frog, the catfish, the turtle, and the snake because he felt they would be among the first creatures to return to the reclaimed site as it slowly came back to life.

Heizer's *Effigy Tumuli Sculptures* also reach in their allusions beyond the postindustrial character of the site. Their title suggests a connection to prehistoric Indian mounds. A tumulus is an artificial hill, often over a grave; many of those of the upper Midwest and the Ohio Valley were made to resemble animals— birds, bears, and serpents. Heizer's reference to prehistory is consistent with his other work, as is his looking to native American rather than to European models for his sources. Striking a remarkable balance, Heizer has remained loyal to his fundamental ambition— the creation of large-scale, geometrically configured earth sculptures outside an art world context—while using a vocabulary that is at once indigenous to the region and conditioned by the recent history of this particular site.

Several projects by other artists are tangentially related to reclamation efforts. In

96. William Bennett (b. 1948). *Jamesville Quarry Sculpture,* work in progress. *Wedge (Stone Boat),* begun 1976. Limestone; 80 x 10 x 6 ft. *Inverted Pyramid* (proposed). 160 x 160 x 20 ft. Jamesville, New York. Photomontage by the artist.

97

98

97. William Bennett. View looking into
Wedge (Stone Boat).

98. William Bennett. View from within
Wedge (Stone Boat).

upstate New York, sculptor William Bennett is utilizing a partially exhausted limestone quarry as a site for a massive environmental work. His purpose is not expressly reclamation; instead, he talks of the quarry as a "found object" and a "powerful space." He has been fascinated by quarries since his days as a graduate student at Indiana University in the early 1970s, when he took his art into the limestone pits around Bloomington. There he began work on a carved relief that soon grew off the single wall onto many others and onto the floor of the pit. In the New York quarry Bennett has dug his work into the ground. Thus far, it consists of a long, triangular wedge that begins at ground level, drops to a depth of six feet and widens to ten. Opposite the point of this wedge, Bennett plans to excavate an inverted pyramid 160 feet square and 20 feet deep, from the bottom of which will rise another, smaller pyramid, this one pointing back to the sky. Recalling the prolonged efforts of Harvey Fite, Bennett has painstakingly lined the floor and walls of the wedge with cut limestone slabs; he plans the same surface for the pyramidal forms. And like Fite, he works in his quarry on his own and only in the warm months. During the rest of the year, his sculptural production includes stone works that frequently take an architectural form.

Michigan sculptor Joseph Kinnebrew has created an architectural sculpture that is an example of reclamation only in the broadest sense of the word. His work is more properly described as an effort at environmental restoration or renewal. A dam in the Grand River at Grand Rapids had been preventing spawning fish from moving farther upstream. The Michigan Department of Natural Resources had plans to build a simple, entirely functional fish ladder when Kinnebrew approached them with a proposal to elaborate and improve the structure. Kinnebrew's fish ladder, completed in 1975, added walkways, seating, and viewing platforms, providing spectators with overlooks of the river, the dam, and the spectacle of migrating fish. And within days of its completion, spawning trout were found over one hundred miles upstream. This project was sponsored by the Arts Council of Greater Grand Rapids, with funds from the Department of Natural Resources, the National Endowment for the Arts, the Michigan Council for the Arts, and several local private foundations.

In Dallas, New York artist Patricia Johanson has completed work on the restoration of a lagoon in Fair Park, near the Dallas Museum of Natural History. At either end, she fashioned complex groupings of painted concrete paths, bridges, and benches, based on the forms of local aquatic plants: *saggitaria platyphylla* (arrowhead) at one end and *pteris multifida* at the other. Among them were introduced actual plants, ranging from water lilies and bulrushes to willow trees. While the concrete forms read as sculptures in their own right, they also serve to stabilize the shoreline and bring visitors close to the newly revived ecosystem. Johanson sounds like many of the earth artists of the late 1960s when she explains her motivation for this work: "The real reason I only design parks and fountains these days is I'm sick of the whole museum/collector/auction house complex with all their self-congratulatory prattle about how much they're doing for culture."[83] Yet rather than removing herself to an unpeopled environment, she is trying, as are many of her contemporaries, to reconcile environmental art with a social purpose.

A similar motivation is behind a project currently under development on a fifty-seven-acre landfill rising one hundred feet out of the Hackensack Meadowlands in Kearny, New Jersey. It is slated to become a park and a work of art entitled *Sky Mound*, designed by Nancy Holt. The triangular site, bounded by Amtrak and New Jersey Transit rail lines and

99

"Pinus Multifida" – Planting Plan
(Parks Through Water, Plants, Fish, + Animals)

Patricia Johanson '82

100

99. Joseph Kinnebrew (b. 1942). *Grand River
Sculpture,* 1975. Concrete; 45 x 35 x 30 ft.
Grand Rapids, Michigan.

100. Patricia Johanson (b. 1940). *Fair Park Lagoon: Pteris Multifida (Planting Plan),* 1982.
Ink, pastel, and conté crayon on paper;
36 x 30 in. Rosa Esman Gallery, New York.

the New Jersey Turnpike, is one of the most
visible of some thirty-five dumps in this wet-
lands area, which for many years has been
the repository of the region's garbage and
industrial waste. Holt's site is one of the few
remaining active landfills; it will be sealed to
contain any toxins and redeveloped as part
of a larger scheme for the reclamation of the
Meadowlands. Her plans call for a grassy, flat-
topped pyramid to be covered with radiating
pathways, smaller earth mounds, and metal
posts and arches, all oriented to significant
solar, lunar, and astronomical events. The work
will combine art with standard landfill-closure
techniques: the pathways will double as a
surface-water drainage system, and the metal
arches will be part of the recovery system for
methane gas released by the decomposing
garbage (the gas will be collected and sold
to a public utility). The project—sponsored
by the Hackensack Meadowlands Development Commission, with additional support
from the National Endowment for the Arts
and the New Jersey State Council on the Arts—
is intended as a model for the creative resolution of the ever-mounting problem of
urban waste management. It is hoped that
Sky Mound will function not only as a park
for human use, but will also become a stop-
over and breeding ground for wildlife.

Clearly, the use of art in land reclamation
and environmental restoration is an idea that
has fired many imaginations. One senses that
enthusiasm for this sort of work comes less
from some quixotic yearning of the artist to
feel needed than from a pressing awareness—
among artists and the general public alike—
of the complex problems generated by waste
disposal and by the continued exploitation
of natural resources. The potential of art to
assist in the renewal of landscape has been
amply demonstrated; it needs now to be developed to the greatest possible advantage.

While artists have thus been pioneering
ways to involve themselves in environmental

restoration efforts, they have also been making
other paths into the public space. Recent
landscape art is at least partially responsible
for generating phenomena known as sited
sculptures. As the term implies, these are
three-dimensional objects carefully situated
in their surroundings. This is not in itself a
new idea: traditional sculpture applied to architecture or monuments centered in public
squares certainly can be said to be sited. Yet
much modern sculpture has had a rootless
character. It has been a thing unto itself, concerned with its own internally generated form
and the properties of its own materials. It has
been sustained by the neutral, characterless
space of the museum and gallery. Land art
helped restore to sculpture a sense that the
surroundings—and most particularly the
landscape—were all-important both in the
formulation of a work and in its perception.
Sited sculpture emerged in the wake of this
restoration and can be said to have descended
in part from land art. More often than not,
sited sculpture is placed in the public domain.
It therefore partakes in the debate about the
public purposes of recent art in the landscape.
Without such evident utilitarian aims as mine
reclamation or landfill closure, however, the
public benefit of sited sculpture is often more
heatedly debated.

Land art, to review, is in large measure about
the landscape itself—its scale, its vistas, its
essentially horizontal character, its topography, and its human and natural history. It is
frequently made from the materials at hand.
It reveals the changing characteristics that a
work assumes in different conditions: diurnal
or nocturnal light, winter glare or summer
haze, full sun or cloud shadow. While any
outdoor work will change appearance under
different conditions, sited sculptures are less
exclusively about the landscape itself. They
are also about mass, form, volume, surface:
that is, some of the traditional concerns of
sculpture. Alternatively, they are manifesta-

tions of the organization of space, both internal and external: that is, architecture. They are still made with a great sensitivity to the surroundings—and often, this is the landscape—but have an internal coherence that land art does not. With sited sculptures, there is often an explicit boundary between the work and the environment. Rather than being forms that have emerged from the landscape, they often have the look of objects that have been set down within it.

Looking back over some of the projects discussed in the initial chapter of this book, one can see the distinctions between land art and sited sculpture emerging even in the early 1970s. Nancy Holt's *Sun Tunnels,* for example, are industrial forms introduced into the landscape, displaying far more of an interest in surface and in positive form than the earlier *Double Negative,* which was composed of empty space. One can also see the phenomenon of sited sculpture emerging in the work of artists not generally associated with land art. Richard Serra is one of these. His sculpture is often formed of massive, rusted steel plates that intrude upon and alter the space in which they are placed, proclaiming their materiality through demonstrations of mass, balance, and stress. Occasionally, these sculptures have been made very suc-

27–29

10

101

104

102

cessfully outdoors. In a wooded glen at the Kröller-Müller Museum in the Netherlands, for example, Serra dedicated a work from 1973 to the memory of Robert Smithson. Entitled *Spin Out (for Robert Smithson),* it consists of three standing plates in a centrifugal arrangement, which disappear into the surrounding slopes. The length and shape of each plate is determined by the contours of the natural setting. Conversely, the plates describe a horizontal cross section of the landscape, like orthogonals in a perspectival rendering. This reciprocity brings *Spin Out* as close as Serra ever came to the aims of the land artists.

Carl Andre is another who sometimes took his sculpture outdoors. In a controversial commission for Hartford, Connecticut, he arranged thirty-six glacial boulders in eight rows on a triangular site. At the apex stands a single stone, the largest of the group. The second row is composed of two slightly smaller boulders; the third, three that are smaller still. This pattern of increased number/ decreased mass is continued through the eight rows. As the numbers increase, so does the interval between the rows. Andre's work often depends on just such mathematically deter-

mined groupings, but his materials are more often industrial, metallic, and modular. Out of a respect for this outdoor setting, he shifted to an irregular, natural material; from a sense of the awkward site emerged the triangular form of the work. This *Stone Field Sculpture* also makes reference to a nearby cemetery: Andre wanted to create a work that would "extend the serenity of the graveyard."[84] Like *Spin Out,* it is an example of the subtle differences between the environmentally determined sculpture and the sculptural manipulation of the environment itself.

Andre's *Stone Field Sculpture* was not welcomed gently to its appointed site. Blasted in letters to the editor in the local press, it quickly became an issue in the 1977 mayoral campaign. It was criticized for its price ($100,000) and for its use of coarse, unworked elements. The controversy eventually spread to the *New Yorker,* the *St. Louis Post-Dispatch,* and *Time* magazine. A similar storm blew up in Seattle over Michael Heizer's sculpture *Adjacent, Against, Upon.* Completed in 1976, it is sited in Myrtle Edwards Park on the Seattle waterfront. It is a combination of natural and architectonic elements—massive granite slabs quarried in the Cascade Mountains, resting

103

near, leaning against, and set upon concrete
plinths that are variously three-, four-, and
five-sided. As such, the work mediates between the natural and architectural landscapes
that compose the view from the site: Puget
Sound and the distant Olympic Peninsula in
one direction, the city in the other.

Controversy notwithstanding, sited sculptures have become the frequent objects of
both corporate and public commissions.
Heizer has produced a fountain, *Levitated
Mass,* for the IBM Corporation in New York.
A granite slab seems to hover over a bed of
rushing water; the fountain's location—Fifty-
sixth Street at Madison Avenue—is indicated
in carved, cryptic inscriptions on the stone
and continued on the stainless steel frame.
For its office building in Bedminster, New
Jersey, A.T.&T. commissioned a sculpture from
104 Beverly Pepper in 1974. Titled *Amphisculpture,*
Pepper's work consists of concentric terraces

stepping down into a shallow bowl that is
bisected by sloping walls and platforms of
concrete. The whole, some 200 feet in diameter, evokes the form of a classical theater.
Athena Tacha's *Streams,* commissioned by the 105
city of Oberlin, Ohio, in 1976, likewise draws
on a classical vocabulary—in this instance,
stone terraces or steps. Tumbling down a slope
on the banks of a creek in a city park, it
throws off classical regularity through the
syncopated placement of risers and treads.
Some risers are higher than others; some
steps longer or wider. Scattered throughout
are irregular boulders that elaborate the visual
rhythms of the steps. Both Pepper's and
Tacha's works, in the manner of much sited
sculpture, combine built form with the use
of landscape contours.

Nancy Holt and Richard Fleischner are two
others who have subsequently distinguished
themselves in the creation of sited sculpture.

106, 107. Richard Fleischner (b. 1944). *Baltimore Project*, 1980. Granite and cor-ten steel; 3 acres. Social Security Administration Center, Woodlawn, Maryland.

Fleischner has explored the creation of outdoor spaces in a way that is at once more subtle and less architectural than Holt's approach. In Roger Williams Park in Providence, Rhode Island, Fleischner built a small bridge over a canal to Cow Island, where he created an environment out of discreet stone elements. Several of these are arrayed along a dominant axis, which conforms to an existing path on the island. Climbing the gentle slope, one comes first to a pink granite slab that is the threshold to the piece; continuing on, one encounters at the crest of the island an open square paved with the same pink granite. From there, two parallel bars of black granite lead down the other side of the island, hugging the ground. To either side of the main square are several other subsidiary elements: a short black granite column to one side balanced by a pink one on the other, and a pair of pink granite steps. Through the combination of all these components, Fleischner brings a remarkable degree of spatial organization to the two-acre island in an elegantly unobtrusive manner.

For a new Social Security Administration building in Woodlawn, Maryland, Fleischner created a similar environment of sculptural forms in 1980. Commissioned by the General Services Administration, the piece occupies a three-acre site. But while Cow Island is relatively open, the Woodlawn site is thickly wooded. Fleischner responded by increasing both the vertical dimensions and the mass of his components. They are again arranged around a central element: in this instance, a platform of rusted steel held horizontal above a slight grade. Up the slope is a kind of portal formed of two facing right angles of pale granite, with a threshold before them. Down the grade, one confronts a high wall of standing steel plates. Hidden behind it is an enigmatic granite cube, like a windowless blockhouse. To one side, serving to lure visitors into this environment, are two sets of

106

107

four tall columns, one on the edge of a grassy area adjacent to the Social Security building, the other slightly into the woods. On the other side is a small plinth and an inverted arch. Again, Fleischner has achieved a deft orchestration of these different elements—vertical and horizontal, granite and steel—and an intriguing balance between passage and closure. He demonstrates an ability (more common to landscape architects than to sculptors) to activate space through just the right proportional and compositional relationships among elements widely scattered in a landscape.

The particular appeal of Holt's work lies in its knowing attempt to reconcile formally distinct, quite architectural sculptures with their surroundings. This is most often achieved through the use of sight lines that lead the eye out into the landscape. Holt's *Rock Rings* was commissioned by Western Washington University and stands on a wooded edge of the campus in Bellingham. Constructed of schist quarried in nearby British Columbia, it is composed of two concentric walls of stone that are perforated with archways and portholes. These windows provide framed vistas over the adjacent meadows and into the trees; the arches are oriented in a north-south direction. The work thus has the effect of placing the observer in the environment. At the same time, however, the strongly architectural character of the work separates inside from outside, creating a cloistered space. One has the sense of being in a secret garden, from which it is possible to look out without being seen. The same effect was produced in a piece commissioned on the occasion of the Thirteenth Olympic Winter Games. Standing in an open field near Lake Placid, Holt's *Thirty Below* is a slender cylinder of brick, thirty feet high and just over nine feet in diameter. Two arches on a north-south axis allow entry to the piece at ground level. To the east and west sides, low berms lead

108

109

110

108

109

110

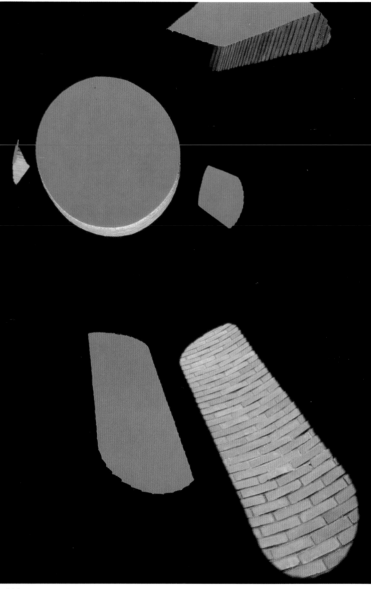

111

108, 109. Nancy Holt (b. 1938). *Stone Enclosure: Rock Rings*, 1977–78. Stone masonry; height: 10 ft., diameters: 40 ft., 20 ft. Western Washington University, Bellingham, Washington.

110, 111. Nancy Holt. *30 Below*, 1980. Brick; height: 30 ft.; diameter: 9 ft. 4 in. Mr. and Mrs. Henry Uihlein, Lake Placid, New York.

111
up to slotted windows that look into and through the piece. From within it, one's principal vista is up, from the darkened interior out to the sky. Shafts of light are thrown upon the inner walls by the perforations of *Thirty Below:* as with the star holes of *Sun Tunnels,* 27–29 forms in light are caught and projected.

The aspect of sited sculpture easiest to separate from land art is that which is most specifically architectural. Siah Armajani has created a number of wooden structures he describes as "reading gardens," with indoor spaces for reading or meditation, but without much obvious relationship to the landscape. Mary Miss and Alice Aycock have both experimented with constructed forms as well. But even architectural structures can bear a significant relationship to their physical and cultural settings. An intriguing case in point is a project by Andrew Leicester for Frostburg State College in Maryland. Frostburg lies in Allegany County, in the mountainous western panhandle of the state. As the site of the first bituminous coal-mining operations in the United States, the region is richly endowed with remains of the industry's 120-year history. Commissioned by the Maryland State Arts Council to create a sculpture for the college campus, Leicester elected to erect a memorial to miners.

115 *Prospect V-III,* as Leicester's work is known, was completed in 1982. It is a wooden structure over 120 feet long and 27 feet high, combining multiple elements that recall the architecture of mines and mining towns. At the outer extreme is a viewing platform that rises above a steep slope and overlooks the George's Creek basin, historical center of the region's coal operations. At the inner extreme is a narrow mine shaft dug for the piece, which serendipitously terminates in a coal seam discovered in the digging. In between are several chambers resembling miners' cottages and detailing the life of the miner. In the first 114 is a coal cart that is also a cradle, set on tracks

that lead irrevocably into the mine. It is surrounded by painted butterflies that metamorphose into black lungs, a reference to the crippling miner's disease. A second represents the miner's maturity, and evokes the tomblike chambers that the miners dig in the coal seam. A third displays the memorabilia of mining, including picks, shovels, and lunch pails as well as photographs and documents. Much of this material, which was intended to suggest the retirement of a miner, was donated to the project by miners, their widows, and families in a gesture of support and enthusiasm for the memorial.

Between this third chamber and the mine shaft is a hexagonal "rotunda," built to re- 113 semble a changing room, with working clothes suspended in the skylit dome. Partially buried in the hillside, it also suggests an archaic beehive tomb. Mining terms are stenciled on the walls, together with glyphs from the Egyptian Book of the Dead. Entrance to the 112 simulated mine is from this final chamber; the shaft is held up by wooden posts and lintels. The cart tracks disappear into the blackness. Glancing back, one overlooks the whole length of the piece and out into the valley.

In addition to receiving donations of mining equipment and memorabilia, Leicester was assisted in planning this memorial by local miners. Septuagenarian Tony Urbas was one of these. "This is something the area has been in need of, something in memory of the miners who worked the area," Urbas told a newspaper reporter. Frostburg College President Dr. Nelson P. Guild agreed with him. "This is about the first thing that has ever been done in this area in recognition of the life of the coal miner," Guild said.[85] There is a special poignance to the placement of this memorial on the campus of Frostburg College. A history of the school reveals that in the late nineteenth century, miners in the Frostburg area were stopped as they left the

112

113

114

112. Andrew Leicester (b. 1948). Entrance into the Rotunda at *Prospect V-III.*

113. Andrew Leicester. The Rotunda, leading into the mine shaft at *Prospect V-III.*

114. Andrew Leicester. The first cottage at *Prospect V-III.*

115. Andrew Leicester. *Prospect V-III,* 1982. Wood and mixed media; 27 x 123 ft. Frostburg State College, Frostburg, Maryland.

115

pits and asked to make contributions for a Normal School. Their donations went toward the purchase of the land on which the college now stands. Adjacent to it is a modern strip mine, the mechanized replacement of the deep pits in which these miners labored. Leicester's *Prospect V-III* demonstrates with particular intelligence the fact that commemorative content, like a purposeful intent, can ease the introduction of contemporary art into the public domain and enhance the public purposes of art in the landscape.

In the early 1980s, an unusual cooperation brought a group of sited sculptures to the grounds of the new Western Regional Center of the National Oceanic and Atmospheric Administration (NOAA) in Seattle. With funds provided by NOAA and with support from the National Endowment for the Arts and the Seattle Arts Commission, five artists—Siah Armajani, Scott Burton, Doug Hollis, Martin Puryear, and George Trakas—were selected to work with the building's architects on an overall scheme for the 114-acre grounds along Lake Washington, the site of a former naval airfield. Their mandate was to study the geography of the site and to plan for future public access to the lakeshore as well as for the placement of their own works.

The design phase of this project continued for about a year and a half. The group identified the pastoral nature of the site and its

116. Siah Armajani (b. 1939). *NOAA Bridges,* 1983. Bronze letters set in aggregate concrete. Western Regional Center of the National Oceanic and Atmospheric Administration, Seattle, Washington.

116

location in a residential neighborhood, near an existing park and a bicycle path leading to downtown Seattle, as primary considerations in their planning. They elected ultimately to connect their individual works along a path that leads down the shore to the park, providing not only passage through the landscape but a vivid experience of the water's edge and vistas over the lake as well. At several points in the planning their ideas were presented to NOAA and to various community groups, which helped build a consensus for the projects far stronger than might be expected for such novel works of public art.

The pieces, completed in 1983, effectively combine each artist's individual vocabulary with an understanding of the overall program for the site. Armajani created a pair of terracotta-colored concrete bridges that span low depressions along the pathway. They continue a series of bridges he has made over the years in different styles that express his interest in indigenous architecture; in this case, the pedimented form is an allusion to American Neoclassicism. These particular bridges take on a relevance to the lakeside setting with their inlaid bronze inscriptions from *Moby Dick,* that most aquatic of novels.

Near one of Armajani's bridges a curving path of triangular brick pavers winds up a

116

117. Doug Hollis (b. 1948). *A Sound Garden*, 1983. 12 towers supporting a tuned organ pipe and a vane; height: 20 ft., diameter of total area: 300 ft. Western Regional Center of the National Oceanic and Atmospheric Administration, Seattle, Washington.

118. George Trakas (b. 1944). *Berth Haven*, 1983. 4 levels of decking wood and cor-ten steel, trees, grasses, and reeds. Western Regional Center of the National Oceanic and Atmospheric Administration, Seattle, Washington.

117

118

119. Scott Burton (b. 1939). *Viewpoint*, 1983. Aggregate concrete, stainless steel, cut and uncut boulders, and grove of crab-apple trees. Western Regional Center of the National Oceanic and Atmospheric Administration, Seattle, Washington.

119

function as viewpoints, though they are vastly different in character. Scott Burton's looks 119 out. One enters through a small grove of trees onto a gridded terrace above the lake. Dispersed at irregular intervals across it are rough-hewn chunks of granite that were dredged up from the lake. They have been saw cut at right angles to form seats, most of which are oriented toward the water. A concrete planter completes the group on the terrace, while stepping stones lead down to the water. Martin Puryear's piece, by comparison, looks in. His *Knoll for NOAA* is a concrete mound forty-five feet in diameter and four and one-half feet high that lies on the crest of a hill adjacent to the building. It was constructed by placing concrete panels end to end to form an ascending spiral, which is most legible from its top. Surrounding the dome are four curved benches whose arcs correspond to that of the knoll. While the piece certainly functions as an overlook, its geometries are centripetal; it consequently reads more strongly as a sculpture than does Burton's terrace. This is not surprising given the nature of Puryear's other work, which generally takes the form of simple, organically suggestive shapes that resolutely proclaim their status as objects, however mysterious.

By comparison, Puryear's *Bodark Arc,* at 121–22 the Nathan Manilow Sculpture Park, Governors State University, University Park, Illinois, dissolves into the landscape. The park is the site of an old farm; Puryear's piece lies in an open field between a windbreak of osage orange—or bodark—trees and a small pond. Puryear inscribed an arc on the ground, little more than a path, that leads from the line of trees to the pond and back again. Where it intersects with the pond, it becomes a curved wooden trestle over the water. Puryear has 122 evocatively described the genesis of this arc and its close connection to the site. "It occurred to me that within its limited radius there was a whole range of the local ecology.

117 gentle slope to Doug Hollis's *Sound Garden*. Visually, this is the most unprepossessing work at NOAA: it seems at first glance to be little more than a collection of metal posts. But each steel tower carries a wind-activated organ pipe that produces its own distinct sound, which varies continually with the intensity of the wind. Set among these towers are angular benches on which to rest as the aeolian harmonies are played.

118 George Trakas's *Berth Haven* lies along the shore, actually projecting into the water. Both in form and material it brings to mind utilitarian marine architecture: tiers of steel and wooden decking are suspended over the lake on steel posts. But its geometric outlines are anything but utilitarian in appearance, and it does much to dramatize the transition from land to lake: native wildflowers are planted along the landward edge, while steps lead down into the water itself.

The two remaining projects at NOAA both

120–22. Martin Puryear (b. 1941). *Bodark Arc*, 1982. Asphalt, wood, stone, and bronze. Chair: bronze. Arch: wood; height: 7 ft. 2 in. Path: wooden bridge and gravel path, radius: 196 ft. Nathan Manilow Sculpture Park, Governors State University, University Park, Illinois. Courtesy of Donald Young Gallery, Chicago.

120

121

122

I used a long arcing path to pull you through 180 degrees of very different landscape realms—a little swamp with cattails, a pond which you cross . . . all beginning and ending in the arcade of tree branches."[86]

Bodark Arc invites a contemplation of other features of the site as well. Just near the mid-point of the arc, a hand-hewn wooden arch, built on the spot, indicates the location of another path. This one leads back to the trees, under which is placed a single small bronze chair, reminiscent, the artist says, of the chairs of African chiefs he saw while in the Peace Corps in West Africa. From this spot, one looks back over the trajectory through the arch and over the lake, which becomes the arrow to the arc's bow. While the crossed arc has appeared in Puryear's sculpture before, here it has a local significance: the osage orange tree was the source of wood for Indian bows; indeed, the alternative name for the tree is a corruption of the French *bois d'arc,* or "bow wood."

The Manilow Sculpture Park is also home to *Field Rotation,* a sited work by Mary Miss built in 1981. Eight rows of circular posts set out in a large field lead insistently to a grassy mound, marked by two metal towers. Sunk within the mound is a stockaded chamber entered by ladder and containing a construction of wooden decking. The acute angles of this chamber's corners together with the radiating posts create a pinwheel effect, as suggested by the project's title. While the Manilow Sculpture Park is administered and supported by a private foundation, it is free and open to the public; moreover, this work, as well as several others in the park, was given some public support—a grant from the National Endowment for the Arts. Miss's and Puryear's sculptures thus continue to address the public possibilities for sculptures sited in the landscape.

Because much recent environmental art has come into being with at least partial public sponsorship, one might forget that on occasion it is still realized through entirely private means. Christo, in his typically exaggerated way, reminds us of this: though his works are public spectacles, they continue to be financed through the private sale of his drawings, collages, and sculptures. His temporary installations engender controversies that are out of proportion to their actual threat to the environment. It may be that this is simply a function of the flamboyance of his projects and their immodest budgets; no doubt it also follows from the vast quantities of publicity that this artist's enterprises invariably generate. When he proposed to install 11,000 banners on twenty-five miles of pathways in New York's Central Park, even the *Public Interest* and the *New York Times* threw themselves into the fray.[87] A *Times* editorial on March 5, 1981, commended the Parks Department for denying Christo a permit to execute this piece, on the grounds that it ran counter to the department's policy of decreasing abuse and encouraging restoration of the park. They also noted that the project's anticipated cost of five million dollars was more than the annual maintenance budget for the park and more than five years' worth of restoration funds. One has to question this moralizing over the cost of a project that was to be privately funded and that might have lent a festival air to a small corner of that grim city. Would it not have been more productive to issue Christo the permit on the condition that he make a substantial contribution to the park's restoration funds?

When Miami granted Christo a permit to surround with 200 feet of floating pink polypropylene eleven of the city's fourteen islands in Biscayne Bay, they received an environmental bonus. Christo agreed to donate $100,000 to Dade County for the Biscayne Bay Preservation Fund, and $50,000 to the City of Miami. In addition, before the vivid pink fabric was unfurled for two weeks in May of 1983,

123

124

the armies of Christo's workers cleared the islands of every scrap of trash. There was an element of self-interest in this: Christo wanted his pink to contrast with the unbroken blue-green waters of the bay and the uncluttered greenery of the islands. He also announced an intention to surround only those islands in the bay that were man-made (the result of dredging a shipping channel), leaving the natural ones unmolested. And he made the usual arrangements for a study of his project's potential threat to the environment, under pressure from a small but vocal group who feared that it would endanger manatees and nesting birds. A section of the pink fabric was floated over an aquarium tank containing manatees; not only did it not disturb them, but it apparently inspired them to amorous activities.[88]

Like Christo's other projects, *Surrounded Islands* was a grand gesture, but civil and even humble in its impermanence. Six and a half million square feet of the woven fabric was folded and attached to pink styrofoam booms, which were towed out to the islands. The booms were anchored 200 feet offshore, and the fabric pulled to land, across the beach, and hooked to earth anchors driven in under the cover of vegetation. The fabric was specially sewn to follow exactly the contours of the islands, except in two instances where Christo surrounded two islands in a single group. The fabric came alive in the water, billowing in the waves and the small tide. One participant recalled seeing a dozen pelicans fly in low over his island and turn a hot pink from the reflection. "That moment was like magic," he said. "And it just might pass for art."[89]

Two more recent works will serve as a coda to this chapter. One is entirely private and temporary, the other a public monument intended for the ages. One is best described as a three-dimensional painting in the landscape, the other as a work of landscape architecture that is also a contemporary sculpture. Both are thus hybrids, demonstrating the fusion of forms that has come in the wake of artistic experimentation in the past two decades. But beyond that, they reveal just how significant and pervasive have the forms and attitudes of land artists become in recent years. What began in the late 1960s as a rejection by just a handful of artists of the then current forms of art has developed into a phenomenon that touches many of the most consequential aspects of art today, from land reclamation to the improvement of public spaces. That the impact of land art can now be felt in the practice of painting and landscape architecture as well only confirms that it has sounded a major chord in contemporary culture.

Alan Wood is a British-born Canadian painter living in Vancouver. Over the past several years, his work has become increasingly three-dimensional. At first, this development amounted only to the application of collage or relief to canvas, but eventually Wood began to build environments out of his paintings, constructing forms of canvas-covered wood that were painted and installed in museum and gallery spaces. At the same time, his subject matter moved from the abstract to the increasingly naturalistic. In particular, he began to draw on the features of his adopted British Columbia landscape: its cathedrals of trees, its waterfalls and mountains, its ocean shores.

In 1980 Wood made his first visit to the Cariboo, the vast, semiarid interior of British Columbia. Having been nurtured on Hollywood westerns as a child in the industrial town of Widnes, near Liverpool, Wood immediately recognized in this landscape the features that had fired his imagination as a youth and that he knew still formed the dominant myth of the West, both in the United States and in Canada. There were the wide open spaces, the sagebrush, and the distant mountains. There, too, were the deserted frontier towns and farmhouses, the irrigation troughs and the snaking fences, the windmills and water tanks. To Wood, the vernacular ranch architecture he encountered was to western Canada "as the Parthenon is to Greece or Elizabethan or Georgian architecture is to Britain": something indigenous and altogether remarkable. The result of this inspiration was a temporary installation at the Emily Carr College of Art in Vancouver in 1981. It included a gate, a corral, a chute, piles of fencing, and an actual fence row disappearing into an illusionistic landscape. All were fabricated of canvas wrapped around wooden supports and colorfully painted.

Wood's enthusiasm for the Western myth did not end there. In 1982 he determined to create an elaborate tribute to ranch architecture, this time in the landscape itself. With the support of many individuals in Vancouver and across Canada, funding was secured and a site was found. Throughout the winter and early spring of 1983 Wood and his crew were busy in a warehouse on the edge of Vancouver, fabricating the components of his three-dimensional painting. These included a life-size water tank and windmill, barns of different sizes, gates, and miles of fencing. Constructed of over 150,000 board-feet of lumber, the components were then knocked down and fed through a homemade machine that wrapped them in a continuous strip of canvas and bathed them with a coat of primer paint. Loaded on flatbeds, these stacks of brilliantly colorful elements were trucked over the Rocky Mountains to Alberta in the late spring.

There, they were reassembled at a working ranch about twenty miles west of Calgary. Approaching the 320-acre site, one was greeted by the sight of a large horse and rider crashing down a hill out of the trees. Like all the components of Wood's *Ranch*, this was made of painted canvas pulled over a wooden frame. From there, one arrived at a large corral and two small pens at the entrance to a large triangular valley. Painted fences ran east and west. To the west lay three kinds of haystacks, again made of canvas-covered wood. One was in the shape of rolled hay, one suggested bales, and the third alluded to the vertical cones that were painted by Claude Monet.

To the east were several other tableaux. On a rolling hill, a seven-bar fence was painted to resemble a rainbow. Below was a blue and yellow bridge and a group of stark white geometric shapes that Wood described as a "still life": a pyramidal windmill, a cylindrical water 126 tank, and conical and triangular feeding troughs. Nearby stood five "receding" barns. 127 They ranged from full size to miniature and were arranged from large to small to simulate diminution over a large distance. The color scheme intentionally confounded this appearance, however: the largest was a cold bluish-white, while the others ranged through a pale blue and mauve to pink and bright red.

From the barns, a trail led east past three tepees to a group of "Old West" façades, 128 including store fronts, hitching posts, and a boardwalk. The façades were held up at the back by an obvious framework, in an explicit reference to movie sets. Two other groups of Western buildings were nearby: a small church with a graveyard and picket fence, and a pioneer homestead, complete with cabin, fence, gate, and outhouse. In the distance, three huge canvas birds seemed to hover over a hilltop, while a fan-shaped installation was meant to suggest the circular fields formed by irrigation from a single, central source. Finally, hidden in the trees was a 125 piece Wood called *Ranchenge*: this was a purple, blue, and orange corallike structure composed of two concentric circles of posts and beams, some standing and others falling. It was inspired both by Stonehenge and by the decaying ruins of an actual corral that Wood had seen on a visit to the Cariboo.

125. Alan Wood (b. 1935). *Ranchenge,* from *Ranch*, 1983 (now dismantled). Wood and painted canvas. Near Calgary, Alberta.

126. Alan Wood. A tableau entitled *Geometry,* including a windmill, a water tank, and feed troughs, from *Ranch*.

127. Alan Wood. *Five Receding Barns,* from *Ranch*.

128. Alan Wood. Storefront façades and church in township, from *Ranch*.

127

26

128

No more different a tribute from Wood's could be imagined than the Vietnam Veterans Memorial. Completed in the autumn of 1982, the memorial provoked a national drama that reproduced in microcosm the conflict engendered by the war itself. Conceived by veterans and paid for with private donations to the Vietnam Veterans Memorial Fund, it is nevertheless an entirely public monument: authorized by Congress, placed on public land, and commemorating the more than 57,000 individuals who died at the request of their government.

The memorial is an elegantly simple one. Its form is an open V-shape with an interior angle of 132 degrees. It is set into the ground, with walls of polished black granite holding up the earth behind it and facing a gradual grassy slope that climbs back up to Constitution Gardens, the Mall, and the other national memorials. The sloping ground gives the walls an elongated, triangular form, as if they were emerging from or receding into the earth in the manner of the Serra in Holland. On the face of the walls are the names of all those who died or are still missing-in-action in the Vietnam War. The names are

given chronologically, beginning at the top right of the memorial's apex, continuing to the far right and then jumping to the extreme left, and culminating at the bottom left of the apex. In the words of Maya Ying Lin, who designed this memorial as a Yale undergraduate student: "Thus the war's beginning and end meet; the war is 'complete.' . . . yet broken by the earth that bounds the angle's open side, and contained by the earth itself."[90]

Lin's design was unanimously selected by a jury from over 1,400 entries submitted in an open competition for the memorial. Competition rules specified, among other things, that the names of the dead and missing should be included in the memorial, and that it should be "contemplative and reflective in character." Lin's design fulfills these requirements with brilliance. Set into the earth, it is sheltered from the ceaseless noise of nearby Constitution Avenue, creating a space that is profoundly calm despite the frenetic surroundings. It is an environmental rather than a conventionally monumental work: its principal axis is horizontal rather than vertical. It accords with its setting in a subtle yet knowing way: the two walls form sight lines that lead

129. Maya Lin (b. 1959). Vietnam Veterans
Memorial, 1982. Black granite; height: 10 ft.,
length of each wall: 250 ft. Constitution Gardens,
Washington, D.C. View toward the Washington
Monument, photographed at the dedication
ceremonies, November 11, 1982.

directly to the Washington Monument in one direction and the Lincoln Memorial in the other. These are both visual and symbolic links. They give the memorial an emphatic sense of belonging on the site, and a contextual continuity with the earlier monuments. To be sure, this is a different sort of memorial: horizontal while those are vertical, black while those are white, spatial while those are architectural. But this commanding alignment allies the Vietnam Memorial with those earlier commemorations of service to the nation.

The best memorials have always had a cathartic function, easing trauma into memory. In this, especially, the Vietnam Veterans Memorial is a stunning success. It is the continual witness of tearful homages to the deceased. Flowers and mementos are regularly left there. These visible expressions of grief are eloquent demonstrations that the individual and collective wounds of Vietnam are still raw, and in need of remedy. The controversy that surrounded the commission was itself a part of a much-needed catharsis. A group of the veterans felt that the memorial was demeaning: they interpreted its blackness and its in-ground setting as implicit condemnations of the war and the sacrifices it required. They were also puzzled by its reductive character — its simple geometry, its abstractness, its unobtrusive horizontality — all of which seemed too much like modern sculpture. Yet Maya Lin's design is in a distinguished tradition of funerary tablets, and no more "abstract" than the Washington Monument. Its blackness and inscribed names serve simply to remind us that people die in wars, irrespective of their cause. As the architecture critic of the *Washington Post* wrote, "Black is indeed the color of sorrow and of mourning, but not of shame."[91] Lin's memorial commemorates sacrifice and death; its perceived antiwar imagery has less to do with her design than with the continued na-

tional conflict about the moral rightness of the war. If we were united in our approval of the war, there would be no cause to look for antiwar sentiment in what is, in any case, a morally neutral statement.

As a concession to those who disapprove of the memorial, plans were approved to place a figurative sculpture at its entry. A grove of trees just away from the end of one of the black walls was chosen as a site for an eight-foot-high bronze sculpture of three infantrymen. Ironically, this may prove to be the more abstract element of the ensemble, divorcing the commemoration from the sacrifice of known individuals. These idealized figures cannot provoke the same sense of wrenching, sorrowful recognition provided by Maya Lin's funerary stele. One imagines that ultimately, once the wounds of Vietnam have healed, the memorial will transcend its specifically commemorative function and stand as an eloquent tribute to all those who have died in our nation's wars.

Scarcely more than a dozen years separate *Double Negative* from the Vietnam Veterans Memorial. If they seem to bear little resemblance to each other, consider this: that they are both meditative spaces, the one a problematic gesture toward the majesty of the earth, the other a recognition of its hallowed function as the receiver of our dead. In between has come an unbounded exploration of the use of art in the landscape to both utilitarian and transcendent ends. If only the Vietnam Veterans Memorial were to endure from this period of brilliance, that would be accomplishment enough. But we have seen more and can rightfully hope for its continuation: the reclamation of our abused landscapes and the renewal through less specifically utilitarian works of our appropriate sense of awe and respect for the extraordinary character of the land.

5. BEYOND EARTHWORKS: THE NEW URBAN LANDSCAPE

Paradoxically, it is in the city that the greatest legacy of the earthworks movement can be seen. While the iconic works of land art — Heizer's *Double Negative* or Smithson's *Spiral Jetty*, for example — were made in the virtually trackless expanses of the American West, quite a few of the most significant recent environmental projects have been incorporated into intensively developed urban spaces. As environmental art, including sited sculpture, has increasingly become the focus of public commissions, more and more of these commissions have been for inner-city locations.

This paradigmatic shift in the location and intention of environmental art in less than two decades results from a number of notable changes in the attitudes of artists and patrons alike. Among artists, the antagonistic posture that prevailed at the end of the 1960s has given way to a more cooperative stance. Many environmental artists now desire not merely an audience for their work but a *public,* with whom they can correspond about the meaning and purpose of their art. In search of this public, many have returned to the city — and to its particular problems and possibilities. Moreover, they have recovered the idea that art can attempt to determine its own social function and thereby attain a prominent position in public discourse. This recovery is not particular to environmental art — there has also been a good deal of politically motivated painting of late. Among environmental artists, however, the notion of public purpose tends to be more generalized, and more subtle. It frequently takes the form of some celebratory, commemorative, or utilitarian function that is deftly blended with the artist's particular aesthetic aims. As an outcome of these changes in the attitudes of artists, one can now legitimately speak of a new and truly public art, rather than merely of contemporary art in public places.

At the same time, the sponsors of public art projects have increasingly turned to environmental art as a way of resolving the many difficulties caused by installing contemporary sculpture in the public space. It has now been over three decades since the federal government began its most recent episode of public art sponsorship, through the Art-in-Architecture program at the General Services Administration (GSA) and the Art in Public Places program at the National Endowment for the Arts.[92] Meanwhile, some seventy-five cities, counties, and states have passed ordinances that allocate up to one percent of their budgets for new construction to be spent on art. There are many rationales offered for these programs. They are educational, inasmuch as they bring an awareness of contemporary art to a wider audience (this, it seems to me, is a variation on an earlier notion that an exposure to art is in some way morally beneficial); they provide opportunities for artists; they stimulate tourism and economic development generally; and they help promote civic identification and pride.

The most compelling rationale for art in public places programs, however, has also proved the most elusive. This is the reintegration of the arts of painting, sculpture, architecture, and landscape design — severed from each other in the modern era — with the aim of creating the best possible public environment. But most sculpture long ago gave up the figurative subjects and narrative content that traditionally assured it a position in the public space and a decorative role in architecture. When the government began again to sponsor public art, the kind of sculpture that was most frequently introduced to public spaces was the monumental, abstract work of such artists as Alexander Calder, Tony Smith, and Mark di Suvero. The expressive aims of this sculpture were often at odds with the architecture with which it was paired, a problem frequently complicated by irreconcilable differences in scale. Moreover, the look of this sculpture was foreign to much of the audience, accustomed as it was to figurative sculptures in public settings. Consequently, viewers were left to grapple with an art that appeared to have little or no public meaning.

Environmental art had not been immune to criticism on these grounds, but the clamor reached its highest pitch over a sculpture by Richard Serra, *Tilted Arc,* installed by the GSA in 1981 on the plaza in front of the Jacob K. Javits Federal Building in lower Manhattan. The sculpture was a 120-foot-long wall of 12-foot-high steel plate that curved slowly across the plaza, tilting slightly off the vertical toward the office building and adjacent courthouse. Almost immediately after the sculpture's installation, tenants of the buildings — notably a judge in the Court of International Trade — complained to the GSA that the piece was visually offensive, that it disrupted the use of the plaza for recreational events, and that it posed an unacceptable security risk because personnel could not see and therefore control what transpired on the other side of the wall.

Many of these same arguments had been made in the mid-1970s in a prolonged but unsuccessful campaign against a sculpture by George Sugarman, *Baltimore Federal.* But what differentiates the two battles and, indeed, made the Serra conflict more complicated than the usual debate over public art (in which reputedly advanced art is pitted against supposedly ignorant philistinism) is the essentially confrontational nature of Serra's art. The artist spelled out the terms of this confrontation even as he was planning the work. "I've found a way to dislocate or alter the decorative function of the plaza and actively bring people into the sculpture's context," he stated in an interview published in 1980. "I plan to build a piece that . . . will cross the entire space, blocking the view from the street to the courthouse and vice versa. . . . After the piece is created, the space will be understood primarily as a function of the sculpture."[93] This language of domi-

nance was transferred to the sculpture itself.

That *Tilted Arc* took formal possession of its rather dreary environment was the principal source of its artistic strength and also of its vulnerability. That its subject was, in large measure, the process of perception as experienced by the moving, reacting body won it few supporters. This brand of phenomenology, while of interest to some in the art world, was evidently neither something to which the public was predisposed nor something for which it was effectively prepared. The efforts of some enthusiasts to make Serra's sculptures stand as revelations of the inhumanity of civic spaces and the brutality of modern working conditions only underlined the reasons *Tilted Arc* generated so much antipathy.[94] The question is whether people are looking for replication of the hostile public environment or for alleviation of it.

In the wake of three days of public hearings in March 1985, during which testimony was heard by both supporters and opponents of *Tilted Arc,* a panel appointed by the regional administrator of the GSA recommended that the sculpture be removed.[95] This recommendation was ratified by the GSA's national director in the fall of that year, and, after an unsuccessful legal effort by the artist to block the decision, the sculpture was dismantled in 1989. Whatever one's opinion of the sculpture, this was a problematic decision. The GSA had entered into a contract with Serra for a sculpture conceived with this particular site in mind, knowing full well the character of his previous work and the precise form this sculpture would take. Breaching the spirit if not the letter of this contract may jeopardize the future willingness of artists to participate in public art programs and set a censorious precedent with far-reaching implications for the freedom of artistic expression. Moreover, as long as *Tilted Arc* remained in place, it was indeed educational, as a forceful reminder of the social impact of public art. If public

131

art programs are to succeed, there must be some effort to develop a language—either in the art or its explication—that is intelligible to at least some of those unfamiliar with contemporary art, thereby narrowing the breach between the art community and the larger public.

Notwithstanding the furor over *Tilted Arc*, environmental art seems more and more determined to make itself welcome in the public space. To begin with, it is made for a particular site, which goes a long way toward resolving issues of scale and setting. This was, however, true of *Tilted Arc* and is thus no guarantee of widespread public empathy. It is rather the demonstrated capacity of environmental art to be contextual—that is, to make reference in its form or content to its surroundings—that governs its true potential as public art. The various sorts of public purpose now being explored by environmental artists—including narrative content, commemoration, environmental restoration, or some form of utility—have been recognized by artists and sponsors alike as a way of changing the widespread perception that the earlier examples of con-

temporary art installed in the public space (*Tilted Arc* being only the best-known example) lacked sufficient—or sufficiently evident—public meaning. As a result, the past few years have seen a remarkable number of new environmental art projects instigated by public art sponsors, including artist-designed parks and plazas and collaborations with building and landscape architects. Some of these projects have been executed in a spare, essentially abstract vocabulary characteristic of late modernist sculpture; others have participated in the recent resurgence of interest in narrative and figurative subject matter.

The involvement of artists in the design of public space has required some modification in their working methods: many of these projects are public not only in their setting but also in their execution. Competitive bidding, public presentation of previous work, hearings on proposals, review by engineers and elected officials—these procedures have long been familiar to architects but less so to sculptors, until recently. Collaborations with other design professionals have generated problems of their own—there may be irrec-

132

oncilable differences between the crisp, thorough planning of architects, for example, and the more intuitive, empirical methods of artists. This is, of course, a generalization, for there are artists who have been quite eager to develop a new role for themselves. It is perhaps enough to say that we are moving away from the stereotype of the solitary artist toward an image of the artist as partner in civic projects. Indeed, this may become the norm. In 1986 the National Endowment for the Arts established a new grant category for projects that involve collaboration between artists and design professionals; and many sponsors now require that plans for art be incorporated into building projects at the outset rather than appended as an afterthought.

The work of Isamu Noguchi can be used to illustrate the transition in public art over the past decade from a preponderance of monumental, abstract, freestanding sculptures to a preponderance of environmental projects. Over the years, Noguchi was the recipient of numerous commissions, both public and private; they were awarded both for environmental designs and for discrete sculptural objects. Among the former are the projects for Chase Manhattan Bank and Yale University mentioned in chapter three. Among the latter are

83, 84

his tubular steel *Sky Gate* in Honolulu, the majestic *Portal* at the Justice Center in Cleveland, and the massive granite *Black Sun* in Volunteer Park, Seattle. But after the mid-1970s many of his commissions were for environmental projects, and most of his patrons were public.

In 1975, for example, the same year that *Sky Gate* was erected in Honolulu, the High Museum in Atlanta approached Noguchi with the idea of creating a play environment in Piedmont Park. The city provided a site within the park that was in need of restoration and secured an Art in Public Places grant; the museum assumed the responsibility for matching the grant, which they accomplished with the assistance of local foundations and charitable organizations. At the time of the Atlanta commission, only one of Noguchi's playground proposals, which date back to the 1930s, had been realized, and that was in Japan. His project in Atlanta places the play sculptures inside a low wall, which protects the playground from the street and also screens out some of the traffic noise. Under a ring of mature oak trees, Noguchi arrayed a group of brightly colored, sturdy play shapes — including slides, swings, cubes, mounds, and several structures for

132. Isamu Noguchi (1904–1988). Aerial view
of Philip A. Hart Plaza, 1972–78. 8 acres.
Detroit, Michigan.

133. Isamu Noguchi. Horace E. Dodge and
Son Memorial Fountain, 1978. Stainless steel
with granite base; height: 24 ft. Philip A.
Hart Plaza, Detroit, Michigan.

133

134. Isamu Noguchi. Bayfront Park (1979–
in progress). 32 acres. City of Miami, Florida.

134

climbing — which are intriguing to children and adults alike.

It is in Detroit that Noguchi's talents in environmental design received their fullest expression. In 1970 Noguchi was asked to submit a proposal for a fountain as part of the plans for a new Civic Center Plaza, bounded by the Detroit River on one side and commercial development on the other, and within sight of Renaissance Center, symbol of the city's commitment to urban revitalization. Noguchi developed a fountain design and submitted it with some suggestions for adjusting the plaza plans to better accommodate his fountain. His suggestions fell on receptive ears, and he was taken on to reform the entire eight-acre site.

132 Hart Plaza, as it is known, is disposed over two levels. It includes restaurant and performance facilities beneath, and open paved and green areas above, together with a large amphitheater that doubles in the winter as a skating rink. At the center is Noguchi's extra-
133 ordinary fountain, a sculptural and technological marvel. It is composed of a tubular ring held twenty-four feet off the ground on two legs, which rise out of a shallow round basin. The flow of water is completely computerized: several dozen programs create a seemingly infinite variety of water patterns generated from above and below, from a fine mist to a massive aquatic column. At the entrance to the plaza is another sculptural object, a twisting aluminum pylon that rises to a height of 120 feet. Both this gleaming column and the computerized fountain have a deliberately machine-tooled, futuristic look. "I wanted to make a new fountain, which represents our time and our relationship to outer space," Noguchi observed.[96] The technological metaphor is also appropriate to a city that is home to the industry that has transformed American life in the twentieth century: the automobile. But the fountain is technology transformed: "a machine becomes a poem," as Noguchi himself put it.[97] It is proof of

Noguchi's continued sculptural inventiveness, while the larger plaza is witness to his sensitivity to the need for physical relief from the claustrophobia of the inner city, which is the most welcome aspect of the new public space. "What is important above all," Noguchi stressed, "is the sense of space that Hart Plaza supplies. An opening to the sky and to the Detroit River. A horizon for people."[98]

Detroit asked for a fountain and received an entire plaza; Miami wanted a new band-
134 shell and got a completely new look for Bay-front Park, which lies between the bay and Biscayne Boulevard, one of the city's principal thoroughfares. Despite its central location, the park was underutilized and run-down. Noguchi saw the park and became convinced that the renewal of the antiquated bandshell would not be adequate to correct the park's problems. He sought and received approval to prepare instead a master plan for eighteen of the park's acres. His proposal called for the removal of an old library building and the addition of an amphitheater, fountains, a children's playground, and a bayside walk, all contained within low berms that would protect the park from the noise and congestion of Biscayne Boulevard. The plans were implemented in stages over the years. The library was demolished, the amphitheater and bayside walk were completed, and a memorial designed by Noguchi was added to the park, honoring the astronauts who perished in the *Challenger* disaster.

Few artists have received the number of commissions or the broad mandate accorded to Noguchi. But others have been engaged in similar kinds of projects. In Rosslyn, Virginia, for example, Nancy Holt was retained
135 to create a small park at one of the major points of entry into this commercial district just across the Potomac River from Washington, D.C. Originally, county planners had thought to have the park and its sculpture designed separately. But the artist-selection

135–37. Nancy Holt (b. 1938). *Dark Star Park*, 1979–84. Granite, earth, sod, winter creeper, crownvetch, willow oak, stone dust, stone masonry, asphalt, steel, water; total area: ⅔ acre. Sphere diameters: 8 ft. (3), 6½ ft. (2). Pool diameters: 18 ft., 15 ft. Large tunnel inner diameter, 10 ft., length: 25 ft. Small tunnel inner diameter, 3 ft., length: 15 ft. Steel poles: inner diameter, 6 in., length: 20 ft. x 16⅔ ft. x ⅝ in. Rosslyn, Virginia.

135

136

137

138. Elyn Zimmerman (b. 1945). *Marabar*, 1984.
Boulders (natural cleft and polished granite)
and water. Plaza: 140 x 60 ft. Pool: 60 ft. x 6
ft. x 18 in. Boulders, height: 2–10½ ft. National Geographic Society Headquarters,
Washington, D.C.

138

panel, reacting to the extremely small site (about one-half acre), felt that landscape and art needed careful integration and recommended Holt as an artist capable of executing a single unified design for both sculpture and open space. Her plans, implemented in late 1983–84, included a high berm pierced by a tunnel entrance and embracing a number of sculptural elements: concrete spheres perched in or near small pools of water, serpentine walls, and paths. The berm itself spills into the entry plaza of the adjacent building, the design of which was modified at Holt's request: a corner of the building was cut back to permit the park to be visible from farther down the street. Sight lines in the berm and several of the concrete globes focus attention on the relationships among the spheres, which pass in and out of view as they are eclipsed by each other. As the chief visual element in the park, these spheres—six and a half and eight feet in diameter—hold their own remarkably well against the scale of the surrounding streets and buildings without overwhelming the pedestrian; they are also a good foil to the angularity of the architecture. Scattered across the ground like an extinguished constellation, they also provide Holt's landscape with a name: *Dark Star Park*.

Holt was able to convince the state to expand her park to include an adjacent traffic island; there she positioned another pair of spheres and a group of poles, the shadows from which line up with an asphalt pattern on the ground early in the morning each August 1, the day in 1860 when one William Henry Ross acquired the land that would become known as Rosslyn. This seems like a rather self-conscious bit of historiography, but it makes for an intriguing visual puzzle. At the moment the park still has a rather exposed feeling, but small groups of willow oaks will eventually grow up and provide some shelter, especially needed in the summer

when the sun bakes this southerly facing site.

Both Holt and Noguchi, while taking into account such factors as topography and function, deployed in their landscapes an essentially abstract, geometric vocabulary consistent with their other sculptural production. There have been other projects in this late modernist idiom that equally maintain a distinct sculptural presence. In 1984, for example, Elyn Zimmerman's *Marabar* became an element in a landscape designed by James Urban for the National Geographic Society Headquarters in Washington, D.C. The project is located between the society's existing office building, designed by Edward Durrell Stone, and a new, essentially L-shaped, terraced structure by David Childs of Skidmore, Owings and Merrill. Zimmerman was commissioned to provide a focus to the space that would also relate to the mission of the institution. She proposed a sculpture of granite rocks and water, suggesting continents and oceans. The artist had long wanted to work with stone at a large scale—in part, she explains, because she had "learned the language of stone" through a geologist brother, and in part as a response to a visit to caves at Ajanta, Ellora, and Elephanta in India. She tracked down a stone of the color and durability she wanted, a mahogany-colored, "dark but not dead," carnelian granite that came from a quarry in South Dakota.

While Zimmerman met several times with Childs to discuss her proposal, it was with the landscape architect that she eventually worked more closely, for she wanted her boulders dispersed throughout the garden. Urban's design for the plaza had gone through several versions by the time the sculpture was added to the plans. Even though he had to modify his design yet again, both he and Zimmerman were well pleased with the results. They went together to examine the boulders, which turned out to be very compatible with the pink Italian granite facing on the building, though not precisely the same shade. They altered the grade and redesigned the lighting. Most important, they were able to change the planned locations of trees and shrubs, adjusting the scale, color, and texture of the plants to accord with the individual stones.

While the boulders have a "found" appearance, they in fact were quarried in massive, rough cubes and fashioned into their present shapes with hammer, wedge, chisel, and blowtorch. "To make something look natural is extremely complicated," acknowledges Zimmerman. Five of the boulders were placed around a rectangular pool in an open paved area between the entrances to the two buildings. Both pool and boulders are placed so that they seem to predate the pavers. The pool, for example, is overhung by the pavers so its sides are not easily seen, making it seem as though there had been a stream on the site that the pavers only partly concealed. Three of the stones, set close together at one end of the pool, are sliced vertically and highly polished, as if by the passing water. The rest of the twelve boulders are dispersed around the garden, some in dense plantings of shrubs, others in a grassy area.

Zimmerman has titled her work *Marabar,* an allusion to the caves in E. M. Forster's novel *A Passage to India.* While Forster's Marabar was the locus of an uncanny, disturbing experience, Zimmerman's is more benign. Yet the title is apt, for it suggests her aim of creating a landscape of the imagination. While Zimmerman was clearly sensitive to functional requirements, especially pedestrian circulation, her sculpture emphatically survives as art.

Other artists have been less concerned with the identity of their work as art. There is a surprising range of expression within Robert Irwin's projects, for example, which he explains as the result of the widely differing spaces in which he works. His prolonged observation of each site yields an awareness of whether the "sculptural gesture" should be "monumental or ephemeral, aggressive or gentle, useful or useless, sculptural, architectural, or simply the planting of a tree, or maybe even doing nothing at all."[99] In 1980 Irwin added a sculptural element to a gateway park in Dallas designed by the landscape-architecture firm of Sasaki/Walker. He was presented with a puzzling site, carved up by several roads, and with the all but completed plans for the park. He responded by suggesting a Serra-like, twelve-foot-high rusted steel wall that would slice through the hilly site, unifying the divided parcels. In places, the full height of the wall is visible; in others, it nearly disappears into the mounds; the wall is interrupted at street crossings and broken elsewhere to allow pedestrian passage.

A markedly different site in Seattle resulted in a very different sort of work, called *Nine Spaces/Nine Trees.* Designed for a plaza at the Public Safety Building, it turns constraint to advantage. As the plaza is supported by columns, it can bear significant weight only on top of them. Using this as the starting point for his design, Irwin placed flowering plum trees in planters that double as benches above the grid of columns. Around each of these he erected pale blue, semitransparent fencing, creating nine equal rooms joining into a large square. At the perimeter of the plaza is a low planter with ground cover.

Scott Burton, too, discounted the importance of an identifiable artistic signature. In 1985 he completed work on *Pearlstone Park* in Baltimore, a more explicitly functional project than any yet discussed. It is an irregularly shaped, approximately one-acre landscape between Meyerhoff Symphony Hall and the Maryland Institute College of Art. Bounded on three sides by streets, the site is constrained on the fourth by a crescent that overlooks a steep slope leading down to the institute. Burton located on this crescent the major sculptural elements of the park, a line of concrete

139

140

139

140

139, 140. Robert Irwin (b. 1928). *Nine Spaces/ Nine Trees,* 1983. Cement planters, plum trees, and blue wire-mesh fencing; 9 rooms of 22 x 22 ft. Seattle, Washington.

141, 142. Scott Burton (1939–1989). *Pearlstone Park,* 1985. Brick and concrete. Baltimore, Maryland.

142, 141 benches and concrete and brick lampposts. While at first glance these look rather clumsy, they relate well to the heavy masonry construction of the old Mount Royal train station, now the College of Art, and to the predominantly brick architecture of the neighborhood. Elsewhere, the park is crossed by diagonal pathways that Burton placed in response to his observations of pedestrian traffic there.

Burton rather self-effacingly described the content of his public works as "lunch hour," noting that in his mind they exist as much to provide public leisure as to make a statement about art. In this sense, their character as art is perceived almost subliminally. He described them as "post-modern in the sense that I don't believe in art as an instrument of social change" (unlike many of the early modernist painters, sculptors, and architects). Yet in Burton's case, as in others, to recognize that this art lacks the capacity to reform society is not to deny its public function, which for *Pearlstone Park* is to facilitate both passage through a landscape and active enjoyment of it. Nor does acknowledging such a public function deny the projects' aesthetic dimensions. *Pearlstone Park* is not an unqualified artistic success — too little of it is articulated either with sculpture or with plants — but the crescent of lamps and benches is an intelligent resolution to the awkward back side of the site.

The balance in *Pearlstone Park,* as in a number of other recent projects, has clearly tipped from an emphasis on individual imagination, as in Zimmerman's *Marabar,* toward an emphasis on social function. A project by Siah Armajani in some ways comparable to Burton's was installed the same year on the College Park campus of the University of Maryland. Like *Pearlstone Park,* Armajani's landscape, *Garden,* is utilitarian in character and understated in appearance. Built adjacent to Tawes

143

141

142

143

Theater, it was intended both as a place for relaxation—especially before theater events and during intermissions—and as a place for informal performances. Consequently, the project is divided into two major components. In one half of the ninety-by-fifty-foot hedged enclosure is a low brick podium or stage, set on the diagonal in a lawn that is surrounded by a square of gray pavement. On two sides of this square are black steel and blond wood benches. The other half of the landscape is centered on a pre-existing tree, around which are two concentric brick pavement squares; as in the podium, the larger one is set on the diagonal. At three corners of the larger square are placed elegant high-backed benches, also in steel and wood. This is a modest project but very satisfying: it is animated by Armajani's use of diamonds within squares and by the fine, if restrained, detailing.

While Burton and Armajani explored the pairing of sculpture and public leisure in their landscapes, Ned Smyth was working on a project employing representational subject matter for symbolic purposes—much as in more traditional public sculpture. Smyth's

144 project, called *Piazza Lavoro/Mythic Source*, was completed in 1984 as part of the redevelopment of a portion of Pittsburgh's Alle-

gheny riverfront into Allegheny Landing Park. It is one of several sculptures acquired or commissioned by local corporations and placed on long-term loan to the Carnegie Institute, which will be responsible for maintaining them.

Smyth's project is composed of two primary elements. *Mythic Source* is a circular plaza at the river's edge, in the center of which is a column of gray concrete aggregate in the abstracted form of a palm tree. Surrounding this, in a pavement of similar concrete aggregate, are tile mosaics of aquatic life. Just up the slope from this, set on a podium of curved steps, is *Piazza Lavoro*, a circular plaza paved in red brick. It too is centered on a columnar tree; on its perimeter are three architectural elements: curved panels with inlaid mosaic figures and palm trees. As the title suggests, *Piazza Lavoro* makes reference to Pittsburgh's long labor history in the mosaic depictions of men and women builders on one pair of panels and of exhausted naked working men on another. As Smyth explains it, these images convey both the satisfaction and anguish of being the builders of civilization.

Smyth skillfully created a bridge from these images of labor, placed closest to the adjacent architecture, to the most prominent landscape feature of the site—the river. The largest of

143. Siah Armajani (b. 1939). *Garden*, 1985. Colored brick, white oak, painted steel, colored aggregate cement; 90 x 50 ft. University of Maryland, College Park.

144. Ned Smyth (b. 1948). *Piazza Lavoro/ Mythic Source*, 1984. Aggregate-cement monoliths inlaid with mosaic figures, aggregate concrete palm trees. Allegheny Landing Park, Pittsburgh, Pennsylvania.

144

145. Anne and Patrick Poirier (both b. 1942). *Promenade Classique*, 1986. Marble, brick, and bronze; 10 acres. Transpotomac Canal Center, Alexandria, Virginia. Photo: Max Mackenzie.

146. Anne and Patrick Poirier. Detail of arrow from *Promenade Classique*, 1986. Bronze; height: 30 ft.

146

the three architectural elements of the upper plaza carries the images of the palm trees; it frames a view of the lower plaza and the river beyond, which together recall the origin of life in the oceans. Smyth likens the upper plaza to an acropolis town, looking down on the water that sustains it. The project thus literally and metaphorically links the urban and the natural landscapes.

Piazza Lavoro/Mythic Source is more openly historicizing and decorative than many other environmental projects. The richly suggestive mixture of architectural styles and mosaic images—especially palm trees and serpentine fish—seems calculated to create a public environment that is visually appealing and symbolically resonant at the same time, and thus to assure the project's public acceptance. Yet the naked human figures are denied real local or historical specificity; the palm trees are geographically anomalous. As such, the piece has less to do with Pittsburgh's particularly gritty history than with a more mythological and comparatively sanitized past. In the absence of such specific, localized meaning, it is possible to mistake a symbolic program for gratuitous decoration. In fairness to Smyth, it must be added that few sculptors were using a classically derived vocabulary when he first began to do so in the mid-1970s. Using that vocabulary then was to recall a previously scorned past and to suggest its potential as a source of form and cultural meaning. By now, however, so many sculptors—and architects—have begun to deploy classical ornament without concern for its original function or meaning that it invites suspicion of merely fashionable intentions.

Similar reservations arise concerning 145 *Promenade Classique* by the French sculptors Anne and Patrick Poirier. The project is the centerpiece of a five-building office and retail development on the Potomac River in Alexandria, Virginia. The Poiriers' contribution was initiated as the buildings were going up

and after a design for the grounds had been devised by the landscape architect Paul Friedberg. Working with Friedberg, the artists modified the design to accommodate their plans. While this is not a public project in every sense—it is on private land and was paid for entirely by the development company—it was intended for public use. "You give a big donation not only to the tenants around you but to the city," observed the corporation manager. "It is something for everybody to enjoy; it is an expensive gift."[100] Not coincidentally, the sculpture contributes to the creation of an "up-scale" atmosphere that attracts the kinds of tenants—and revenues—desirable to the developers.

The Poiriers' project is not a single sculpture but a series of incidents along a promenade that leads from the center of the buildings to the river. In a circle formed by the entry road is a cluster of marble boulders in a grove of white birch trees. At one edge is a thirty-foot bronze arrow set in a ring of fine, high jets 146 of water—as if the water had been released by the plunging arrow. Water also springs from a lower row of jets and pours down

147. Ned Smyth (b. 1948). *Landfall 39°49′N 75°31′W,* 1988. Exposed aggregate poured-concrete structures, blue slate, and paved brick; ⅓ acre. Commissioned by the Christina Gateway Joint Venture, a joint venture of The Linpro Company and Delle Donne & Associates, Wilmington, Delaware.

stepped basins before seeming to reappear across the drive in a long, rectangular pool. This pool is dominated by a rough-hewn marble boulder that reveals itself, on the other side, to be a human mouth spouting a broad sheet of water. Looking toward the river, two more boulders flank an opening in the terrace wall; they are inscribed with the Latin phrase "the eye of memory." These are, predictably, fashioned into eyes on the other side. A cascade pours between these eyes down to a basin filled with more fragments of monumental sculpture and playfully miniaturized architectural relics. Below, steps flanked by a pair of mouths lead down to the Potomac, where a forty-foot marble obelisk stands sentinel on the shore.

The Poiriers' classicism has overtones not only of the ancient world, but also of the Renaissance and of the nineteenth-century recovery of the past through archaeology. These overtones are appropriate enough in the neighborhood of the capital city, in which there is ample visual evidence of our culture's effort to define and legitimize itself through attachment to the classical past. Yet this analogy to Washington is somewhat incidental to *Promenade Classique,* which follows a long-established pattern in the Poiriers' work of archaeological fragments picturesquely disposed. The only certain reference to Washington is the obelisk, a miniature counterpart to the Washington Monument just visible up the river. Apart from this, it is not clear that the work aspires to any particular meaning relevant to its site. Instead, the project seems to reach for a mythic character that it doesn't quite grasp, especially not in this commercial precinct—although its decorative appeal is considerable.

In other instances, artists have been more concerned about their imagery's local pertinence. For a new park in Wilmington, Delaware, commissioned on the occasion of the city's 350th anniversary, Ned Smyth chose as the central elements of his design two features that allude to the founding and development of the city. One is a pair of boats that recalls the arrival of the original Swedish settlers of Wilmington. A group of flags flies in one; in the other stands a row of Smyth's schematized palm trees. The other main feature of the park is a cluster of building façades of different sizes and types—domestic, ecclesiastical, and commercial—intended, he says, as "a monument of urban growth." Some of the gables and cornices are similar to those on surviving buildings still visible from the site. He sought for this project, by comparison with *Piazza Lavoro/Mythic Source,* a more "localized, American" imagery that would blend myth with history and thus be "not so removed." Smyth's project, called *Landfall,* stands between the train and bus stations and a new commercial development that will eventually include four high-rise buildings.

Perhaps the most successful use to date of locally relevant—even reverent—imagery is Andrew Leicester's gateway to Sawyer Point Park in Cincinnati. The park, a new twenty-two-acre multiuse landscape on the Ohio River in downtown Cincinnati, was constructed as part of the city's bicentennial observances in 1988. Leicester was selected in an invitational competition to design a prominent entrance to the park, which would be paid for through private contributions. As he had done for his *Prospect V-III* in Frostburg, Leicester immersed himself in local history while planning the Cincinnati project. He kept a notebook in which he recorded information on the city's political, commercial, and cultural past, as well as its geology and topography. In this notebook, too, he began to develop the images that would be featured in the gateway.

The principal feature of Leicester's project—executed in cooperation with MS & R Architects, Minneapolis—is a 750-foot-long earthen mound that runs parallel to the river. On its top the *Ohio River Walk* follows a 450-foot

watercourse that maps the configuration of the river from its beginnings in Pittsburgh to its junction with the Mississippi in Cairo, Illinois. At the center, just where Cincinnati appears on the map, the mound is cut by
149 fifteen-foot-high brick-faced walls in the shape of a canal lock, which commemorates the fact that this spot was the terminus of a canal that ran from Toledo, on Lake Erie, to the Ohio—a fact that was crucial to Cincinnati's early economic development. While this lock provides direct, ground-level access to the park, the walkway passes above it over a schematized suspension bridge, a tribute to John Roebling's handsome construction that spans the Ohio nearby, a predecessor to his more famous Brooklyn Bridge. The suspension cables of Leicester's bridge are held in
151 the mouths of fishes; its twenty-foot towers metamorphose into riverboat smokestacks, from which emerge four-foot-high winged
152 pigs (fabricated by Minneapolis sculptor Douglas Freeman). These are a reference to Cincinnati's role in the nineteenth century as pork butcher to the world, which earned it the nickname *Porkopolis*.

On the surfaces of the lock and on adjacent retaining walls are a number of other locally pertinent images, executed in brick of various colors. One represents the Cincinnati Arch, an anticline of sedimentary rock on which Cincinnati was built. Embedded in this wall are both glazed stoneware "fossils" and reproductions of Indian artifacts unearthed in the Ohio Valley. Through the lock, on axis with it, is one of the other principal commemorative features of the gateway. In the center of a circular plaza defined by four pairs of smokestacks stands the sixty-five-foot *Flood Column*, crowned by a bronze arc. This column marks the level the river reached in the three major floods of the past century, including that of 1937 when it crested at eighty feet. In all, as a passage in Leicester's notebook asserts, "the work is a 'map' of the Ohio River system's history."

Notwithstanding the fact that they are a very small part of the entire gateway complex, the pigs enraged quite a few Cincinnatians, who were apparently still smarting from the indignities their city has endured over the years through its association with swine. Per-

148

149

148. Andrew Leicester (b. 1948). *Cincinnati Gateway,* 1988. Polychrome brick, patinated bronze, cast iron, steel, and water; 480 x 145 x 65 ft. Sawyer Point Park, Cincinnati, Ohio.

149. Andrew Leicester. Entrance to *Cincinnati Gateway.*

150. Andrew Leicester. Detail of *Ohio River Walk* from *Cincinnati Gateway.* Cast-iron and steel columns; height: 38 ft.

151. Douglas Freeman. Detail of fish from Andrew Leicester's *Cincinnati Gateway.* Patinated bronze; diameter: 2 ft., height: 2 ft.

152

152. Douglas Freeman. Detail of winged pig from Andrew Leicester's *Cincinnati Gateway*. Patinated bronze; height: 4 ft.

153. Richard Fleischner (b. 1944). Wiesner Building plazas, 1980–85 . Granite, teak, painted steel, plants, and lighting; 2½ acres. Massachusetts Institute of Technology, Cambridge.

haps the most notable of these came from the novelist Frances Trollope, who lived in Cincinnati from 1828 to 1831 and later wrote in her very unflattering *Domestic Manners of the Americans*, "I'm sure I should have liked Cincinnati much better if the people had not dealt so very largely in hogs." Recalling a walk she took up a hill that promised a fine prospect and fresh air, she noted: "We found the brook we had to cross, at its foot, red with the stream from a pig slaughterhouse; while our noses . . . were greeted by odors that I will not describe, and which I heartily hope my readers cannot imagine; our feet, that on leaving the city had expected to press the flowery sod, literally got entangled in pigs' tails and jawbones: and thus the prettiest walk in the neighborhood was interdicted forever."

Certain present-day Cincinnatians felt that Leicester's winged pigs were a joke at their expense; moreover, they were concerned that the swine would become a symbol of the city and revive the long-suppressed appellation Porkopolis. While Leicester did indeed intend his pigs partly in fun—they are a play on, among other things, the celebrated winged lions atop the columns in the Piazza San Marco in Venice—he is also serious about their importance to his theme and to the history of Cincinnati. Not only were pigs economically significant in their own right, but their ren-

dered fat gave rise to another of the city's major industries, the production of soap. The controversy eventually reached well beyond Cincinnati, occasioning much wry commentary. An Associated Press piece that ran in the *Chicago Tribune* led off with a paraphrase of a song from *The Music Man*: "They've got big trouble in this Ohio River city, with a capital 'T' and that rhymes with 'P' and that stands for pigs." The *Wall Street Journal* carried a headline that left no doubt about where it stood in the Serra debate: "Perhaps New York Would Accept the Pigs in Trade for 'Tilted Arc.' "[101]

The battle between enthusiasts and antagonists came to a head when a member of the city council, apparently with an eye on higher office, called a special public hearing to review the matter. Proponents turned it into a rousing pro-pig rally. They arrived carrying banners and cardboard winged-pig cutouts on sticks. Several swine enthusiasts on the council wore pig hats and snouts to show their support. Two live pigs were even in attendance, presumably to endorse the project: one small one—some remember it as wearing wings—sat politely in its owner's lap through the three-hour hearing; a large Vietnamese one—with "thick black bristles and more folds than an accordion," according to the *Cincinnati Post*—was brought in from the city zoo.[102] The pro-pork forces carried the day, and the project, pigs and all, was dedicated on June 1, 1988. "The real victory is Cincinnati's," ran an editorial in the *Post*. "The Queen City . . . has shown the poise to acknowledge, with a touch of whimsy, the pigs in her past."[103]

Leicester designed his gateway independently and thus had considerable creative latitude. This is less true for artists who become involved in direct collaborations with building and landscape architects. In what was to have been a test case of how well collaboration might work, six artists were selected in 1979 to collaborate with architect

153

I. M. Pei on the design of the new Arts and Media Technology building at the Massachusetts Institute of Technology in Cambridge. Only three artists stuck with the project to the end, which in itself is an indication of trouble. A writer who followed the process closely observed that "the purpose of this project mandated . . . an integrative aesthetic approach," but that one of the artists who bowed out felt that "the role of art should be to invade space and not to disappear into it."[104] Whether these difficulties were a matter of program or personality is fruitless to debate: what seems clear is that some types of art as well as some artistic personalities still do not thrive in the public space, especially when so closely conjoined with architecture. This is not necessarily the fault of the artist—the presumption that art will invariably be polite to architecture is a fantasy many architects and planners still cherish.

When the MIT building was finally completed in 1985, its interior and exterior skin included bands of color suggested by the painter Kenneth Noland. Inside, Scott Burton designed a set of elegantly curved benches and railings for an atrium stairwell. Outside,

Richard Fleischner, who was originally commissioned to work on a sculpture court, assumed responsibility for the landscaping of the entire two-and-a-half-acre site. He had to contend with a changing grade and with the fact that the arts building was not on axis with those around it. He resolved these difficulties by dividing the space into two elevations with a central stair that is on axis with the Health Sciences/Health Services building to one side and on the diagonal with the arts building. He also had to contend with heavy traffic, which he addressed with the generous use of multicolored granite pavers in several different patterns and, again, on different axes.

Fleischner's design goes a long way toward reconciling the various buildings and pulling the space together. The artist credits his success to his rather intuitive approach. He spent a great deal of time at the site, observing its features and anticipating its use. There is a distinction, according to Fleischner, between the process that leads to a work of art and the process that leads to what he skeptically calls "a design situation." He likens the difference to recording a recipe while you are cooking, as opposed to writing it down without trying it; the former situation, he says, is "plastic, and allows for a different way of looking." Not wanting to be limited by his drawings, he has expressed his need to feel free to adjust things as they are built. While some modification of a plan is no doubt possible in the process of construction, the notion of extensive changes is bound to give fright to architects and clients alike. It suggests again the many differences yet to be resolved between the approaches of artists and architects.

If the MIT episode suggests the difficulties of collaboration, a group of projects at Battery Park City in New York may represent its true possibilities. Constructed since 1980, Battery Park City is a mixed commercial and residential complex on ninety-two acres of landfill along the Hudson River in lower Manhattan. Developed by the Battery Park City Authority, a public agency created by the New York State legislature, the site was organized in accordance with a 1979 master plan prepared by the architects and planners Alexander Cooper and Stanton Eckstut. Their plan determined the basic streetscape—essentially integrated with the existing grid of lower Manhattan—and allocated approximately thirty percent of the site for public open space, much of it along the river. Subsequent design guidelines mandated a variety of building types and scales—with the buildings linked by certain common features—in an effort to avoid a monotonous, "superblock" appearance while still creating a coherent neighborhood. Within this overall plan, in which the whole was more important than any of the parts, parcels were leased to a variety of private corporations for development.

Although the 1979 master plan did not specifically mention art, it called for the creation of a number of "special places" all along a 155 mile-and-a-quarter-long esplanade, ultimately designed by Cooper, Eckstut down to the details of benches, lampposts, and railings, with plantings by Hanna/Olin, landscape ar-

chitects. Calling open space "the most treasured public resource in high-density Manhattan" and the Hudson River waterfront "Lower Manhattan's greatest potential recreational amenity," the plan suggested punctuating the esplanade, which runs beside the river the entire length of the site, with specially designed parks and plazas.[105] The landfill, completed in 1976 but not built upon until 1980, was the site for several years of a series of temporary installations called Art on the Beach. Given this history, it is not surprising that in 1981 planning began for a permanent incorporation of art into Battery Park City.

That year, a pro-bono Fine Arts Committee was appointed to assist the Authority in selecting artists, identifying sites for their works, and reviewing their proposals. Art projects were to be financed with money earmarked for open space in the infrastructure budget, generated through the sale of bonds and from "pilot payments" made by developers to the Authority in lieu of taxes. A publication prepared by Cooper, Eckstut in association with the Authority offered both economic and quality-of-life justifications for this program: "In addition to increasing economic benefits for both public and private developments, the program's objective is to enhance the quality of the open spaces and the enjoyment of people visiting, working and living at Battery Park City."[106] While art here, as is so often the case, was intended to benefit the commercial tenants as well as the predominantly upper-income residents, an unusual arrangement was made to spread the economic gain beyond Battery Park City: a portion of lease revenues generated there has been set aside for the construction of low- and middle-income housing elsewhere in the city.[107]

In formulating their plans, the Fine Arts Committee took into consideration the idea of "special places" as recommended in the original plan, which were now to be identified with art. They commissioned several artists

to create site-specific works for the esplanade at the terminus of the cross streets. Ned Smyth was given a site at the end of Albany Street; his project, *The Upper Room* — a rectangular colonnaded court of concrete aggregate and mosaic tile — was completed in the spring of 1987. R. M. Fischer created a fanciful metal gateway arch for a site farther down the esplanade at the entrance to Rector Park. Richard Artschwager was selected for a triangular site at the end of West Thames Street; he fashioned a group of high-backed granite chairs, wooden chaise lounges, and tables that resemble raised tree grates.

Three major precincts received even more elaborate treatment: North Cove, South Cove, and South Park — officially known as Robert F. Wagner, Jr., Park and designed by Machado and Silvetti Architects, with landscape architects Hanna/Olin and garden designer Lynden Miller. North Cove is the commercial heart of Battery Park City, located directly across West Street from the World Trade Center. Grandly called World Financial Center, the complex includes some six million square feet of offices as well as retail space and an 130 indoor "winter garden" with palm trees — all in four (there may yet be five) granite- and glass-sheathed towers designed by Cesar Pelli. For the design of a three-and-a-half-acre plaza around North Cove and between these buildings, Scott Burton and Siah Armajani were chosen in a limited competition to collaborate with Pelli and landscape architect Paul Friedberg. Both Burton and Armajani insisted that this was a "true collaboration," with all parties participating in all aspects of the design. "We utilized different people's expertise," Armajani reported, "but everybody worked on everything." This accounts for the fact that within an overall design that bears the stamp of no one person, certain signature elements nevertheless stand out — happily, to my mind. (These particular artists generally have placed too much emphasis on submerg-

ing their artistic personalities in a functional or collaborative program.)

The North Cove plaza is divided into two 156 sections. A garden area to the south includes, among other features, an oval lawn surrounded by a colonnade of cherry trees. An open plaza to the north is organized in an L shape around a multicolored checkerboard of granite pavers. To either side are blue granite fountains that spill a continuous sheet of water. Behind the fountains stand double rows of sycamores, fast-growing, broad-leafed trees that provide ample shade. Below them, rows of steps lead down to round stone tables and seats, all made in pink granite. These tables and benches recall Burton's work in Baltimore as well as at the Equitable Center in midtown Manhattan. The perimeter of the plaza is bounded with green lattice fencing; its center is marked with a torchère — an enormous conical stained-glass and bronze lamp on a column. Curved ramps lead from either side of the torchère down to the water's edge; inscribed on their fence balustrades are quotations about New York from Walt Whitman ("City of the World . . .") and contemporary poet Frank O'Hara ("One need never leave the confines of New York . . ."). This conceit recalls the similar use of texts by Armajani on his bridges for NOAA, among 116 many other projects.

The civic importance of the North Cove precinct was strengthened in 1995 by the addition of the Belvedere, a small park at its northern edge. On axis with the Winter Garden, the Belvedere is the terminus of a New Jersey commuter ferry that brings passengers to the financial district; it also marks the transition between North Cove and the large, Olmsted-inspired Hudson River Park to the north. The Belvedere was designed by architect Steven Goldberg of Mitchell/Giurgola and landscape architect Susan Child of Child Associates. It is disposed over two levels that are separated by a handsome, battered-stone wall,

156. Scott Burton (1939–1989) and Siah Armajani
(b. 1939), with Cesar Pelli and M. Paul Friedberg.
Aerial view of North Cove, 1988. Battery Park City,
New York.

156

157. Martin Puryear (b. 1941). *Stainless Steel Pylons,* 1995. Granite, stainless steel, and lighting, north pylon, height: 72 ft. 3 in.; south pylon, height: 56 ft. 8 in. For the Belvedere at Battery Park City, New York, designed by Mitchell/Giurgola Architects with Child Associates, Landscape Architects.

157

which turns the corner from the North Cove yacht basin to the esplanade. Broad stairs pierce the wall at the site of the ferry terminal, providing direct access to the plaza in front of the World Financial Center. The upper level is planted with a bosque of English oaks that repeats the grid of palms in the Winter Garden.

As at other important sites at Battery Park City, the Authority commissioned sculpture to provide an emblem for the park and to mark the locus of the ferry terminal. After a limited competition, Martin Puryear was selected to design a pair of stainless-steel pylons that glow with reflected light by day and with artificial illumination by night. Distant cousins of Brancusi's *Endless Column,* Puryear's sculptures are, in the words of the artist, "about what the *Endless Column* is not." Like their antecedent, Puryear's pylons are composed of repeated elements, but their units are not identical. In one pylon, the elements diminish in height and breadth as they climb; in the other, they become more squat and beamy toward the ground. One sculpture is an open, spiraling lattice; the other is solid. The two are different heights: the open one stretches to some seventy-two feet, while the solid is compressed to about fixty-six. Even the bases are different. The lattice stands on an elegant cylinder, whereas the closed form seems to compress its base, causing it to bow like a barrel. As Puryear says of the pylons: "One is about airiness, light, levitation. The other is about gravity." But both are dramatically lit from within, which intensifies the perception of their shifting patterns.

While the plaza at North Cove is formal and fundamentally geometric, the landscape at South Cove received a more natural treatment. Although the two projects are equivalent in size, South Cove is in a residential rather than a commercial setting and is thus open to more intricate landscaping. Designed collaboratively by landscape architect Susan Child, sculptor Mary Miss, and architect Stanton

Eckstut, the project draws on both the natural and historical aspects of a cove. The inland terminus of this cove is marked by dense plantings of honey locust, wild azalea and roses, blueberry, and beach grass surrounding informal groups of boulders that spill down to the water. While this landscape recalls a natural inlet, other features of the design are associated with the history of the waterfront, especially the wooden piles and decking.

At one end of the cove, several elements combine to form the architectural heart of the area. There, the shoreline walk curves around to meet the water at the outer limit of the cove — another wonderful, densely planted section with a variety of pines, wild roses, and beach grass. A wooden jetty continues out over the water, curving in on itself and nearly closing the circle; its decking ends partway out to reveal the supporting structure beneath. The diameter of this circle is marked by an arched bridge with a raised viewing platform to one side. The bridge, like the jetty, gives views of the structure beneath — this time, the concrete decking on which the whole Battery Park landfill rests. This seems a particularly self-conscious element in a design that otherwise aspires to naturalness and historical verisimilitude; but it serves as reminder that this landscape is, after all, artificial and that nature in the city is fundamentally a cultural construct. While the design of North Cove is basically consistent with the geometry of the setting, it remains to be seen how that of South Cove will work with the residential units built right up on it. On its own, however, it achieves considerable success, both in its imaginative plantings and in its historical evocations. This is a landscape with distinct architectural, sculptural, and horticultural elements, all of them appealing.

In many respects, the landscape at Battery Park City is exemplary. Although the commercial precinct around the North Cove is overbuilt, there is an overall sense of a coherent

155

neighborhood achieved partially through the architecture but also through the open-space design, which knits the string of parks and plazas together along the esplanade. The art at Battery Park City has come into being as an expression of the same commitment to coherent urbanism and good design that characterizes the project as a whole. It does its part in creating a visually intriguing environment; in the North and South Cove projects it also contributes to reinforcing the maritime character of the place. Moreover, it is clear that the Authority is committed to maintaining all the open spaces, including the art, in the best possible condition: it has established a separate not-for-profit agency to be responsible for maintenance, funded through an assessment on residential units.

In all, Battery Park City — together with many of the other projects discussed in this chapter — suggests the great advances that have recently been achieved in the creation of the artistically improved public landscape. There is no question that art, as it has become more responsive to its physical setting and its cultural context, has gained an important element of public relevance: as a form of civic expression, public art created for specific sites has emphatically improved. There is little doubt in my mind that this art has had a beneficial impact on the public space. Environmental art has taken the lead not only in making those spaces more satisfying visually, but also in restoring some element of public meaning to them. Sculpture has been faster certainly than landscape architecture but arguably also faster than architecture to recover the narrative, commemorative, and even symbolic possibilities inherent in environmental design. It is for this reason, it seems to me, that so many environmental projects were, for a time, given to artists alone; now that the practices of architecture and landscape design are catching up with sculpture, some artists are beginning to work comfortably with designers.

Yet what has been good for public art and for the public space has not necessarily been good for art itself. As the breach between public art and the larger community has narrowed, the gap has widened between two forms of art: that produced in the studio for the artist's personal satisfaction and destined for the gallery, the museum, and the private collector on the one hand, and that produced for the public space on the other. This schism is apparent even within the work of individual artists: both Martin Puryear and Scott Burton have made a distinction between their studio and their public work. Indeed, Puryear goes so far as to describe many of his public projects — such as his fountain and garden pavilion for a commercial development in Bethesda, Maryland — as "amenities" rather than sculptures; the latter are generally more convincing as art than the former.[108] Burton put the conflict in terms of the need to balance his imagination with the social role of his sculpture: too much imagination, he said, is threatening. "If it is too self-conscious, people are resentful."

The schism is also apparent in the roster of compelling artists who have won little or no place in the public space. While Richard Serra may represent the phenomenon of the good sculptor who, by virtue of his antagonistic stance, makes a bad public artist, there are other, nonconfrontational artists who have as yet been passed over for public commissions. For instance, there is Charles Simonds, at one extreme, and John Duff and the late Chris Wilmarth at the other. It may be that the strongly fantastical quality of Simonds's work and the subtle poetry of Duff's and Wilmarth's are simply too much at odds with the notion of public communication. Other artists have categorically refused to work in the public space because of the constraints they feel it places on them; they are ceding their position there to artists who are more willing to adapt to the social and architectural context.

The schism may be on the brink of institutionalization, as public art sponsors turn increasingly to art that seeks accommodation with the public. There seems to be, for the moment at least, something inimical in the practice of public art to the language of either transcendence or social criticism. In the best of all possible worlds, there would be a place for all sorts of art in the public space: I, for one, would not want our public agencies to prescribe or proscribe certain types of art, mandating that they invariably be functional, for example, or incorporate historical content.

All this suggests that those of us accustomed to more personal gratifications from art will have to acquire new standards for appreciating public art, just as artists will have to content themselves with the knowledge that, whatever the limitations on their creative latitude, working in the public space has other satisfactions. And these are considerable. If we have learned anything at all from the debates over public art — whether over the Richard Serra in New York or the Andrew Leicester in Cincinnati — it is that people care deeply about the character of their public spaces. They seem eager for an experience of communality that goes beyond the exchange of money for goods in the suburban shopping mall that has lately passed for public life in America. They want a public landscape on which they can meet, one that satisfies the requirements of function and the appetite for visual splendor, but one that also triggers the memory and fires the imagination, one, moreover, that suggests some common culture in a society that has not yet entirely resolved the matter of how to be a whole while still being respectful of all the parts.

Few recent works of public art attain all these goals, but this, it seems to me, is the high purpose to which the best of them are directed — although it remains to be seen if they can attain this communal purpose while retaining the particular magic of art. If our public officials, architects, planners, and artists have failed in recent decades to provide a landscape that permits, or even promotes, an experience of public life, then we must pay heed to the mounting evidence that many people want this situation rectified. We owe it, at least in part, to a recent generation of public artists that a new form of communal experience and a new concept of public life may be in sight.

158. Joseph Beuys (1921–1986). *I Like America and America Likes Me,* 1974, at René Block Gallery, New York. Courtesy of Ronald Feldman Fine Arts, New York.

6. THE GREENING OF ART

In 1971, the year after Michael Heizer completed *Double Negative,* the German artist Joseph Beuys waded fully clothed into a marsh at the edge of the Zuider Zee in the Netherlands, until little more of him was visible than the top of his trademark hat. This *Bog Action,* as he called it, was meant to dramatize his concern for the widespread destruction of wetland ecosystems in the country as shallow seas were being drained to produce new land.

Beuys was an artist for whom the morally and socially engaged act was entirely synonymous with art; his life was his art. *Bog Action* was just one of many initiatives he made on behalf of environmental causes as part of his broader political life. Later in 1971, for instance, Beuys and a small army of supporters swept with birch brooms a section of a Düsseldorf forest, Grafenberger Wald, to protest the planned cutting of trees to accommodate the expansion of a tennis club. He did numerous solo performances affirming his empathy for animals — notably, *I Like America and America Likes Me* (1974), in which he lived with a coyote for five days in a New York gallery. In 1979 Beuys ran unsuccessfully for the European Parliament as a candidate of the Green party; in 1983 — in a project anticipating Mel Chin's *Revival Field* — he proposed using special plants to reduce the concentration of toxic chemicals in the badly polluted mud flats along the Elbe River near Hamburg. Nothing came of this idea, but his equally ambitious project to plant seven thousand oak trees in the West German city of Kassel was brought to completion. Instigated on the occasion of the Documenta 7 exhibition in 1982, the action was completed when the last tree was planted at the opening of Documenta 8 in 1987. Although Beuys died before this vast urban reforestation project was completed, *7,000 Oaks* lives on as one of the world's largest "green" sculptures.[109]

Heizer and Beuys were working in dissimi-lar landscapes and in different cultural circumstances — one in the relatively unpopulated expanses of the western United States, the other in one of the most densely populated and intensively industrialized regions on earth. But they also represent the opposite ends of a continuum of artists' attitudes toward nature. Whereas Heizer was using the earth as a neutral surface on which to act and as the source of raw materials for his sculptures, Beuys — like his English contemporaries Richard Long and Hamish Fulton — was staking out a more conspicuously empathic relationship to landscape. He also provided a model of the artist as environmental activist and cultural critic, a model that has grown increasingly influential as the years have passed. By submerging himself in a bog, for example, Beuys was affirming a conception of nature as a living system of which we are a part and which we modify, for better or for worse, with our actions. Landscape in this view is a cultural artifact, subject to the vagaries of politics as much as to the laws of nature. No intervention in the landscape is independent of either social or ecological implications. Beuys made it his mission to reveal some of the places where those interventions were problematic and to propose some modest remediations.

Beuys was not alone in hoping that his art might help repair the landscape, as demonstrated by the nearly contemporaneous mine-reclamation projects by Robert Smithson, Herbert Bayer, and Heizer, among others. But their primary intent was to make art, not to direct attention to environmental ills. Other European and American artists practiced a form of ecological activism more akin to that of Beuys; all were expressing the increased environmental awareness that has characterized the past several decades. The German-born artist Hans Haacke, for example, began working with natural materials and processes in the mid-1960s: making ice sculptures, floating balloons in the air, using water to create

159. Dennis Oppenheim (b. 1938). *Cancelled Crop* stage of *Directed Seeding/Cancelled Crop,* 1969. Wheat field, harvester, seed, and grain, 505 x 876 ft. Temporary installation, Finsterwolde, the Netherlands.

160. Alan Sonfist (b. 1946). *Circles of Time,* 1989. Trees, stones, bronze sculpture, and natural landscaping, diameter: 200 ft. Collection of Villa Celle Art Spaces, Florence. Photograph by the artist.

treated, filtered, and released into a tank containing goldfish.

By the early 1970s, a related sensibility had begun to emerge in the United States in the work of artists such as Dennis Oppenheim, Helen Mayer Harrison and Newton Harrison, Ana Mendieta, and Alan Sonfist. Starting in 1968, Oppenheim executed a series of ephemeral projects intended to make manifest the political and economic structures that shape the landscape. The most interesting of them took the form of inscriptions: *Time Line,* for example, was a three-mile-long drawing made with a snowmobile on the frozen surface of the Saint John River along the border between the United States and Canada. Not only did it underscore the way the landscape is carved into political jurisdictions but it also marked a boundary between the Atlantic and Eastern time zones. Oppenheim's *Directed Seeding/Cancelled Crop* (1969) was a commentary on the tendency to see the landscape only in terms of the commodities it can produce. At Oppenheim's instruction, a field in Holland was seeded with wheat and later harvested in the shape of the letter X. All further processing was halted. "In this case the material is planted and cultivated for the sole purpose of withholding it from a product-oriented system," Oppenheim explained.[110]

Also in 1969, Alan Sonfist started planning for a piece that would add a small patch of forest to the dense urban environment of lower Manhattan. Planted in 1977, his *Time Landscape* is a re-creation of the forest that was indigenous to Manhattan before the arrival of Europeans transformed the island forever. The piece is problematic in several respects. It is meant to be wild, hence it is unkempt. It implies the existence of an "innocent" nature prior to colonization, whereas we now know that the precolonial forest was altered by Native American habitation even before the arrival of settlers.[111] And it reinforces the un-

159

mist and erosion. By the turn of the decade, however, Haacke had evidently come to realize that natural systems were almost invariably modified by human actions, and he began to concentrate on revealing the detrimental impact of those actions on the landscape. In 1970, in a project called *Beach Pollution,* he collected all the trash on a 600-foot section of Spanish beach. Two years later came *Rhine Water Purification Plant,* in which polluted water from the Rhine was trucked to the Museum Haus Lange in Krefeld, then

159

fortunate implication that nature is something apart from culture: a chain-link fence encloses the project, rendering *Time Landscape* inaccessible as well as unattractive.

160 Sonfist has gone on to make much more engaging variations on this theme — in particular, the version commissioned by Giuliano Gori for the notable collection of site-specific art at his villa, Fattoria di Celle, in Pistoia, Italy. Calling the piece *Circles of Time,* Sonfist created an emblematic history of the Tuscan landscape in a three-acre composition of concentric rings. At the center of the circles is a re-creation of the indigenous but now obliterated Tuscan forest. Surrounding this is a garden featuring herbs known to have been cultivated by the Etruscans; it is guarded by bronze stick figures cast from the limbs of endangered trees. Around this is a ring of laurels, through which passages are cut to permit access to the interior. A broad band of stones constitutes the outermost ring, suggestive of Roman roads and medieval streets. The whole is set on a slope in a working orchard, which connects the composition to present-day uses of the Tuscan landscape.

Beginning in the late 1960s, Helen Mayer Harrison and Newton Harrison traveled the world to study ecological and biodiversity problems ranging from the salinization of fresh water in California to the effect of chemical pollution on Yugoslav forests. They became virtual ambassadors-at-large to the environment. "Our work begins when we perceive an anomaly in the environment that is the result of opposing beliefs or contradictory metaphors," they told an interviewer in 1987. "Moments when reality no longer appears seamless and the cost of belief has become outrageous offer the opportunity to create new spaces — first in the mind and thereafter in everyday life."[112] Their art takes a wide range of forms, from the creation of portable farming systems for museum installation to the study of entire ecosystems, using maps, drawings, photographs, videotapes, and even poetry to analyze environmental conflicts and recommend possible resolutions.

Like Long and Fulton, the Harrisons joined in the reaction against more monumental earthworks. "Think of the vast energy put into big cuts and shapes in the desert that are inherently gestural," Newton Harrison said. "They are transactional with museum space, not with the earth. They are involved primarily with forms."[113] The Harrisons' own work, by comparison, blurred the boundaries between art and science. One of their first projects, for example, involved a study of the mating behavior of a Southeast Asian crab, *Scylla serrata*

161

161

forskal, which they carried out as a museum installation with the support of a Sea Grant from the Scripps Oceanographic Institute (a grant typically reserved for biologists and oceanographers). They went on to examine whole ecosystems — in one project moving a segment of endangered meadow in Germany, destined to be plowed under for development, to the roof of the Kunst- und Ausstellungshalle in Bonn. In another, they created a memorial to vanishing California floodplain ecosystems as a permanent public art project for the Santa Monica Beach Promenade.

The Harrisons' recent work has grown in scope, addressing the contested landscapes that compose whole countries, even continents. *Vision for the Green Heart of Holland* proposes a "Central Park" for the Netherlands, which would protect the natural and farming communities at the center of the nation from the development pressures being exerted by the ring of cities surrounding it. The proposal suggests the considerable impact that art might have on social policy and thereby on the physical environment. Commissioned by the Cultural Council of South Holland, the Harrisons'

Vision covers a region of some 618 square
miles (1,600 square kilometers) with a population of about 5.5 million people. The project became the focus of a museum exhibition,
then of a poster that was mailed to all the
public officials, schools, and architects in the
region. The main points in the Harrisons' proposal were subsequently incorporated into a
draft planning document by the national min-
ister of the environment. Although the document is still subject to review, the Harrisons'
ideas seem well on their way to becoming
national policy. In the same spirit, the two
have also proposed creating a forest preserve
in Tibet to protect the headwaters of Asia's
great rivers.

Other artists have found different ways to
assert their sense of personal identification
with the earth. Like Charles Simonds — for
whom the landscape, the body, and architecture are all forms of dwelling — the late
Cuban-born sculptor and performance artist
Ana Mendieta drew analogies between the
body and the earth, but in a more insistently
feminist way. In a series called The Tree of
Life, she covered her naked body with clay
and stood against the trunk of a tree, suggesting the affinity she felt between her vitality
and that of the plant, and the dependence of
both on the earth. She also created numerous
effigy figures in the ground, shaping the image of her own body in mud, flowers, or gun-
powder and wood. Some of these she would
sprinkle with blood, others she would ignite,
implying the violence that she felt had been
perpetrated against both women and the earth
by a predominantly patriarchal culture. Undoubtedly it was Mendieta's desire to escape
the emphatically masculine history of art that
led her to reach all the way back to ancient
fertility figures as inspiration. Although she
was certainly successful in asserting an affinity
between the creative powers of women and
those of the earth, she also risked reinforcing
an old duality in which nature is imagined to

162

be female and culture is perceived to be male — and the latter presumed to be superior.

Mendieta's work foreshadowed several gender-based transformations in the practice of environmental art. In terms of sheer numbers, it would increasingly become the province of women. More important, their growing presence through the 1980s and 1990s would bring subtle changes to the discourse about landscape. Many women joined in the critique of the first generation of earth artists, seeing in their high technology and heavy equipment a degree of macho posturing. Many more evidenced a commitment to environmental stewardship. I don't subscribe to the notion that there is a "women's art," nor would I say that women are inherently any more or less capable than men as guardians of nature. At the risk of generalizing, however, I would say that women are more attuned to its gender implications. Some, like Mendieta, explore the way that dualities between male and female are replicated in the distinctions between culture and nature or intellect and instinct. Others have become self-conscious about the traditional associations between women and caretaking, especially in the home and garden. Paradoxically, much recent environmental art by women both reiterates and subverts these dualities: as we shall see with the work of Meg Webster, Karen McCoy, and Lorna Jordan, for example, it is at once more domestic, gardenesque, and nurturing than work by men, even as it chafes against these stereotypes.

Whether through ecological intervention, horticulture, or the evocation of ancient ritual, sculptors such as Mendieta, Sonfist, and the Harrisons developed in America the role for which Beuys had provided the model — that of the artist as environmental activist and social critic. Many of them merged art with other pursuits, including anthropology, science, garden design, and landscape architecture. In so doing, however, they have raised questions about whether they were stepping beyond the limits of their competence and whether their work might not be better if executed by someone from another discipline. These are questions to be faced by all artists who would be environmentalists. As their work has shaded toward ecological activism, it has not only had trouble asserting its identity as art, it has sometimes seemed to trespass on the territory of others.

Notwithstanding these difficulties, what might be termed "green art" has emerged as one of the most significant new trends in late twentieth-century sculpture. No doubt this is an expression of a deepening and ever more pervasive sense of anxiety about the potentially catastrophic effects of unchecked population growth, industrial development, and resource consumption on global climate and health. Artists can hardly be expected to resolve all our environmental ills. There is some cause to wonder if they should try at all, if the result is neither good art nor good design nor good science. Moreover, their efforts must seem small compared to the magnitude of the problems. It seems to me fair to ask if they are making a real difference or merely expressing their own feelings of frustration and guilt at being part of a culture of conspicuous consumption, pollution, and waste.

In fairness to these artists, solutions to large problems are often local and incremental, and artists surely have a part to play in determining them. More important, art has the power to give voice to myth, if not to help shape it. We need desperately now to revive some old myths — myths about culture being embedded in nature, for example, and about the possibility of people living in greater empathy with their environment. And we need to articulate some new myths — myths in which the considerable forces of technology would be marshaled to fix, not to create, problems, and in which nurture would replace domination as the guiding notion in our earthly affairs. We

163. Michael Singer (b. 1945). *First Gate Ritual Series 5/80,* 1980. Pine, rock, and spruce branches, 3 x 24 x 20 ft. Riehen, Switzerland. Photograph by the artist.

163

are still a long way from the land ethic articulated half a century ago by the conservationist Aldo Leopold in his trenchant book *A Sand County Almanac* (1949). Our relationship with the earth, now as then, seems governed more by expedience than by sound planning. "There is as yet no ethic dealing with man's relation to land and to the animals and plants which grow upon it," Leopold wrote. "Land, like Odysseus' slave-girls, is still property. The land-relation is still strictly economic, entailing privileges but not obligations."

Leopold called for human activities to be regarded in the light of a deceptively simple equation. "Examine each question in terms of what is ethically and esthetically right, as well as what is economically expedient. A thing is right when it tends to preserve the integrity, stability, and beauty of the biotic community. It is wrong when it tends otherwise."[114] Judgments about what is ethically and aesthetically right are subject to endless discussion. But to the extent that aesthetics plays a part in the land ethic, artists can surely be instrumental in advancing the debate. It would be no little accomplishment if art were to assist in the critical process of cultural redefinition, even as it continues to offer us some of its familiar visual gratifications.

Thus far, the artists who have been most successful at integrating art with environmental activism have used strategies familiar to us from recent public art projects. They have often collaborated with people from other disciplines, and they have developed distinctions, in theory and in practice, between their studio art and their projects in the landscape. Michael Singer provides a particularly interesting case in point, creating distinct kinds of sculptures in different settings and entirely changing his manner of working to fit the public context, where he has emerged as a visionary architect and planner. He has a long history as an environmental sculptor, dating back to some ephemeral constructions of

wood or reeds that he created in the mid-1970s in ponds near his home in southern Vermont and in the salt marshes of Long Island Sound and the Chesapeake Bay. More than simple responses to a site, these were expressions of Singer's immersion in a particular place. "In order to experience and learn from the natural environment," he explained, "I felt the need to yield to it, respect it, to observe, learn, and then work with it." These were meditations on landscape, with titles — such as First Gate Ritual Series — that alluded to his almost ceremonial connections with nature. 163

At the same time, Singer has made robust constructions for indoor settings, which often define a passage or an enclosure. These too are contemplative spaces in which to study the fragmented stone or hewn wood that signify larger nature. They can seem almost memorializing in function, and Singer has used related structures in public commissions with a commemorative purpose. The city of Stuttgart, Germany, for example, retained Singer

164

164. Michael Singer. *Ritual Series/Retellings: A Place to Remember Those Who Survived,* 1994. Plantings, brownstone, granite, fieldstone, bronze, and patterned concrete, approximately one acre. Stuttgart, Germany.

in Warsaw in 1945: "The world in its entirety is a narrow bridge, and the main thing is not to be afraid." Singer recalls with evident gratification a conversation among the German, Turkish, and American workmen who were helping him build this memorial garden. One asked, "Who are the survivors?" Another responded, "I guess we all are."

Singer has also been called upon to work on a number of public infrastructure projects, several of which have been geared toward environmental remediation. In 1989, through the Phoenix Percent-for-Art program, he was hired to collaborate with the artist Linnea Glatt on the design of a solid-waste transfer and recycling facility, which was to be built on the 166 site of a landfill that had reached its capacity at the edge of the city. This project necessitated the creation of a new dump in a distant desert location, as well as a facility where garbage could be transferred from standard sanitation trucks to the massive vehicles that would carry it away. Ordinarily, a waste depot would not be considered a civic space and, in fact, this transfer and recycling facility was originally planned as a utilitarian shed with no public access. But the city's director of public works, Ron Jensen, felt that the project offered a wonderful opportunity to educate the public about the workings of their city, perhaps encouraging them to conserve and recycle in the process — thus saving the city both hauling costs and landfill space. So he made the unusual suggestion to the Phoenix Arts Commission that they select artists to head a design team charged with imagining a new kind of public place, where people could observe the parade of their waste and learn about its impact on the environment.

Putting aside the original plans for the facility, Singer and Glatt worked with the designers and planners Sterling McMurrin and Richard Epstein; the architect Dino Sakellar; and the engineering firm of Black and Veatch, Inc., to come up with plans for the entire

in 1993 to design a one-acre garden within a larger city park in conjunction with an international garden exposition. Noting that the site lay over rubble from World War II bombings, Singer elected to create a generalized memorial to armed conflict and to the particular burdens of those who must rebuild their lives and reconcile themselves to history.

164, 165   Calling the piece *Ritual Series/Retellings: A Place to Remember Those Who Survived,* Singer worked with two streams found on the site, supplemented by three new wells. He designed a sequence of spaces around these water sources, including a shadowy glade of willow and ferns, through which the water runs in a granite rill. The streams all converge in a sunny area framed by a stone-and-wood enclosure, entwined with clematis and ivy. Here water flows over and around stone slabs, past low-growing plantings of wild ginger and moneywort. Inscribed on a granite tablet in this garden is a quotation from a poem written about 1800 by Rabbi Nachman of Bratslav, which was found scratched on a ghetto wall

165. Michael Singer. *Ritual Series/Retellings: A Place to Remember Those Who Survived.*

166. Michael Singer and Linnea Glatt, with Sterling McMurrin, Richard Epstein, Dino Sakellar, and Black and Veatch, Inc. 27th Avenue Solid Waste Management Facility, 1993, west elevation. Phoenix.

165

166

twenty-five-acre site — including roads and
landscaping — and a design for a 100,000-
square-foot, $18 million transfer and recycling
building. This was a far cry from the meditative structures that had previously been
Singer's forte, but the project gave him another way to pursue his goal of connecting
people with an experience of nature. The team
designed three approach roads. One is for the
approximately five hundred large trucks per
day that convey trash in and out of the facility. Another is for "self-haul": the people who
bring their own trash and recyclables. The
third, for visitors and administrators, leads over
the mile-long, six-story-high capped landfill
that had necessitated the project in the first
place, after becoming filled to capacity.

The building itself is surprisingly handsome,
with gray cement-block walls that are stepped
like a ziggurat and softened with drought-
tolerant plantings of rosemary, sage, yellow
Lady Banksia roses, bougainvillea, and cat's-
claw in the terraced intervals. The rosemary
drapes, while the roses, bougainvillea, and
cat's-claw climb, creating hanging gardens.
"The landscape [is] much more than a gratui-
tously decorated area," Singer wrote in a description of the project. "It is a means to fuse
the natural and built environments." The edi-
fice is capped with a 480-foot sage green steel
truss that is visible for miles around. The truss
negates the need for interior supports, which
frees the entire two-acre space for the huge
machines that sort the trash. This spectacle
is visible from catwalks and from an exterior
amphitheater where visitors can peer in
through large glass panels. The whole effect
is at once archaic and futuristic, suggesting an
ancient temple consecrated to a postindustrial phenomenon — the culture of excess
and obsolescence.

Singer's success in this venture has led to
his involvement in several other public infrastructure projects. In Grand Rapids, Michigan,
he designed a river walk and flood-control

wall completed in 1996; in New Haven,
Connecticut, he led a team that developed
a master plan for a waterfront park at Long
Wharf, which will entail the reuse of a de-
funct sewage-treatment facility as a center for
vocational education in aquaculture; and in
Prague he is at work on a plan to preserve
Troja Island and restore the surrounding Vltava
River environment. While his assumption of
widely disparate roles in different contexts —
sculptor, landscape architect, environmental
planner, civil engineer — has raised a few eye-
brows, it is becoming more typical for artists.

Like Singer, the sculptor Mierle Laderman
Ukeles has been engaged in a project involving a solid-waste transfer station. For some
twenty years Ukeles has been an unpaid
artist-in-residence with the Department of
Sanitation in New York City, trying to promote public appreciation of the heroic efforts
made by trash collectors and recognition of
their importance to the health of the urban
environment. She has constructed temporary
tributes to them in recycled materials, such as
*Ceremonial Arch Honoring Service Workers
in the New Service Economy.* At her urging,
the new marine transfer station at Fifty-ninth
Street on the west side of Manhattan has been
engineered to be a public space, with catwalks and observation decks so the public can
watch the loading of garbage on barges bound
for the Fresh Kills Landfill on Staten Island. It is
her ambition to create permanent sculptures
in recycled materials for the facility, signify-
ing possible other uses for some of the trash
we daily commit to the ground. Calling the
project *Flow City,* Ukeles has also proposed a
wall of video monitors that will broadcast in
real time the activities at city landfills.

Mel Chin has become something of an expert in botany for a project he has developed
with the scientist Rufus Cheney, a heavy-
metals expert in the Environmental Chemistry
Laboratory at the USDA's Agricultural Research
Service in Beltsville, Maryland. *Revival Field,*

168. Mierle Ukeles (b. 1939). *Ceremonial Arch Honoring Service Workers in the New Service Economy*, 1988. Steel arch with materials donated from New York City agencies, including gloves, lights, grass, straps, springs, and asphalt, 11 ft. x 8 ft. x 8 ft. 8 in. (overall structure), plus glove branches ranging from 2 to 4 ft. long. Temporary installation, New York Public Library.

168

169. Mel Chin (b. 1951). *Revival Field* (aerial view), 1990–93 (photographed 1993). Plants and industrial fencing on a hazardous-waste landfill, approximately 60 x 60 x 9 ft. Pig's Eye Landfill, Saint Paul.

169

as this series of growing sculptures is called, began when Chin happened upon an article about hyperaccumulators — plants that selectively absorb heavy metals from toxic soils as they grow. Touted as a form of "green remediation" and as a low-tech, on-site alternative to more costly forms of decontamination, these plants had yet to be proved effective in field trials. Recognizing the need to bring scientists, public agencies, and the necessary capital together, Chin approached Chaney with the unusual proposal that he help orchestrate test plantings as an art project. Chin secured the support of the National Endowment for the Arts and the Walker Art Center in Minneapolis and a site at the Pig's Eye Landfill in Saint Paul, which was contaminated with cadmium, zinc, and lead. Between 1990 and 1993, annual plantings of six hyperaccumulators were set out at the landfill in a circular pattern divided by two walkways, evoking the crosshairs on a rifle scope and suggesting that the earth was targeted for restoration.

At the end of each growing season, plants were harvested and tested for the presence of heavy metals. At the end of the three-year period it was determined that they were indeed removing contaminants from the soil, although not fast enough to achieve significant cleansing. Meanwhile, another *Revival Field* was established at a site in Palmerton, Pennsylvania, that had been designated by the federal Environmental Protection Agency as a top priority for remediation. There the soil contains heavy concentrations of zinc and cadmium, probably from a smelter that operated between about 1890 and 1980. The most promising zinc and cadmium hyperaccumulators, including Alpine pennycress *(Thlaspi caerulescens),* are being tested at Palmerton in a variety of soil conditions. Laboratory work has also begun on the next challenging phase of the project — the development of high-biomass, high-uptake "superaccumulators," which would remove heavy metals at a much

faster rate. The possibility is being explored that these plants could be harvested and burned, and the metals recovered and recycled. Still other plant species are being sought that might help clean nuclear waste sites by absorbing uranium, cesium, strontium, and other radioactive isotopes.

Chin acknowledges that his work on these projects is a far cry from his studio sculptures, which are beautifully crafted constructions, often made of wood, with enormous aesthetic appeal. By comparison, a *Revival Field* is not an object but a process, an effort to "sculpt a site's ecology." The series relates, he says, to "my interest in alchemy and my understanding of transformative processes and the mutable nature of materials. The contaminated soil is transformed back into rich earth, capable of sustaining a diverse ecosystem."[115]

Chin's insistence that his *Revival Fields* be seen not as static images but as part of a landscape in transformation is underscored by a related drawing called *Revival Ramp*. It depicts the evolution of a hypothetical site along a stream, beginning at the bottom with a copse of trees lifted from a drawing by Leonardo da Vinci. Moving up through what Chin describes as "a five-hundred-year loop," the landscape passes through agricultural and industrial phases, becoming contaminated with heavy metals by smelting in the latter. The landscape then divides into three branches, becoming a "ramp of possibilities." In one unlikely alternative, the landscape is restored to its original condition. In another, it continues to be degraded. In a third, not yet fully imagined alternative, some middle way is found in which the working landscape is restored to health and productivity. "The future is open-ended," Chin admits, but he clearly hopes that the processes he has helped bring to light will one day contribute to environmental restoration on a large scale.

As the projects by Singer and Chin suggest, some form of environmental awareness — if

172

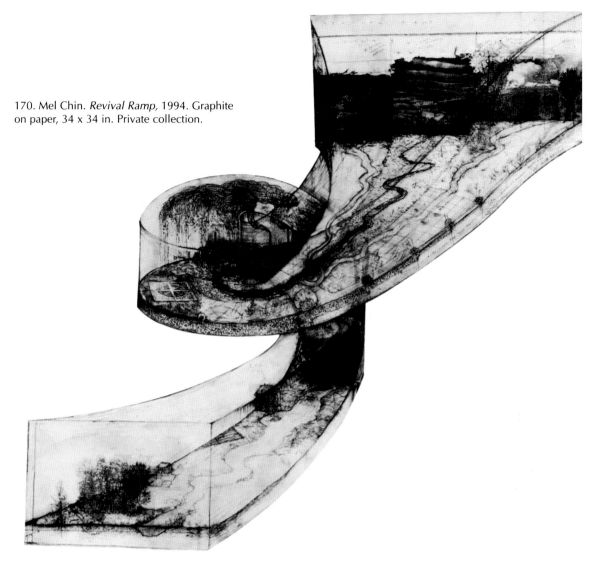

170. Mel Chin. *Revival Ramp,* 1994. Graphite on paper, 34 x 34 in. Private collection.

170

not remediation — has become more common to public art in recent years. Elyn Zimmerman, Lorna Jordan, and Jim Sanborn stand out among the many artists who have created for the public space works that engage various natural processes and systems. Zimmerman typically works with stone and water, creating sheltered oases on urban plazas — exemplified by *Marabar,* her project for the National Geographic Society. In some instances, however, her sculptures are a literal bridge between culture and nature. *Keystone Island,* for example, rises from a mangrove swamp adjacent to a new county courthouse on the north side of Miami. Her piece creates a subtle naturalistic counterpoint to the high-

138

171

tech architecture of the building, designed by the Miami firm Arquitectonica.

The architects had established an axis from the entrance of the courthouse to the rear of the site; it terminated abruptly at the edge of a small tidal lagoon bordered by mangroves. Zimmerman extended the axis over a bridge of her design to a small island she created of coral rock (also known as *keystone*). The material was mined at a now-closed quarry on Key Largo; it is the same stone used in the gardens at Vizcaya, a Renaissance-inspired villa south of Miami, where Zimmerman had first observed with pleasure the way it changes color as it weathers. She designed the island to be some fifty feet in diameter and to rise

171. Elyn Zimmerman (b. 1945). *Keystone Island,* 1989. Limestone, concrete, and water, height: 11 ft., diameter: 50 ft. Dade County Justice Center, North Miami, Florida. Dade County Art in Public Places.

171

172. Lorna Jordan (b. 1954), *Waterworks Gardens: The Grotto,* 1996. Third of five public garden rooms in the King County East Division Reclamation Plant, Renton, Washington. Stone mosaic, shotcrete, water seeps, pools, fountain, benches, and plants, 8 acres.

172

about ten feet from the high-tide line. Steps lead down from either side of the bridge to a walkway that skirts the island. The path passes a small pool on the island that is open to the lagoon; fish can be seen darting between the two bodies of water. Without undue self-consciousness, the project brings visitors face to face with the local ecosystem: with the mangroves and marine life that inhabit the lagoon and with the calcified coral that is the foundation for most of South Florida. Just as significantly, the piece serves as a reminder that at the edges and in the interstices of urban environments are natural systems awaiting discovery and explication. Nature isn't something distinct from culture but permeates the built environment — albeit in a highly transmuted and often debased form.

172, 173 Lorna Jordan's *Waterworks Gardens* restored such a battered ecosystem. Located next to a vast wastewater treatment facility in Renton, Washington, the gardens purify oil-laced and silty storm-water runoff — up to 2,000 gallons a minute collected from 50 acres of roads and parking lots. In the absence of Jordan's project, this water would have been treated along with sewage (an expensive process representing an instance of overkill). Or it would have been collected and filtered in bland detention ponds. Jordan's eight-acre project, commissioned through the King County Metro Arts Program and designed in conjunction with Seattle landscape architects Jones and Jones, turned this problem into an attractive public environment enriched with a subtle narrative.

In plan, the gardens resemble a blooming plant, with leaf- and flower-shaped ponds along stemlike paths; they tell a story about the power of natural systems to cleanse themselves. Particle pollution settles from the water in the first ponds, then trickles into a marsh where filtration is completed among native wetland species including sedges, rushes, yellow iris, and red-twig dogwood arranged in

colorful bands. In between, the water bubbles through a fantastic grotto featuring concrete stalactites overhanging tumbled granite and marble inlay. The floor of the grotto resembles an enormous seedpod, which sends its shoots up the walls. A classical form that reappeared in Renaissance gardens, the grotto is historically linked to sacred springs; here, it represents the rebirth in purified form of the degraded water. Jordan has managed to reconcile history, ecology, and the requirements of public infrastructure and access in this project, which is no small achievement.   172

Jim Sanborn has executed both public and private works in the landscape. Among the former is a piece called *Coastline,* outside the   174 buildings that house the National Oceanic and Atmospheric Administration (NOAA) offices in Silver Spring, Maryland. His sculpture forms the dramatic centerpiece to a small park outside the complex. It is a semicircular pool about seventy feet long and twenty-five feet wide, bordered on the straight edge by a seven-foot wall of striated granite. Using a reduced version of the pumps that propel waves

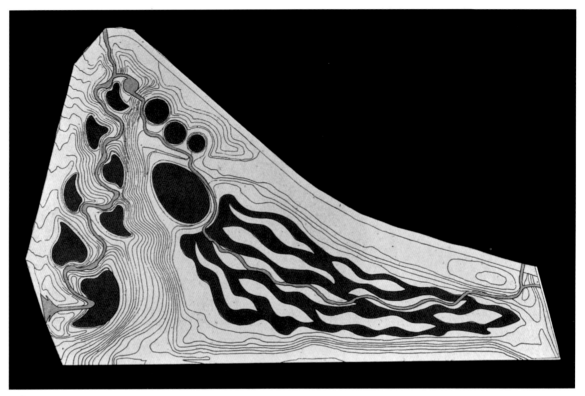

173

in amusement parks and calling on the advice of a coastal scientist, Sanborn created variegated patterns of computer-driven swells directed at the granite wall. At times, gentle "lake" waves lap against it at four-second intervals; at others, great oceanic surges break upon it every seven seconds. It's all a simulation, but it is appropriately suggestive as well, reminding us that the landscape is a cultural artifact. At the same time, *Coastline* acknowledges the physical power and mythic potency of the place where water meets the land.

Sanborn's private projects have included Topographic Projections, a series of large-scale but ephemeral light installations in the high deserts of Utah and New Mexico. Using a 2,500-watt projector he built himself, powered by a mobile generator, he directs beams of light through films bearing computer-generated designs, spreading an image sometimes 3,000 feet wide and 2,000 feet high onto darkened mountain ranges half a mile away. These he photographs with a large-format camera, using prolonged exposures, recording not just the projected patterns but also star trails and the tracks of passing aircraft. Sometimes the projected images have been words (*lux,* the Latin word for "light," for example), but more often they have been grids — an allusion, Sanborn says, to the fundamental geometries of geological structure and to cultural patterns such as surveys that have been imposed on the landscape irrespective of its true topographies. His projections set up an interesting dialogue with the work of earlier earth artists like Smithson and

175

176

174. Jim Sanborn (b. 1945). *Coastline
(Wave Pool for NOAA),* 1995. Granite, water,
and wave generator, 6 x 70 x 30 ft. National
Oceanic and Atmospheric Administration,
Silver Spring, Maryland.

174

175. Jim Sanborn. *Topographic Projection
(Shiprock, New Mexico),* October 1995.
Projected light, 1,700 x 2,500 x 500 ft.
Temporary installation, Shiprock, New Mexico.
Photograph by the artist.

175

176. Martin Puryear (b. 1941). *Camera Obscura*, 1994. Wood, height: 20 ft. Temporary installation, Denver.

Heizer. Sanborn grapples, as they did, with the wondrous scale of the Western landscape and the imposing geological processes it records. At the same time, however, his brief illuminations have only a minimal impact on delicate desert ecosystems.

The temporary project, often created in conjunction with an exhibition, has become one of the main opportunities in recent years for exploring the intersection of art and ecology. For many artists, the virtue of such work is not only that it is effaced with time but also that it allows them to work in places where they might not be able to place a permanent piece. It also permits them to be more provocative or experimental than a permanent public project ordinarily does.

176   Martin Puryear's *Camera Obscura,* for example, executed for the 1994 exhibition *Landscape as Metaphor* at the Denver Art Museum, had a much higher emotional pitch than public projects such as his pylons for Battery Park City. *Camera Obscura* was composed of an aged cherry tree cut from an abandoned orchard and hung by a chain from a structure that resembled a gallows. The title, which refers to the antique device that projects images upside down, was meant to reveal the artist's ambition for the sculpture: "to present an inverted reality." More specifically, Puryear says, the piece was intended to convey "the idea of landscape as a cultural construct, different from nature. Landscape is nature under the hand of man, or with man looking at it." But the sculpture clearly called to mind a lynching — an intimation that was strengthened when sap ran down the branches and caused the tree to blossom in death. One couldn't escape the sense that the sculpture represented the casual violence being perpetrated against nature as the world's great forests face oblivion. Nor could one avoid the perception that — in profound if unspecified ways — this violence is somehow analogous to the brutal lynchings of African Americans,

176

which are among the sorriest episodes of modern American history. So while the sculpture was meant to evoke the daily, even casual manipulations of nature that compose our landscapes, it came to stand for more vicious transactions with the earth. In all, *Camera Obscura* might be taken as representing some of the subtlety and intellectual complexity of recent art in the landscape, in which historical and cultural references often intertwine with expressions of environmental concern.

Karen McCoy has also put the temporary installation to provocative use, aspiring to the same rich mixture of allusions. "I always try to let a sense of place shape my work," she says. But that requires more than topography or ecology. "It involves a process of remembering, imagining, and contemplating historical and present-day uses of the land." The

177. Karen McCoy (b. 1951). *Floating Pyramid for Providence: A Consideration of Cultural Notions of Wealth and Value,* 1995. 3,000 clamshells, wood, cement, and steel pyramid: 10 x 10 x 8 ft.; steel barge: 12 x 12 x 2 ft. Temporary installation for the exhibition *Convergence 8,* Roger Williams Park, Providence, Rhode Island. Photograph by the artist.

177

177 complexities of McCoy's ephemeral *Floating Pyramid,* a 1995 project for Roger Williams Park in Providence, Rhode Island, are suggested by its subtitle: *A Consideration of Cultural Notions of Wealth and Value.* Ten feet square and eight feet tall, the pyramid was made of clamshells piled on a steel float. For McCoy, the shells were an allusion to wampum — strings of white and purple beads made from whelk and quahog shells that were the traditional currency of Native Americans in the region. At the same time, they suggested the importance of shellfish to the New England economy. The pyramid made multiple references: to a shell mound, possibly a burial, found by archaeologists at nearby Warwick; to the "triangle trade," in which slaves were shipped to the Caribbean and traded for molasses that was made into rum in the American colonies, which was in turn traded for slaves in Africa; and to a triadic theory of property value, in which land is appraised according to who owns it, who uses it, and who profits from it. Though she admitted that "not all these references are something the casual observer will take in," McCoy hoped the visual appeal of the sculpture would lure people into contemplating cultural differences in how worth is perceived.

178 An earlier project, *Considering Mother's Mantle,* was also formed in response to the many physical and cultural layers of the landscape in which it was made — Stone Quarry Hill Art Park at Cazenovia, near Syracuse, New York. It began with McCoy's observation of the many lines that traversed the site. She made note of a pattern of marsh grasses in a pond, which grew out of glacial grooves oriented north to south in the bedrock. Looking out over the landscape, she saw these lines echoed in the grid of farm fields. Taking a compass and some string, she staked out a grid over the water and rearranged spiky arrowhead plants in broken patterns along these lines. She then extended the axes into adjacent fields, transplanting or cutting grasses to mark them. Along the extended lines, she created other visual events, including circles of braided grasses and a cluster of woven grapevines, the latter meant to evoke a Native American dugout that had been found submerged in a local lake. McCoy's title is an illusion to the soil mantle, the thin layer of productive earth that lies over bedrock and that bears the marks of the overlapping, sometimes competing effects of nature and culture.

The North Carolina artist Patrick Dougherty also survives almost entirely on temporary projects for museums and sculpture parks. Dougherty, who lives in a hand-built house surrounded by a swept-dirt yard in the woods near Chapel Hill, travels the world making vast, energetic fabrications of freshly cut and bundled saplings of willow, pine, or — most often — maple. Exploiting the suppleness and tensile strength of green wood, he weaves the sticks together to resemble cyclones, serpents, or animated haystacks, without using any hardware or fasteners. In 1992 Dougherty went to Japan on an exchange fellowship sponsored by the Japan–United States Friendship Commission and administered by the National Endowment for the Arts. There he had the opportunity to work in the garden of the Rinjyo-in Temple in Chiba, where he built a swirling, tubular shape out of bamboo, which 179 climbed up an oak tree and dissipated like smoke in the branches. Most of Dougherty's sculptures employ windblown natural forms, but a few are architectural. For example, *Sittin'* 180 *Pretty,* a project for the South Carolina Botanical Garden in Clemson, brought to mind a neoclassical garden temple.

Like Sonfist and Singer — and like David Nash before them — Meg Webster has worked with living plants. To experience her sculptures is to return to one's senses; she often makes simple cones of salt, beds of earth and moss, or chambers of hay that reward sight, invite touch, and exude scent.

181

178

179

180

181

178. Karen McCoy. *Considering Mother's Mantle: To the Memory of Terry Ryan LeVeque,* 1992. Transplanted arrowhead plants, 40 x 50 ft. Stone Quarry Hill Art Park, Cazenovia, New York. Collection of Dorothy and Robert Reister. Photograph by the artist.

179. Patrick Dougherty (b. 1945). *Untitled,* 1992. Bamboo, height: 25 ft., diameter: 10 ft. Temporary installation, Rinjyo-in Temple, Chiba, Japan.

180. Patrick Dougherty. *Sittin' Pretty,* 1996. Saplings, height: 28 ft., diameter: 20 ft. Temporary installation, South Carolina Botanical Garden, Clemson University, Clemson, South Carolina.

181. Meg Webster (b. 1944). *Glen,* 1988. Earth, steel, plants, and fieldstone, 11 ft. 10 in. x 42 ft. x 42 ft. 6 in. Temporary loan to the Minneapolis Sculpture Garden, Walker Art Center.

But her intent is not simply to provide a sensory experience. Provoked by a growing fear of ecological crisis, she is determined to reconnect us with our surroundings, to make us see good earth, clean water, and healthy plants as essential to our lives. Her planted pieces — such as *Glen,* a temporary project for the Minneapolis Sculpture Garden at the Walker Art Center — "are about caring for nature," she explains. *Glen* was a secret garden in a cone of earth, entered through a narrow passage; plants filled it with leaves and blossoms of various colors and textures. "Plants [made] the space," Webster observed, "but I am not really interested in composing plants the way a landscape architect would. The plants express enterprise and caring. They connect people to the earth and to growth."

In a more offbeat manner, Stan Herd has also affirmed his connections with the land and with nurture. The son and grandson of farmers, Herd (who grew up on his family's home place in southwestern Kansas) found a

181

182. Stan Herd (b. 1950). *Absolut Landmark* (photographed with light snow), January 1991. Planted and mown crops—including soybeans, clover, sorghum, oats, and wheat—and plowed ground, 20 acres. Temporary installation, Johnson County near Lawrence, Kansas.

way to marry his enthusiasm for art with his knowledge of agriculture. He began in the early 1980s to plant 160-acre portraits in wheat and maize of important local figures, including the Kiowa war chief Satanta and the humorist Will Rogers. In 1985 came perhaps his most famous image, *Sunflower Still Life,* a variation on a Vincent van Gogh painting that Herd made of real sunflowers; it was filmed by Charles Kuralt for "The CBS Evening News" and featured in the opening pages of the book *A Day in the Life of America* (1986). Until recently, Herd has executed his projects without financial backing. Since neither environmental art nor farming is a reliable way to make a living — and a combination of the two even less so — the artist has lived on the economic edge. Herd has consequently accepted a number of commissions for corporate clients. One of the most interesting was for Absolut vodka, which involved multiple plantings that yielded a sequence of differently textured and colored images. In the spring of 1989 he planted an eighteen-acre field with clover and oats, which mature at different times, creating a green then a golden bottle on a quilted field. Later, the image was re-created in fall plantings of milo and soybeans; in the winter, it was a ghostly field of stubble. Herd remains somewhat apologetic for his corporate work, although what he achieved by isolating and enlarging the commercial image is not unlike what Andy Warhol was celebrated for doing.

His interest in the history of Native Americans in the Great Plains led Herd to become involved in a collaborative project with the students and faculty at Haskell Indian Nations University in Lawrence, Kansas, near his present home. At the instigation of Dan Wildcat, chair of the Natural and Social Sciences Department, he was invited to create a planted piece on campus to coincide with the Columbus quincentennial. After consultations with the faculty, it was determined that the image would be a medicine wheel, designed by the Native American artist Leslie Evans and his Haskell students, in the form of a circle divided by lines indicating the four cardinal directions. Attached to one side would be a triangular birdlike shape based on a Pre-Columbian design. The project was inaugurated in a ceremony on October 3, 1992, followed by a "flame spirit run," in which runners bearing torches set out from the circle in four directions — toward the two coasts, toward Canada and Mexico — to symbolize the enduring Native American presence in contemporary culture.

The Circle also expresses the artist's evolving concern about the impact of modern agricultural practices on the midwestern landscape. Under the tutelage of the environmentalist Wes Jackson and others at the Land Institute in Salina, Kansas, Herd has become more skeptical of agribusiness, with its reliance on chemicals and petroleum and its wholesale disruption by plowing of indigenous plant communities. *The Circle* was one of Herd's first pieces to be made without plowing — it was instead mowed from an existing field of cultivated brome grass, supplemented by site-specific hand plantings of evergreen trees and wildflowers. It was also one of his first permanent works, setting the stage for several later projects, including a permanent portrait of Amelia Earhart for her hometown of Atchison, Kansas. Herd is also at work on a temporary project inspired by Grant Wood — a landscape within a landscape — just off the end of the runway at the airport in Cedar Rapids, Iowa, commissioned for the state's sesquicentennial.

Perhaps the most ambitious growing sculpture of the late twentieth century is the 340,000-square-foot garden conceived by Robert Irwin for the Getty Center in Los Angeles — the billion-dollar museum and research complex designed by Richard Meier, which opened in late 1997. According to Irwin, he and Meier "went head-to-head for over a

185

183. Stan Herd with Leslie Evans. *The Circle* (aerial view), May 1992. Etched and mown grass, stone, and wood poles, 2 acres. Haskell Indian Nations University, Lawrence, Kansas.

184. Robert Irwin. *Color Drawing of the Central Garden*, 1995 (drawing by Spurlock Poirier Landscape Architects). Colored pencil, 4 x 6 in. Commissioned for the J. Paul Getty Center, Los Angeles.

184

year" and ultimately realized that they could not work together. Irwin came to feel that, first, "in order to be important, the garden had to make its own decisions, apart from the architecture." Second, it needed scale. As Irwin put it, "I had to make a few key gestures to hold the space." Third, it had to respond to the formal, geometric character of the architecture — as Irwin said, "how to get from that to the texture, pattern, and detail you expect in a garden."

Irwin resolved to re-create a canyon that the architect had obliterated in preparing the site for his buildings. A stream meanders down this restored slope, spilling over a beveled wall of split-faced carnelian granite and ending in a pool set into a large terraced bowl. This amphitheater is the visual centerpiece of 185 the garden. Derived from classical sources, it is a fairly standard sculptural device — remember Beverly Pepper's *Amphisculpture* 104 and Robert Morris's untitled King County 89

185. Robert Irwin (b. 1928). *Model for the Central Garden,* 1995. Commissioned for the J. Paul Getty Center, Los Angeles.

185

reclamation project. There is some irony to Irwin's historicizing, since he began his career as a Minimalist painter who was attuned to the subtleties of perceptual psychology and openly dismissive of historical precedent. Here, however, he acknowledges the futility of trying to escape history. "How does someone like me interact with a tradition that's been going on for centuries?" he asks. "You're not going to reinvent the garden. But you can bring a new perspective to how things are put together."

In this spirit Irwin has made some unexpected moves within the amphitheater. It is planted with rings of pale-violet-flowered crepe myrtles and overlooks a maze of azaleas, which appears to float in the pool. The maze is particularly unusual, composed of three interlocking circles, each planted in several concentric rings and each a different color of azalea — one white, one red, and one pink. The slope above the amphitheater is planted with London plane trees. These are not naturalistic — over a period of ten years, they will be pruned and trained to grow into a canopy that is rigidly geometric on the outside but more informal on the inside. Speaking of the plane trees and the crepe myrtle to a reporter from the *Los Angeles Times*, Irwin said: "Both these trees have beautiful trunk structures, and ultimately they're the most important element of the garden. If we succeed in getting them to take the shape I envision, it will be something you'd come a thousand miles to see."[116] Along with the amphitheater, these trees are the bones of the garden, fleshed out by flowering plants in the summer.

Irwin acknowledges that it is unusual for an artist to land such a big garden commission. "In hiring me rather than a landscape architect, [the Getty Center] made an adventurous choice that most supposedly avant-garde places aren't willing to make." He brings a lot of artistic expertise to the project, having developed much of the theoretical

language of environmental sculpture, especially in his 1985 book *Being and Circumstance.* There he described the gradients of an art project's effect on the landscape, from one that seeks to dominate a site to those that are more site-specific or site-generated and thus more attuned to the physical or cultural forces that shape a particular place.[117] He put these ideas to work in his own pieces, such as *Nine Spaces/Nine Trees* in Seattle. At the same time, Irwin accumulated a great deal of practical experience in planning public projects. He spent much of the later 1980s involved with the redesign and expansion of the Miami Airport, though his ideas were never realized because of a change in airport administration.

139, 140

What Irwin is doing at the Getty runs against the grain of much recent landscape architecture. Although his design is contextual in the sense that it responds to Meier's architecture, it seems in some respects to refute Irwin's own notions of site-generated art. At a time when many in California and the Southwest are turning to drought-tolerant species as a way to avoid the high economic and environmental costs of non-native plants, Irwin's garden is unabashedly lush and exotic. The artist has identified some seven hundred varieties of plants for possible incorporation into the garden as it matures over the coming decade. Some are types known to thrive in the southern California climate, including bougainvillea and roses, but Irwin says that others will be surprises. He has selected some plants for their scent — freesias, sage, and gardenias, for example. Others have been chosen expressly for their power to evoke another place. The plane tree, Irwin says, is "the only local tree that has the stature of the great East Coast trees."

Irwin concedes that he is pushing the envelope in the Getty garden but insists that what he is doing is not out of bounds. He has hired fourteen consultants, ranging from civil and

186

187

188

190

soils engineers to arborists and horticulturists, and he is working closely with Richard Naranjo, the head gardener at the Getty Museum in Malibu. Irwin is orchestrating test plantings at fields near his home in San Diego and at the Getty to see how different non-natives will survive. "At the moment, people talk about native plants as if it's the only ethical way to make a garden, but ninety-nine percent of the California landscape is not native. Gardens are about another kind of experience," he insists. "They're about joy. . . . Not only does the Getty have the money to create an extravagant garden, they also have the funds and the willingness to maintain it." Given the ambition of Irwin's scheme, only time will tell if even the Getty is up to the task.

Just as sculptors are trespassing on the territory of landscape architects, so are designers beginning to use the vocabulary of recent sculpture. Two San Francisco Bay Area landscape architects, Peter Walker and George Hargreaves, for example, are shaping landforms in ways similar to those favored by earth artists. Walker's exploration of the sculptural dimensions of landscape architecture dates back at least to his *Tanner Fountain* (1984) on the campus at Harvard University — a circular composition of 159 stones, sixty feet in diameter, that recalls work by Carl Andre or Richard Long. More carefully designed than anything by those sculptors, it is set into an interlocking pattern of grass, concrete, and asphalt paving and incorporates a mist fountain designed with the artist Joan Brigham. Walker also created a sculptural landscape at the Center for Advanced Science and Technology — a complex designed by Arata Isozaki for Harima, a new town established as a center for scientific research in the mountains near Kobe, Japan. The landscape includes several "homages to mountains," a wry commentary on the hills that were leveled to build the town. In a courtyard inside the complex are large turf and stone mounds, set in a bed of raked gravel overlaid with lines of stone and charred wood. Outside are clusters of small hillocks, each with a juniper tree planted at the top to suggest a plume of volcanic smoke. Ironically, these hills are highly engineered, even as they evoke ancient prototypes. Walker describes his work at the center as "Japanese gardens made in a scientific way, using modern technology."

Hargreaves has been even more consciously impelled by the example of recent sculpture. As a student at Harvard University's Graduate School of Design in the late 1970s, he came across photographs of Smithson's earthworks. They struck him then, he recalls, "as beacons on the parched field of landscape design." Like a number of his fellow students and even some of his teachers (Peter Walker was one), Hargreaves was searching for a way beyond what he perceived as the formulaic language of landscape architecture — beyond, he later explained, the reflexive use of the English picturesque for public parks and the dependence on the balanced, asymmetrical geometries of modernism for urban plazas. "For the first time," Hargreaves has said, "I understood that designed landscapes could be extraordinarily meaningful. The Smithson works reintroduced the concept of landscape as idea — something lost in the pursuit of the functional landscape — and opened a door to a world not yet fully explored and still expanding."[118]

Initially inspired by Smithson, Hargreaves came to see additional implications for design in other aspects of contemporary art. In the repetitive units of Minimalist sculpture, for example, in which a finite grid suggests endless extrapolation in every direction, he saw the possibilities of what he termed "open-ended" composition. From Richard Serra as much as from Smithson, he learned an empathy for derelict urban spaces and gritty industrial materials. In Serra's work he also observed the operations of chance — as in his sculptures made by flinging molten lead against a wall. And from Irwin, he learned the language to describe site-generated art.

Over the past decade Hargreaves — with the help of his colleagues at Hargreaves Associates — has put all these ideas to work in a series of challenging public projects. In the spirit of Smithson he has developed a concern — even an enthusiasm — for the restoration of abused landscapes. His Candlestick Point Cultural Park, completed in 1993, is built on rubble pushed into San Francisco Bay. Byxbee Park, also on the bay in nearby Palo Alto, is a thirty-acre former landfill that lies over garbage as much as sixty feet deep. And the Guadalupe River Park, a three-mile greenway that snakes through the heart of San Jose, was devised as an alternative to an Army Corps of Engineers flood-control project, using terraced banks and dispersed landforms to control runoff rather than channeling the river into unsightly concrete culverts. Hargreaves restored these sites with particular attention to the structural and symbolic use of sculptural form. The exposed peninsula that became Candlestick Point Cultural Park includes a funnel-shaped entry (a "windgate") oriented to the prevailing gales, a lawn pitched toward the water (thus enhancing views of the bay), shallow channels that reach inland and fill with water at high tide, and a series of berms designed to give shelter from the wind. These elements compose what Hargreaves describes as a "theater of the environment" — a place to observe the natural forces that have shaped the landscape.

The Guadalupe River and Byxbee Parks might also be designated "theaters of the environment" because of the way they heighten the spectator's awareness of natural processes. At the former — downstream from the city center, where the Guadalupe River is unconstrained by dense development — the river edge has been reshaped to suggest the braided character of Western streams. On grassy banks above the low-water channel (where the river flows when it is not in flood), Hargreaves has shaped graceful berms that resemble sandbars in a river, with their narrow ends pointed upstream in accordance with hydraulic principles. Hargreaves aptly describes these berms as "a deconstructed levy"; they will encourage floodwater to spread out and slow down in emulation of a natural river system. Plantings reinforce the attention to riparian ecology: California sycamores near the water, oaks and acacias on the adjacent slopes.

At Byxbee Park, designed in collaboration with the artists Peter Richards and Michael Oppenheimer, two forms of sculpture have been deployed. On the one hand, there are Hargreaves's signature earthworks. At the crest of the site, a landgate — an opening in a long, prominent berm — marks the transition from the windward to the leeward side of the park. Nearby are clusters of low hillocks, seemingly shaped by the wind. On the other hand, there are compositions of prefabricated elements. One is a grid of truncated telephone poles, their tops — like De Maria's *Lightning Field* — forming an imaginary plane above the sloping ground. Evoking the repeated units of Minimalist sculpture, these poles extend the park visually and conceptually into the surrounding landscape.

Like those artists more concerned with process than with product, Hargreaves is willing to relinquish some control over his designs, establishing the outlines but letting nature manage many of the details. Because neither Candlestick Point nor Byxbee Park could be irrigated — for environmental and economic reasons — Hargreaves used native, drought-resistant species of grasses and wildflowers. These are being allowed to migrate around the parks, establishing their own communities wherever growing conditions suit them best. Similarly, Hargreaves anticipates that volunteer shrubs and eventually trees will invade these landscapes. Water will also reshape his

188

189

parks in dramatic and subtle ways: floods have already inundated Guadalupe River Park, while at Byxbee moisture is collecting in low places and establishing colonies of damp-loving plants. Hargreaves describes this approach as "radically different" from conventional design, in which more control is exercised over the final result to make it look beautiful or refined. "I'm setting up a framework on the land," Hargreaves says. "Then vegetation, people, and water wash over it. This is completely different from what I was brought up to do. It's a cousin of [Serra's] lead pours: you set up the process, but you don't control the end product." The results of this approach, as Hargreaves acknowledges, are landscapes that are paradoxically "natural, but not natural looking."

The same paradox is evident in the environmental art of Maya Lin. She too shows a familiarity with the syntax of recent sculpture: her *Vietnam Veterans Memorial,* for example, clearly reveals a debt to Serra's monumental abstract sculptures, such as *Spin Out (for Robert Smithson),* that reveal shifting topographies. And she sounds very much like Irwin when she insists, "What I introduce into the land does not try to dominate or overwhelm the existing landscape, but instead tries to work with it, producing a new experience."[119] But Lin has developed a more personal idiom in recent sculptural projects, one that suggests affinities with Hargreaves's idea that the landscape is a dynamic place. The fluidity of both our cultural and our natural surroundings is evoked in the forms she uses. *Groundswell,* for example, at the Wexner Center for the Arts at Ohio State University in Columbus, is named for sudden risings or crestings in the ocean. Forty-six tons of pale green crushed glass were poured into mounds and then shaped by hand. The piece is disposed over three levels at the Wexner, in what Lin calls the "residual spaces" of Peter Eisenman's building: on a roof, outside the main entry,

and in a light well below grade outside sealed café windows. Instability is implicit in the material she has selected — the glass has already been shattered, and it looks as if it could continue to settle. Further, *Groundswell* evokes the ebb and flow of cultural history — reminiscent of Japanese dry-stone gardens, the poured glass also recalls the burial and effigy mounds of the Hopewell Indians, who once inhabited this area of Ohio.

Wave Field, for the Aerospace Engineering Building at the University of Michigan, Ann Arbor, relates to fluid dynamics, which is central to the physics of flight. The piece was inspired by a photograph that Lin saw while reading up on aerodynamics — a close-cropped image of a pattern of ocean waves. This inspiration gave rise to a rectangular field of low grassy mounds. Like waves, each is slightly different in height or breadth. "It is this fascination with evolving states, whether social and historical constructs or erosion properties of the natural environment, that permeates the entire body of [my] work." Although her sculpture is often abstract, she keeps it at a human scale. "The *Wave Field* is designed so that you can sit inside a wave and read a book." Acknowledging that she has also been inspired by the environmental movement, Lin proposes that the way to begin repairing the harm we have done to the environment is by healing the breach between nature and culture. "Most importantly," she says, "[my work] represents a relationship in which we are a part of nature not separate from it."

The British architectural theorist Charles Jencks has also turned to landscape to express ideas about the dynamic character of nature. "I have never understood why architects, painters, and philosophers — following Plato — have thought that the ultimate reality behind things lies in straight lines, right angles, and perfect, geometric solids," Jencks recently wrote. "Nature is basically curved, warped, undulating, jagged, zigzag, and sometimes

189. George Hargreaves and Hargreaves Associates. Byxbee Park, 1988–92. Native grasses, earth, telephone poles, and highway barriers, 35 acres. City of Palo Alto, California.

189

190. Maya Lin (b. 1959). *Wave Field,* 1995.
Earth and grass, 100 x 100 ft. Commissioned for
the Francois Xavier Bagnoud Aerospace
Engineering Building, University of Michigan,
Ann Arbor.

191

beautifully crinkly." Jencks has given visual form to this conviction in a series of gardens begun in 1989 in the Borders area of Scotland, which were designed with his late wife, Maggie Keswick.

193 The most prominent features in the gardens are two sinuous hills overlooking a pair of serpentine lakes. Jencks was responsible for the design of the former; his wife, for the latter. One hill is a spiral mound, nicknamed "the snail"; the second is a reversing curve pp. 2–3 known as "the snake" that brackets the water on one side and a cow pasture on the other. Both Jencks and his wife meant to suggest more with these forms than animal morphology, however. Maggie Keswick was a scholar of Chinese landscape design; for her, the forms were evocative of the ancient art of geomancy — divining the forces of nature in geological structure. As Jencks explained it, "Chinese landscape painters, following Taoist monks and philosophers, saw hills and mountains as 'the bones of the earth' energized with the 'vital breath' of subterranean dragons." Jencks himself intended the mounds to evoke the emerging sciences of complexity and chaos theory, which he was researching for his book *The Architecture of the Jumping Universe* (1995). He piled dirt on the spiral until it nearly disintegrated in landslides, to recall the notion in complexity theory that creativity occurs at the edge between order and chaos. The reversing curves of the snake imply the idea of "enfolding," by which unlike things are joined in smooth transitions.

In a number of garden gates, Jencks represented the actions of soliton waves, the pulses of energy that underlie phenomena such as tidal waves, nerve impulses, and superconductors. Bands of metal in these gates curve and twist, like colliding or overlapping surges. These images recur elsewhere in the garden — terraces on the snake mound fold like the bands of metal in the gates, for example. A curious smaller garden features beds

of gravel colliding with bands of turf; both 192 are interrupted by curving rock walls. All these elements are meant to reinforce an image of nature as unpredictable, creative, and dynamic, periodically leaping to new and surprising levels of order within apparent confusion. It is Jencks's contention that artists must address these new conceptions of the world if their work is to remain compelling. In words that might apply to Hargreaves or Lin, he insists, "It is time artists and designers reclaimed a territory that was customarily theirs and the obligations to portray a more interesting, beautiful, dynamic, and tragic universe."[120]

Martha Schwartz has also straddled the line between artist and landscape architect. Though primarily known as a landscape designer, she has received a number of public art commissions, including a project at the Miami Airport for the Metro-Dade Art in Public Places Program. Called *Miami Sound Wall* (1996), the piece replaced conventional sound buffering proposed for the edge of the airport with an artistically improved product. Schwartz had holes punched in the prefabricated concrete panels and filled the holes with colored glass, which is illuminated by the sun. She also scalloped the top of the wall and made undulating shapes in the earth in front of it, creating wavelike patterns that stretch for about a mile between the airport and a neighboring residential community.

After the 1989 demise of *Tilted Arc,* Schwartz landed a more visible and contentious commission that obliged her to refine her ideas about sculpture and the public space. She was asked by the Art in Architecture Program at the General Services Administration to propose a redesign for Federal Plaza in lower Manhattan, where Serra's sculpture had once stood. She initially had some reservations about taking on the project but found that her attitude changed as she studied the space and the way it was used. "At first, I was outraged [by what had happened

192

193

194

192. Charles Jencks (b. 1939). *Symmetry Break Terrace,* in *Landscape of Waves,* 1992–94. Earth, gravel, and turf, six acres overall. Scotland.

193. Charles Jencks. *Snail Mound* (left) and *Snake Mound,* in *Landscape of Waves.* Earth and turf, *Snake Mound,* length: 900 ft.; *Snail Mound,* height: 45 ft.

194. Martha Schwartz (b. 1950). *Untitled,* 1996. New York City park benches, asphalt block pavers, raised grass panels, metal hoop fence, lights, fog machines, concrete, 40,500 square ft. Federal Plaza, New York. Commissioned by the General Services Administration (GSA).

to *Tilted Arc*]," she recalls. "But I came to feel sorry for the people who had to use the space. The sculpture was very confrontational. The obligations of public art are different from those of the gallery or the museum." Focusing on the social life of the place led her to conceive what she terms "an antithetical kind of piece." Recalling the words of Scott Burton, she decided to "shape the space for the way people actually use it: to eat lunch."

Like Serra, Schwartz had to contend with a degraded architectural context. Federal Plaza was an uninspired modernist space — a paved forecourt that was barren except for a fountain that didn't work and a pair of bulky raised planters at diagonally opposite corners, which isolated the space from the street. Because the plaza was the roof of a parking garage, it could not support the weight of trees; because it faced north and east, it was frequently in shadow. Although Schwartz couldn't change the plaza's orientation or its lack of structural support, she was able to remove the planters to improve visual and physical access to the space. She also eliminated the fountain, which occupied the sunniest and consequently most useful part of the site. And although she couldn't alter the flat surface of the plaza, she could animate it. This she achieved by threading a double row of park benches back-to-back in great arcs through the space, evoking a baroque parterre. The benches loop across the entire plaza, providing lunchers with a variety of seating options as the sun and shadows shift.

To remedy the lack of plantings, Schwartz designed turf mounds six feet tall and eighteen feet in diameter, which are nestled on the interior curves of the benches. They provide what she calls "small centers of visual gravity around which the swirls of benches seem to circle." Their high relief also provides more greenery. Each mound incorporates a mist fountain that will operate on hot days; at night each will be illuminated with a

green light. Schwartz has used color liberally to enliven the space: dark mauve for the concrete pad on which the benches rest, blue enamel for the drinking fountains, and orange for the wire-mesh trash baskets.

Without question, Schwartz's Federal Plaza is more user friendly than Serra's; she has entirely replaced the metaphors of conflict with those of leisure. But there is something to be lamented in the complete erasure of the site's contested history. Rather than creating the antithesis of *Tilted Arc*, Schwartz and her patrons at the GSA might have aimed for a synthesis that remade the plaza in a new image but carried some sign of the past. That past is too important to forget, for it dramatized the conflict over how public culture is to be defined in a democratic society. We need to continue to acknowledge disputes over the artistic character and social function of public space if we are going to construct a more tolerant and pluralist culture. Although Schwartz represents a different profession from most public artists, her project at Federal Plaza sounds a familiar theme — the reconciliation of sculptural ambitions with the social requirements of the civic space.

Given the growing hybridization of sculpture and landscape architecture, it is possible to overemphasize their connections at the expense of their differences. These are considerable, though difficult to generalize. Sculptors are typically more attuned to the symbolic possibilities of form — its power to evoke history or to provoke the emotions. Landscape architects, on the other hand, are usually more attentive to details — to the use of appropriate materials, to soil types, and to drainage — and typically have a better knowledge of plants. And for all their talk about context, artists often end up being more insistent about their aesthetic prerogatives. The contrast between Irwin and Hargreaves might be taken as particularly instructive. Although the latter was openly inspired by the former, it is

194

Hargreaves who has turned out to be more attentive to the social and environmental conditions in which he works, while Irwin has created a mildly reactionary design that addresses itself openly to the history of gardens.

Ultimately, the issue of whose approach to nature is more "correct" is somewhat beside the point. Whatever the nuances of their particular approaches to nature, artists and landscape architects alike have provided dramatic proof that the landscape is one of the primary forums of cultural expression, where social and environmental as well as aesthetic values are articulated. Every work that engages the landscape underscores the crucial connections between nature and culture and helps to revitalize — and, with any luck, improve — that relationship. Both environmental sculpture and landscape architecture can help us decode our multiple, often conflicting attitudes toward nature, reviving old myths when appropriate and shaping new paradigms when necessary. Though both environmental sculpture and landscape architecture have their more and less successful examples, they can surely help us improve our aesthetic relationship with the land. In so doing, they may yet contribute to replacing the metaphors of domination with those of cooperation and nurture. Together, they might finally bring us closer to the ethic of landscape that has evaded us for so long.

NOTES

Complete citations for sources given here in abbreviated form can be found in the bibliography.

1. In addition to *The End of Nature* (New York: Random House, 1989), notable recent efforts to assess the relationship of humans to the environment include Alexander Wilson, *The Culture of Nature: North American Landscape from Disney to the Exxon Valdez* (Cambridge: Blackwell, 1992), and the anthology edited by William Cronon, *Uncommon Ground: Toward Reinventing Nature* (New York: W. W. Norton, 1995). Smithson's essay "A Tour of the Monuments of Passaic, New Jersey" is in Nancy Holt, ed., *The Writings of Robert Smithson*, pp. 52–57.

2. Ralph Waldo Emerson, "Nature," 1836, in Brooks Atkinson, ed., *The Complete Essays and Other Writings of Ralph Waldo Emerson* (New York: Modern Library, 1950), p. 34.

3. Thomas Jefferson, "Notes on Virginia," 1782, in Paul Leicester Ford, ed., *The Writings of Thomas Jefferson* (New York: G. P. Putnam's Sons, 1894), vol. 3, p. 271.

4. Ibid., p. 268.

5. Those who have read J. B. Jackson's excellent essay, "Jefferson, Thoreau & After," will recognize my indebtedness to him here. *Landscape* 15 (Winter 1965–66): 25–27; reprinted in Ervin H. Zube, ed., *Landscapes: Selected Writings of J. B. Jackson* (Amherst: University of Massachusetts Press, 1970), pp. 1–9.

6. Henry David Thoreau, "Walking," in Henry S. Canby, ed., *The Work of Thoreau* (Boston: Houghton Mifflin, 1937), pp. 659–60.

7. For a thorough treatment of the breadth of Olmsted's achievement, see Albert Fein, *Frederick Law Olmsted and the American Environmental Tradition* (New York: George Braziller, 1972).

8. Unless otherwise noted, all quotations are from conversations with the artists.

9. Michael Heizer, "The Art of Michael Heizer," p. 34.

10. Heizer, in Howard Junker, "The New Sculpture: Getting Down to the Nitty Gritty," p. 42.

11. Heizer, "Art," p. 37.

12. Published in Robert Hobbs, *Robert Smithson: Sculpture*, p. 238.

13. Joseph Masheck, "The Panama Canal and Some Other Works of Art," p. 41.

14. Michael Auping, "Michael Heizer: The Ecology and Economics of 'Earth Art,'" *Artweek* 8 (June 18, 1977): 1.

15. Heizer, in Douglas Davis, "The Earth Mover," *Newsweek,* p. 113.

16. Discussed in Elizabeth Baker, "Artworks on the Land," p. 94.

17. Others in this exhibition included Richard Long, Robert Morris, and Dennis Oppenheim.

18. From Alexander Pope, "Epistle to Lord Burlington," 1731.

19. Particularly curious are his characterizations of the picturesque theories of Uvedale Price as a "democratic dialectic between the sylvan and the industrial," and of Olmsted's work as a "Jeffersonian rural reality in the metropolis." See Robert Smithson, "Frederick Law Olmsted and the Dialectical Landscape," *Artforum* 11 (February 1973): 62–68; reprinted in Holt, *Writings*, pp. 117–28.

20. Originally published in Gyorgy Kepes, ed., *Arts of the Environment*, pp. 222–32; reprinted in Holt, *Writings*, pp. 109–16. All quotations from the latter source.

21. Robert Smithson, "A Sedimentation of the Mind: Earth Projects," *Artforum* 7 (September 1968): 45, reprinted in Holt, *Writings*, p. 82.

22. Samuel Beckett, quoted by Smithson in his film *Spiral Jetty,* and used by Liza Bear and Nancy Holt in "Robert Smithson's Amarillo Ramp," pp. 18–19.

23. Smithson, "Spiral Jetty," in Holt, *Writings,* p. 111.

24. See Robert Smithson and Gregoire Müller, ". . . The Earth, Subject to Cataclysms, Is a Cruel Master," *Arts Magazine* 46 (November 1971): 36–41; reprinted in Holt, *Writings,* pp. 179–85.

25. Smithson, "Untitled, 1971," in Holt, *Writings,* p. 220.

26. Smithson, "Proposal, 1972," ibid., p. 221.

27. Ibid., p. 220.

28. Robert Morris, "The Art of Existence, Three Extra-Visual Artists: Works in Progress," *Artforum* 9 (January 1971): 28.

29. Robert Morris, "Aligned with Nazca," p. 39.

30. Robert Morris, "Some Notes on the Phenomenology of Making: The Search for the Motivated," *Artforum* 8 (April 1970): 66.

31. In *Grand Rapids Project: Robert Morris,* n.p.

32. Ibid.

33. Christo, in *The Golden Door: Artist-Immigrants of America, 1876–1976,* exhibition catalog (Washington, D.C.: Hirshhorn Museum and Sculpture Garden, 1976), p. 389.

34. See Alfred Frankenstein, "Christo's 'Fence,' Beauty or Betrayal?" pp. 58–61.

35. Nancy Holt, "Sun Tunnels," p. 36.

36. I should say that a comparable sensibility was not unknown to America during the same years. See chapter 6.

37. Unless otherwise noted, quotations from Richard Long are from a statement published in *Aspects of British Art Today,* exhibition catalog (Tokyo: Asahi Shimbun, 1982), p. 174.

38. Richard Long, *Five, Six, Pick Up Sticks, Seven, Eight, Lay Them Straight* (London: Anthony d'Offay, 1980), n.p.

39. Fulton, in Michael Auping, "An Interview with Hamish Fulton," in *Common Ground: Five Artists in the Florida Landscape,* p. 87.

40. Unless otherwise noted, quotations from Hamish Fulton are from a statement published in *Aspects of British Art Today,* p. 115.

41. Fulton, in Auping, "Interview," pp. 86–87.

42. Unless otherwise noted, quotations from David Nash are from *Loosely Held Grain,* exhibition catalog (Bristol, England: Arnolfini Gallery, 1976), n.p.

43. See Michael Charlesworth, "Alexander Pope's Garden at Twickenham: An Architectural Design Proposed," *Journal of Garden History* 7 (January 1987): 60.

44. From a statement in *Fletched Over Ash,* n.p., published on the occasion of Nash's exhibition at AIR Gallery, London, 1978.

45. Nash, in Hugh Adams, "Natural Acts," in *Sixty Seasons: David Nash,* p. 27.

46. Originally published in Charles Simonds, *Three Peoples* (Genoa, Italy: Samanedizione, 1975); reprinted in John H. Neff, *Charles Simonds,* pp. 35–38.

47. Rémy Inglis Hall, trans., *The Wandering Jew and Other Stories* (London: Hart-Davis, 1967), pp. 3–14.

48. See Robert Goldwater, *Primitivism in Modern Art* (New York and London: Harper and Brothers, 1938; revised New York: Vintage Books, 1966).

49. Arshile Gorky, from a letter dated February 17, 1947; reprinted in K. Mooradian, ed., "A Special Issue on Arshile Gorky," *Ararat* (New York) 12 (Fall 1971): 39.

50. Barnett Newman, from the announcement of an exhibition at Betty Parsons Gallery, New York, in 1947; quoted in Ralph Pomeroy, *Stamos* (New York: Harry N. Abrams, 1974), p. 19.

51. Adolph Gottlieb and Mark Rothko, from a letter to the editor, *New York Times,* June 13, 1943, section 2, p. 9.

52. See especially the essays and selections of artists' writings in *The Natural Paradise: Painting in America 1800–1950,* exhibition catalog (New York: Museum of Modern Art, 1976).

53. Christopher Hussey, *The Picturesque* (New York and London: Putnam's, 1927; reprinted Hamden, Conn.: Archon Books, 1967), pp. 58–59.

54. For thorough discussions of the sources of the picturesque, see Hunt and Willis, eds., *The Genius of the Place,* and Christopher Hussey, *English Gardens and Landscapes 1700–1750* (London: Country Life, 1967).

55. Recent speculation on the iconographic program at Stourhead is summarized in Kimberly Rorschach, *The Early Georgian Landscape Garden,* exhibition catalog (New Haven: Yale Center for British Art, 1983), pp. 75–77.

56. Ian Hamilton Finlay, "Unconnected Sentences on Gardening," in *Nature Over Again after Poussin,* p. 21.

57. Unless otherwise noted, quotations from Finlay are from correspondence with the author.

58. The exhibition was held at Collins Exhibition Hall, University of Strathclyde, Glasgow, in 1980.

59. Stephen Bann, "Introduction," in *Nature Over Again after Poussin,* p. 9.

60. A more complete description of Stonypath can be found in Stephen Bann, "A Description of Stonypath."

61. Finlay, "Unconnected Sentences on Gardening," p. 22.

62. For a more extended discussion on this theme, see Sidney Geist, *Brancusi: The Kiss.*

63. See Barbu Brezianu, *Brancusi in Romania,* pp. 128–54.

64. Brancusi, ibid., p. 130.

65. Ibid., p. 131.

66. Constantin Brancusi, from a letter dated February 11, 1935, quoted in Geist, *The Kiss,* p. 76.

67. Isamu Noguchi, "Noguchi on Brancusi," p. 29.

68. Noguchi, in Sam Hunter, *Isamu Noguchi* (New York: Abbeville Press, 1978), p. 35.

69. Noguchi, "Noguchi on Brancusi," p. 29.

70. Isamu Noguchi, *A Sculptor's World,* p. 16.

71. Ibid., p. 159.

72. Noguchi, in Hunter, *Noguchi,* p. 56.

73. Hunter, *Noguchi,* p. 111.

74. Jan van der Marck, *Herbert Bayer: From Type to Landscape,* p. 40.

75. Smithson, "A Sedimentation of the Mind: Earth Projects"; reprinted in Holt, *Writings,* pp. 85–86, 91.

76. The artists were Herbert Bayer, Iain Baxter, Richard Fleischner, Lawrence Hanson, Mary Miss, Dennis Oppenheim, and Beverly Pepper.

77. Total project costs (excluding indirect costs) on the Morris project were $145,800; estimates for conventional reclamation ranged from $132,000 to $190,000. Figures from a report by the King County Arts Commission to the National Endowment for the Arts; reported in Dolores Tarzan, "Earthworks Are Good Economics," *Seattle Times,* October 17, 1979, p. A8.

78. Robert Morris, "Robert Morris Keynote Address," in *Earthworks: Land Reclamation as Sculpture,* p. 16.

79. Bayer, in "Dedication of Earthworks Park in Kent Is September 4," *The Arts* 11 (newsletter of the King County Arts Commission, August 1982): 2.

80. From a press release of the Kent Parks and Recreation Department, August 13, 1982.

81. From an undated press release prepared by Stan Dolega.

82. Heizer, in David Bourdon, "Working with Earth, Michael Heizer Makes Art as Big as All Outdoors," *Smithsonian* 17 (April 1986): 74.

83. Johanson, in *Patricia Johanson: Drawings and Models for Environmental Projects, 1969–1986* (Pittsfield, Mass.: Berkshire Museum, 1987), p. 11.

84. Andre, in Diane Henry, "Some Residents of Hartford Are Throwing Stones," *New York Times,* September 5, 1977, p. 21.

85. Both quotations are from an Associated Press story, "Former Coal Miner's Dream Comes True with Monument Dedication at Frostburg," circulated from Baltimore, October 11, 1982.

86. Puryear, in Hugh M. Davies and Helaine Posner, *Martin Puryear* (Amherst: University Gallery, University of Massachusetts, 1984), p. 32.

87. See Nathan Glazer, "Christo in Central Park—And in Harlem," *Public Interest,* no. 68 (Summer 1982): 70–77, and "Closing Christo's Gates," *New York Times,* March 5, 1981, p. A22.

88. Reported by William Dunlap, a painter from McLean, Virginia, who worked on the project.

89. William Dunlap, "Surrounding of Island 12," *Washington Post,* May 15, 1983, p. K5.

90. Lin, in Benjamin Forgey, "Model of Simplicity," p. C4.

91. Benjamin Forgey, "Monumental 'Absurdity,'" *Washington Post,* March 6, 1982, p. C5.

92. For a detailed history of the G.S.A. program, see Donald Thalacker, *The Place of Art in the World of Architecture* (New York: Chelsea House, 1980); on the Endowment's history see John Beardsley, *Art in Public Places,* and Stacy Paleologos Harris, ed., *Insights/On Sites: Perspectives on Art in Public Places.*

93. Serra, in Richard Serra, *Richard Serra: Interviews, Etc., 1970–1980* (Yonkers, N.Y.: Hudson River Museum, 1980), p. 168.

94. See especially Douglas Crimp, "Serra's Public Sculpture: Redefining Site Specificity" in Rosalind Krauss, *Richard Serra/Sculpture* (New York: Museum of Modern Art, 1986), pp. 40–56.

95. For a good account of the hearings and of the controversy in general, see Robert Storr, "'Tilted Arc': Enemy of the People?" *Art in America,* pp. 90–97.

96. Noguchi, in Nancy Foote, "Sightings on Siting," in *Urban Encounters: Art, Architecture, Audience,* p. 32.

97. Noguchi, in Hunter, *Noguchi,* p. 165.

98. Noguchi, in *Isamu Noguchi: The Sculpture of Spaces,* p. 29.

99. Robert Irwin, *Being and Circumstance,* p. 27.

100. Julian Redele, manager of Savage/Fogarty Corporation, in Georgia Sargeant, "Promenade Classique," p. 23.

101. "Porcine Plan Evokes Squealing in Cincinnati," *Chicago Tribune,* January 12, 1988, p. 4; Clare Ansberry, "Perhaps New York Would Accept the Pigs in Trade for 'Tilted Arc,'" *Wall Street Journal,* January 19, 1988, section 2, p. 33.

102. Lew Moores, "Cincinnati Voices Its Pig Beefs," *Cincinnati Post,* January 13, 1988, p. 1B.

103. "Let the Pigs Soar," *Cincinnati Post,* January 13, 1988, p. 6A.

104. Kathy Halbreich, "The Social Dimension: Art That's More 'As' Than 'On,'" in Harris, *Insights/On Sites,* p. 58.

105. Alexander Cooper Associates, *Battery Park City: Draft Summary Report and 1979 Master Plan* (New York: Battery Park City Authority, 1979), p. 64.

106. Cooper, Eckstut Associates in association with Battery Park City Authority, *Battery Place Residential Area: Design Guidelines* (New York: Battery Park City Authority, 1985), pp. 14–15.

107. Jeffrey Schmalz, "New York Reaches Accord on Housing," *New York Times,* December 27, 1987, section 1, pp. 1, 36.

108. On Puryear's notion of amenities, see Patricia Fuller, "Martin Puryear: Public Places, Personal Visions," in *Martin Puryear* (Chicago: Chicago Public Library Cultural Center, 1987), p. 41; also Michael Brenson, "Maverick Sculptor Makes Good," p. 90.

109. For more on Beuys's Actions, see Heiner Stachelhaus, *Joseph Beuys* (New York: Abbeville Press, 1991), pp. 144–49.

110. Oppenheim, in Lucy Lippard, *Overlay: Contemporary Art and the Art of Prehistory,* p. 53.

111. On the transformation in the precolonial and colonial landscapes, see William Cronon, *Changes in the Land: Indians, Colonists, and the Ecology of New England* (New York: Hill and Wang, 1983).

112. Helen Mayer Harrison and Newton Harrison, interview, *Nobody Told Us When to Stop Thinking* (New York: Grey Art Gallery of New York University, 1987).

113. Newton Harrison, in Grace Glueck, "The Earth Is Their Palette," in Alan Sonfist, ed., *Art in the Land,* p. 182.

114. Aldo Leopold, "The Land Ethic," in *A Sand County Almanac* (New York: Oxford University Press, 1949; reprint ed., 1989), pp. 203, 224–25.

115. Chin, in Don Comis, "Revival Field," *Agricultural Research* 43 (November 1995): 9.

116. Irwin, in Kristine McKenna, "Uncommon Grounds," *Los Angeles Times,* April 7, 1996, *Calendar,* pp. 3, 83–85. Subsequent quotations are also from this source; previous quotations are from my conversation with the artist in August 1996.

117. For more on Irwin's ideas about site-generated art, see his book *Being and Circumstance,* especially the introduction.

118. For Hargreaves's critique of the conventions of landscape architects, see especially his essay "Post Modernism Looks Beyond Itself," *Landscape Architecture* 73 (July 1983): 60–65; quotations are from Hargreaves, "Most Influential Landscapes," *Landscape Journal* 12 (Fall 1993): 177.

119. Quotations by Maya Lin are from an unpublished typescript of a talk she gave at the annual meeting of the Industrial Design Society of America, in Santa Fe, September 1995.

120. Quotations by Charles Jencks are from his essay "Landscape of Waves," *Prospect Magazine,* Scotland's Architecture issue (Winter 1996): 2–5.

ARTISTS' STATEMENTS

Walter De Maria

The Lightning Field

Some Facts, Notes, Data, Information, Statistics and Statements:

The Lightning Field is a permanent work.

The land is not the setting for the work but a part of the work.

The sum of the facts does not constitute the work or determine its esthetics.

Because the sky-ground relationship is central to the work, viewing *The Lightning Field* from the air is of no value.

Part of the essential content of the work is the ratio of people to the space: a small number of people to a large amount of space.

It is intended that the work be viewed alone, or in the company of a very small number of people, over at least a 24-hour period.

The light is as important as the lightning.

The period of primary lightning activity is from late May through September.

There are approximately 60 days per year when thunder and lightning activity can be witnessed from *The Lightning Field*.

The invisible is real.

The observed ratio of lightning storms which pass over the sculpture has been approximately 3 per 30 days during the lightning season.

No photograph, group of photographs or other recorded images can completely represent *The Lightning Field*.

Isolation is the essence of Land Art.

Walter De Maria, "The Lightning Field," p. 58.

Ian Hamilton Finlay

Unconnected Sentences on Gardening

A garden is not an object but a process.

Flowers in a garden are an acceptable eccentricity.

Poussin and Salvator: Cops and Robbers.

Modern sculpture is *wilfully* ignorant.

Ethical Battles are 18th Century Gardens continued by other means.

What our culture proposed as the *general* it now treats as an eccentricity.

Ecology is Nature-Philosophy *secularised*.

Technology—Epic Convenience.

The murmur of innumerable bills was known to most great gardeners.

Superior gardens are composed of Glooms and Solitudes and not of plants and trees.

Weather is the chief content of a garden.

Installing is the hard toil of garden making, *placing* is its pleasure.

Garden centres must become the Jacobin Clubs of the new Revolution.

Public funding of the arts should be confined to nations with heroic ideologies.

Grand conceptions are inhuman to small inhuman minds.

Certain gardens are described as retreats when they are really attacks.

Our earth is carnivorous.

Embark on a garden with a Vision but *never* with a plan.

Ian Hamilton Finlay, *Nature Over Again After Poussin*, pp. 21–22.

Richard Fleischner

The project I built in Baltimore covered a two-and-a-half year span. I probably went down there thirty times before anything was fabricated and worked on the site with sticks, strings, anything that established planes and distances for me. When they felt right in relation to existing elements, I measured them and they were drawn and engineered by others.

It is very seldom that I'm not involved in the fabrication and construction of these things. And I'm normally working with people who are much more skilled than the particular crafts involved. There are many people involved with me who are craftsmen and builders in their own right and who, on their own time, make very beautiful things that are the result of their own intentions. It's analogous to the theater or dance. If something works, it's because of the interaction of all of us.

Lois Tarlow, "Alternative Space: Richard Fleischner," interview, *Art New England* 4 (April 1983): 15.

Andy Goldsworthy

I have become aware of how nature is in a state of change, and that change is the key to understanding. I want my art to be sensitive and alert to changes in material, season and weather.

A rock is not independent of its surroundings. The way it sits tells how it came to be there. The energy and space around a rock is as important as the energy and space within. The weather; rain, sun, snow, hail, mist, calm, is that external space made visible. When I touch a rock, I am touching and working the space around it. In an effort to understand why that rock is there and where it is going I do not take it away from the area in which I found it.

Sometimes a work is at its best when most threatened by the weather. A balanced rock is given enormous tension and force by a wind that might cause its collapse. I have worked with colourful leaves, delicate grasses and feathers made extra vivid by a dark rain-laden sky that cast no shadow. Had it rained the work would have become mud-splattered and washed away.

I make one or two pieces of work each day I go out. From a month's work two or three pieces are successful. The "mistakes" are very important. Each new work is a result of knowledge accumulated through past work. A good work is the result of being in the right place at the right time with the right material.

Letter to the author, June 14, 1983.

Nancy Holt

My work also is about putting function back into art. I want to emphasize that I'm tired of the isolation of aesthetics. There has been a lot of aestheticizing going on, and it was very much part of the Conceptual Art movement—there were artists during the sixties who would go around and select things in the environment saying that they were works of art, or take photographs of them so that they could be transformed into art. So, there was a whole movement to aestheticise the environment.

Right along some of my work has had a functional aspect, like indicating sun cycles or astronomical alignments, and with the park I'm working on now in Washington, D.C. I have to think about people sitting down and having enough room for baby carriages and so on. So by doing that I'm making art more functional. Art needs to be a more necessary part of the world, of society.

From an interview with Nancy Holt in Micky Donnelly, *Circa* (Belfast) 11 (July–August 1983), p. 9.

Maya Lin

The worst thing in the world would have been indifference to my piece. The monument may lack an American flag, but you're surrounded by America, by the Washington Monument and the Lincoln Memorial. I don't design pure objects like those. I work with the landscape, and I hope that the object and the land are equal players.

The piece itself is apolitical in the sense that it doesn't comment directly on the war—only on the men that died. For some people—especially right-wing politicians—that's political enough. It's like the emperor's new clothes. What people see, or don't see is their own projection.

Classical Greek temples were never white. They were highly colored. At some point much later, someone decided that white signified classical architecture. Black for me is a lot more peaceful and gentle than white. White marble may be very beautiful, but you can't read anything on it. I wanted something that would be soft on the eyes, and turn into a mirror if you polished it. The point is to see yourself reflected in the names. Also the mirror image doubles and triples the space. I thought black was a beautiful color and appropriate for the design.

In a world of phallic memorials that rise upwards, the memorial certainly does have a female sensibility. I didn't set out to conquer the earth, or overpower it, the way Western man usually does. I don't think I've made a passive piece, but neither is it a memorial to the idea of war.

Elizabeth Hess, "A Tale of Two Memorials," p. 123.

David Nash

Earlier, I used woodmill wood, regular standard units; later, greenwood, fresh from the tree; now, the tree itself. The more I look at the tree, the more I see the tree: Its space and location, its volume and structure, its engineering and balance. More than that, I see the uniqueness of each single tree, and beyond that still I see it as a great emblem of life. A potent vibrant tower, a whirling prayer wheel of natural energy.

Fletched Over Ash, n.p., published on the occasion of Nash's exhibition at AIR Gallery, London, 1978.

James Pierce

I find that earthworking is an economical and relatively harmless means of satisfying desires for control, security and immortality while reliving the history of the race and discovering one's humanity in physical union with nature.

My work is always tempered by the "genius

of the place," as Alexander Pope would say. I work with the landscape, not against it. This is not only true in a visual sense, but my medium is the landscape itself, its earth, rocks, and trees. I work in these materials because I feel their elemental power and because they cost nothing and are long lasting. I accept them as they are and do not alter their basic nature. The earthworks are literally alive with insects, birds and even an occasional mammal. These lifeforms add an everchanging variety of color, texture, and movement to an underlying simplicity of form. The discipline imposed by this essential simplicity is a constant spur to invention, as the original stimulus is sometimes surprisingly altered to satisfy requirements of support, slope, drainage, and exposure. In earthworking, unlike painting, not everything is possible. You know when to stop.

Letter to the author, November 8, 1976.

Robert Smithson

Across the country there are many mining areas, disused quarries and polluted lakes and rivers. One practical solution for the utilization of such devastated places would be land and water re-cycling in terms of "earth art." Recently, when I was in Holland, I worked in a sand quarry that was slated for redevelopment. The Dutch are especially aware of the physical landscape. A dialectic between land reclamation and mining usage must be established. The artist and the miner must become conscious of themselves as natural agents. In effect, this extends to all kinds of mining and building. When the miner or builder loses sight of what he is doing through the abstractions of technology he cannot practically cope with necessity. The world needs coal and highways, but we do not need the results of strip-mining or highway trusts. Economics, when abstracted from the world, is blind to natural processes. Art can become a resource, that mediates between the ecologist and the industrialist. Ecology and industry are not one-way streets, rather they should be cross-roads. Art can help to provide the needed dialectic between them. A lesson can be learned from the Indian cliff dwellings and earthworks mounds. Here we see nature and necessity in consort.

"Untitled, 1971," in Nancy Holt, ed., *The Writings of Robert Smithson*, p. 220.

James Turrell

Roden Crater Project

You can note, when standing on an open plain, that the sky is not limitless and has a definable shape and a sense of enclosure, often referred to as celestial vaulting. Then, when lying down, you can note a difference in the sense of shape. Clearly, these limits are malleable. To work with the limits of the space of the sky and its sense of interior sizing, a hemispherically shaped, dished space, about 400 to 1000 feet above a plain, was sought. It was necessary that this space be on a plain so that some preliminary sense of celestial vaulting could be experienced. A crater-shaped space was desired so that it could be formed to effect changes in the perception of the size and shape of the sky. The height above the plain was important, so that the slight quality of concave curvature to the earth experienced by pilots at low altitudes would increase the sense of celestial vaulting after you emerged from the crater space. A high-altitude site with infrequent cloud cover was also sought, so that the deeper blue of the sky could be utilized to support a close-in sense of celestial vaulting while in the bottom of the crater. Either a solitary cinder cone or a butte would satisfy these requirements.

All the Western states were flown, looking for possible sites. The search itself altered many ideas regarding the piece and also generated ideas for future works. Roden Crater, a volcano on the edge of the Painted Desert, was decided upon. The form of the volcano and its surroundings also changed my thinking about the piece. Obviously, this particular geological feature was selected not only because it met the requirements for the work, but also because the volcano itself is a powerful entity.

Rather than impose a plan upon the landscape, it was decided to work in phase with the surroundings. The site is a volcano, and will remain so. But it will be worked enough so that the desired experience will be heightened and ordered. This could also allow the piece to exist without beginning or end.

James Turrell: Light and Space, p. 42.

LOCATIONS OF SELECTED WORKS

Carl Andre. *Stone Field Sculpture,* 1977. Hartford Public Green, Main and Gold Streets, Hartford, Connecticut.

Siah Armajani. *NOAA Bridges,* 1983. On the grounds of the Western Regional Center of the National Oceanic and Atmospheric Administration, 7600 Sand Point Way N.E., Seattle.
——. *Untitled,* 1985. Adjacent to Tawes Theater on the campus of the University of Maryland, College Park.
——. *World Financial Center Plaza* (with Scott Burton, et al.). At the World Financial Center, on the Hudson River at the intersection of West and Liberty Streets, Battery Park City, New York.
——. *Irene Hixon Whitney Bridge,* 1988. Minneapolis Sculpture Garden, Walker Art Center.
——. *North Shore Esplanade Tower and Bridge,* 1996. Near the Saint George Ferry Terminal, Staten Island, New York.
——. *Olympic Tower and Bridge,* 1996. Olympic Stadium, Atlanta.

Herbert Bayer. *Earth Mound* and *Marble Garden,* 1955. Aspen Meadows, Aspen Institute for Humanistic Studies, Aspen, Colorado.
——. *Mill Creek Canyon Earthworks,* 1982. Mill Creek Canyon Park, Titus and Canyon Streets, Kent, Washington.

William Bennett. *Jamesville Quarry Sculpture,* work in progress. Jamesville, New York. For additional information, contact the artist at Department of Fine Arts, University of Virginia, Charlottesville, Virginia 22903.

Scott Burton. *Viewpoint,* 1983. On the grounds of the Western Regional Center of the National Oceanic and Atmospheric Administration, 7600 Sand Point Way N.E., Seattle.

——. *Pearlstone Park,* 1985. Across from Meyerhoff Symphony Hall at the intersection of Preston and Howard Streets, Baltimore.
——. Sculpture for the Equitable Center, 1986. The Equitable Life Assurance Society, in the Seventh Avenue lobby and on the north and south plazas on Sixth Avenue between 51st and 52nd Streets, New York.
——. *World Financial Center Plaza* (with Siah Armajani, et al.). At the World Financial Center, on the Hudson River at the intersection of West and Liberty Streets, Battery Park City, New York.

Walter De Maria. *Las Vegas Piece,* 1969. For information, contact Dia Art Foundation, 141 Wooster Street, #3A, New York 10012.
——. *The Lightning Field,* 1971–77. To arrange a visit, write Dia Art Foundation, Box 207, Quemado, New Mexico 87829.

Stan Dolega. Reclamation project, 1981. One-half mile east of Hanna, Wyoming, off Wyoming Highway 30 (follow signs to the city dump).

Ian Hamilton Finlay. *Stonypath,* begun 1967. *Stonypath* is open by appointment between May and September. Write to Stonypath, Dunsyre, Lanarkshire, Scotland.
——. *Five Columns for the Kröller-Müller,* 1981. In the garden of the Rijksmuseum Kröller-Müller, Otterlo, the Netherlands.

Harvey Fite. *Opus 40,* 1939–76. For directions and a schedule of open days, write Friends of Opus 40, 7480 Fite Road, Saugerties, New York 12477.

Richard Fleischner. *Sod Maze,* 1974. On the grounds of Château-sur-Mer, Bellevue Avenue, Newport, Rhode Island.
——. *Cow Island Project,* 1978. Roger Williams Park, Ninth and Elmwood Avenue, Providence, Rhode Island.
——. *Baltimore Project,* 1980. Social Security Administration Center, 6401 Security Boulevard, Woodlawn, Maryland.
——. *M.I.T. Project,* 1980–85. Between the Wiesner and Health Sciences/Health Services buildings on the campus of the Massachusetts Institute of Technology, Cambridge.

——. *Saint Louis Project,* 1988–89. South Park and Laumeier Sculpture Park, Saint Louis.
——. *Saint Paul Project,* 1988–91. East Capitol Plaza, Saint Paul.

George Hargreaves. Candlestick Point Cultural Park, 1985–93. San Francisco. Exit U.S. 101 at Candlestick Park, adjacent to the stadium and state park.
——. Byxbee Park, 1988–92. Palo Alto, California. On San Francisco Bay, east of U.S. 101 at the Embarcadero exit.
——. Guadalupe River Park, begun 1988. San Jose, California. The park can be entered from either Hedding or Taylor Street at the Guadalupe River Parkway; the Riverwalk, in downtown San Jose, is best approached from Woz Way at the Children's Discovery Museum.

Helen Mayer Harrison and Newton Harrison. *California Wash: A Memorial,* 1989–96. At the terminus of Pico Boulevard at the Santa Monica Beach Promenade, Santa Monica, California.

Michael Heizer. *Double Negative,* 1969–70. *Double Negative* is reached by driving north from Overton, Nevada, to the Overton airport. There, bear right onto a road that, after about two miles, climbs steeply up the western escarpment of the Mormon Mesa. Drive about three miles to nearly the other side of the mesa. Just before the road makes a 90-degree turn to the right and drops down the far side of the mesa, another road diagonals off to the left. Bear left on this road, which leads northeast slightly over a mile to *Double Negative.* There are other tracks that cross this last road, so this section of the trip can be confusing. *Double Negative* is in the third scallop of the escarpment north of where the road drops down the eastern edge of the mesa. See USGS map "Overton Quadrangle," 15-minute series.
——. *Complex One City,* 1972–76. For further information on this work, contact Knoedler Contemporary Art, 19 East 70th Street, New York 10021.
——. *Adjacent, Against, Upon,* 1976. Myrtle Edwards Park, Alaskan Way between West Bay and West Thomas, Seattle.
——. *Levitated Mass,* 1983. IBM Corporation, Madison Avenue at 56th Street, New York.
——. *Effigy Tumuli Sculptures,* 1985. Adjacent

to Buffalo Rock State Park, two miles west of Ottawa, Illinois. From Ottawa, west on Route 6, south on Boyce Memorial Drive, west on Dee Bennett Road to entrance to the state park.

Doug Hollis. *A Sound Garden,* 1983. On the grounds of the Western Regional Center of the National Oceanic and Atmospheric Administration, 7600 Sand Point Way N.E., Seattle.

Nancy Holt. *Sun Tunnels,* 1973–76. Lucin, Utah, the town nearest to *Sun Tunnels,* can be approached from the south by leaving Interstate 80 at Oasis, Nevada, and driving north on Route 30 through Montello. It can also be reached from the east by leaving Interstate 80N at Snowville, Utah, and heading west on Route 30 through Park Valley and Rosette. In either case, turn south off Route 30 about seventeen miles northeast of Montello (at "Grouse Creek Junction") onto a gravel road that leads four miles into Lucin. Continue south from Lucin two and one-half miles, then bear left, driving east. *Sun Tunnels* should begin to be visible off to the right at this point. After two miles, bear right one-half mile to *Sun Tunnels.* See USGS maps "Lucin Quadrangle" and "Pigeon Mountain Quadrangle," 7.5-minute series.
———. *Rock Rings,* 1979. On the campus of Western Washington University, Bellingham.
———. *Dark Star Park,* 1983–84. At the intersection of Fort Meyer Drive and Arlington Boulevard (Route 50), on the southern edge of Rosslyn, Arlington, Virginia.

Robert Irwin. *Untitled,* 1980. Steel wall for East Portal Park, Carpenter Plaza, Dallas.
———. *Nine Spaces/Nine Trees,* 1983. Public Safety Building, Fourth Avenue and Cherry Street, Seattle.
———. *Central Garden,* 1997. Getty Center, off Interstate 405 (the San Diego Freeway) in the Sepulveda Pass, Los Angeles. Parking reservations required; call 310-440-7300.

Patricia Johanson. *Fair Park Lagoon,* 1986. Near the Dallas Museum of Natural History, Fair Park, Dallas.

Lorna Jordan. *Waterworks Gardens,* 1996. East Division Reclamation Plant, 1200 Monster Road S.W., Renton, Washington. From Seattle, take I-5 south to Martin Luther King, Jr. Way. Turn right at the second light on 68th Avenue South. Go one mile to the intersection of Monster Road; gardens are on the corner and can be entered from Monster Road.

Joseph Kinnebrew. *Grand River Sculpture,* 1975. Bank of Grand River at 600 Front Street, N.W., Grand Rapids, Michigan.

Andrew Leicester. *Prospect V-III,* 1982. On the campus of Frostburg State College, Frostburg, Maryland. Write or call 301-689-4000 for open hours.
———. *Cincinnati Gateway,* 1988. At the entrance to Bicentennial Commons, at Sawyer Point on the Ohio River, Eggleston Avenue at Pete Rose Way, Cincinnati.

Maya Lin. *Vietnam Veterans Memorial,* 1982. Constitution Gardens, Constitution Avenue at 21st Street, N.W., Washington, D.C.
———. *Civil Rights Memorial,* 1989. At the entrance to the Southern Poverty Law Center, Montgomery, Alabama.
———. *Groundswell,* 1993. Wexner Center for the Arts, Ohio State University, Columbus.
———. *The Womens' Table,* 1993. Yale University, New Haven, Connecticut.
———. *Wave Field,* 1995. Francois Xavier Bagnoud Aerospace Engineering Building, University of Michigan, Ann Arbor.

Mary Miss. *Field Rotation,* 1981. At the Nathan Manilow Sculpture Park, Governors State University, University Park, Illinois. For directions and further information, call 312-534-5368.
———. *South Cove* (with Susan Child, et al.), 1988. At the Hudson River off West Street at Second Place, Battery Park City, New York.
———. *Greenwood Pond: Double Site,* 1996. Greenwood Park, Des Moines, Iowa.

Robert Morris. *Observatory,* 1971; reconstructed 1977. *Observatory* is located along the road from Lelystad to Swifterbant, northeast of Amsterdam, the Netherlands. It is at the junction of Houtribweg and Swifteringweg about midway between the two towns. Maps and details on bus service from Amsterdam have been published in *Robert Morris's Observatory in* *Oostelijk Flevoland* by the Stedelijk Museum, Amsterdam, 1977.
———. *Grand Rapids Project,* 1973–74. Belknap Park, Coldbrook Road, Grand Rapids, Michigan.
———. Untitled reclamation project for King County, Washington, 1979. The site is ten miles south of Seattle and one-half mile east of Interstate 5 at the intersection of 40th Place South and South 216th Street. Exit I-5 at South 200th Street, turn east, follow Military Road to South 216th, and bear left.

Isamu Noguchi. *Marble Garden,* 1960–64. Beinecke Library, on the campus of Yale University, New Haven, Connecticut.
———. *Chase Manhattan Bank Plaza Garden,* 1961–64. Chase Manhattan Bank, 1 Chase Manhattan Plaza, New York.
———. *Playscapes,* 1975. In Piedmont Park, Atlanta.
———. *Hart Plaza,* 1972–78. Jefferson and Auditorium Drive, Detroit.

Beverly Pepper. *Amphisculpture,* 1974–77. On the grounds of the AT&T Corporation Headquarters, Routes 202/206 North, Bedminster, New Jersey.

James Pierce. *Pratt Farm,* begun 1970. For information on visiting Pierce's garden of history, write to the artist at 14 Pearl Street, Camden, Maine 04843.

Anne and Patrick Poirier. Promenade Classique, 1986. TransPotomac Center, North Fairfax at First Street, Alexandria, Virginia.

Martin Puryear. *Bodark Arc,* 1982. At the Nathan Manilow Sculpture Park, Governors State University, University Park, Illinois. For directions and further information, call 312-534-5368.
———. *Knoll for NOAA,* 1983. On the grounds of the Western Regional Center of the National Oceanic and Atmospheric Administration, 7600 Sand Point Way N.E., Seattle.
———. *Pavilion in the Trees,* 1993. West Fairmount Park, Philadelphia.
———. *Pylons,* 1995. At the Belvedere, adjacent to North Cove at World Financial Center, West and Liberty Streets, Battery Park City, New York.

Jim Sanborn. *Coastline,* 1993. Eastern Headquarters, National Oceanic and Atmospheric Administration, East-West Highway, Silver Spring, Maryland.

————. *Paleos,* 1993. Department of Biology, Massachusetts Institute of Technology, Ames Street, Cambridge.

————. *Indian Run Park,* 1994. United States Courthouse, Cherrywood Lane, Greenbelt, Maryland.

Martha Schwartz. Center for Innovative Technology, 1986–88. Route 28 at the Dulles Airport Access Road, Fairfax County, Virginia.

————. Rio Shopping Center, 1988. Piedmont and North Avenues, Atlanta.

————. The Citadel Grand Allée, 1990–91. An entry court at an office and retail complex, City of Commerce, California.

————. *Miami Soundwall,* 1996. North edge of Miami International Airport.

————. Federal Plaza, 1996. Jacob K. Javits Building, Lafayette and Worth Streets, New York.

————. Minneapolis Federal Courthouse Plaza, 1996. Third Avenue and Fourth Street, Minneapolis.

Richard Serra. *Spin Out (For Robert Smithson),* 1973. In the garden at the Rijksmuseum Kröller-Müller, Otterlo, the Netherlands.

————. *Schunnemunk Fork,* 1990–91. On the grounds of the Storm King Art Center, Mountainville, New York.

Michael Singer. 27th Avenue Solid Waste Transfer and Recycling Center, 1989–93. 27th Avenue and Lower Buckeye Road, Phoenix.

————. *Ritual Series/Retellings: A Place to Remember Those Who Survived,* 1993. Killesberg Park, Stuttgart, Germany.

————. Interior garden and inlaid stone flooring, 1994. Concourse C, Denver International Airport, Denver.

————. *Grand Rapids Riverwalk and Floodwall,* 1996. Along the east bank of the Grand River, Grand Rapids, Michigan.

Robert Smithson. *Spiral Jetty,* 1970. *Spiral Jetty*

is reached by driving west from Brigham City, Utah, on Route 84. At Corrine, about five miles west of Brigham City, bear left onto Route 83. Continue for about eighteen miles to Lampo Junction, and bear left toward Promontory and the Golden Spike National Historic Site. Continue west on a dirt road down Promontory Hollow after passing the Golden Spike Historic Site. About six miles west of the historic site, as Promontory Hollow begins to open up onto Rozel Flat, the road will fork. Bear left about a mile and a half to another fork ("Pipeline Point"). Bear right, and drive across Rozel Flat toward the Great Salt Lake, which will begin to be visible in the distance between Promontory Mountains on the left and Rozel Hills on the right. The road will curve around the east side of the Rozel Hills and end at an abandoned oil drilling site marked by a straight jetty. *Spiral Jetty* is a mile up the shore to the right from there, and can be reached on foot or on a very rough road just up the hill from the drilling site. It is a total of about fifteen miles from the historic site to *Spiral Jetty.* See USGS map "Great Salt Lake City and Vicinity." As *Spiral Jetty* is often submerged, it is advisable to check with the Chamber of Commerce in Brigham City before going to the site to determine if the water is above the 1970 level.

Ned Smyth. *Piazza Lavoro/Mythic Source,* 1984. Allegheny Landing Park at North Shore Center, Federal Street at the 6th Street Bridge, Pittsburgh.

————. *The Upper Room,* 1987. On the esplanade at Albany Street, Battery Park City, New York.

————. *Landfall 39°49'N75°31'W,* 1988. Across from the Amtrak and bus stations at the intersection of Martin Luther King Boulevard, North Walnut and French Streets, Wilmington, Delaware.

Athena Tacha. *Streams,* 1976. On the banks of Plum Creek, Vine Street Park, Oberlin, Ohio.

George Trakas. *Berth Haven,* 1983. On the grounds of the Western Regional Center of the

National Oceanic and Atmospheric Administration, 7600 Sand Point Way N.E., Seattle.

James Turrell. *Roden Crater Project,* work in progress. For further information, contact the Skystone Foundation, Box 725, Flagstaff, Arizona 86002.

Peter Walker. *Tanner Fountain,* 1984. At the Science Center on the campus of Harvard University, Cambridge, Massachusetts.

————. Site planning and gardens, IBM Solana, 1984–93. Westlake and Southlake, Texas.

————. Plaza Tower and Town Center Park, completed 1991. Bristol Street and Town Center Drive (and just across Anton Boulevard from Noguchi's *California Scenario),* Costa Mesa, California.

————. Marugame Station Plaza, completed 1992. Marugame City, Kagawa Prefecture, Japan.

————. Gardens for the Center for Advanced Science and Technology, completed 1993; and Town Park, under construction. Harima Science Garden City, Hyogo Prefecture, Japan.

Elyn Zimmerman. *Marabar,* 1984. At the National Geographic Society, M Street between 16th and 17th Streets, N.W., Washington, D.C.

————. *Keystone Island,* 1989. Dade County Justice Center, North Biscayne Boulevard, North Miami, Florida.

————. *Sanctuary,* 1990. H. Lee Moffitt Cancer Center and Research Institute, University of South Florida, Tampa.

————. *Lithos,* 1991. 865 South Figueroa Street, Los Angeles.

————. *First Market Plaza,* 1991. 525 Market Street, San Francisco.

————. *Charles W. Ireland Sculpture Garden,* 1994. Birmingham Museum of Art, Birmingham, Alabama. Zimmerman collaborated with architect Edward Larabee Barnes on the design of the garden, which includes her sculpture *Lithos II.*

————. *World Trade Center Memorial,* 1995. On the plaza at the World Trade Center, New York.

SELECTED BIBLIOGRAPHY

This is a concise rather than an exhaustive listing. Individual bibliographies for those artists discussed at length in the text follow the general one. Sources that discuss more than one artist are included in the general bibliography and are not repeated in the individual listings. The general bibliography includes books, exhibition catalogs, and periodicals. Special issues of periodicals that include more than one essay on the subject are listed under the title of the issue or the name of the special editor; individual essays within such issues are not also listed by author. The general bibliography also contains some pertinent monographic essays on artists discussed briefly or not at all in the text. For a more complete bibliography on the subject through 1982, see Patricia Pate Havlice, *Earth-Scale Art: A Bibliography, Directory of Artists, and Index of Reproductions* (Jefferson, N.C., and London: McFarland and Company, 1984).

General

Adams, David. "Joseph Beuys: Pioneer of a Radical Ecology." *Art Journal* 51 (Summer 1992): 26–34.

Alloway, Lawrence. "Site Inspection." *Artforum* 15 (October 1976): 49–55.

Anderson, Wayne. *American Sculpture in Process: 1930–1970.* Boston: New York Graphic Society, 1975.

Auping, Michael. *Common Ground: Five Artists in the Florida Landscape,* exhibition catalog. Sarasota, Fla.: John and Mable Ringling Museum of Art, 1982. Includes Hamish Fulton, Helen and Newton Harrison, Michael Singer, and Alan Sonfist.

"Art Outdoors," special issue. *Studio International* 193 (March–April 1977): 82–130. Includes essays by Lucy R. Lippard, Nancy D. Rosen, and Andrew Causey.

Baker, Elizabeth. "Artworks on the Land." *Art in America* 64 (January–February 1976): 92–96.

Beardsley, John. *Probing the Earth: Contemporary Land Projects,* exhibition catalog. Washington, D.C.: Smithsonian Institution Press, 1977. Published for the Hirshhorn Museum and Sculpture Garden.

———. *Art in Public Places: A Survey of Community-Sponsored Projects Supported by the National Endowment for the Arts.* Washington, D.C.: Partners for Livable Places, 1981.

———. "Personal Sensibilities in Public Places." *Artforum* 19 (Summer 1981): 43–45.

Berkson, Bill. "Seattle Sites." *Art in America* 74 (July 1986): 68–83, 133–35.

Bongartz, Roy. "It's Called Earth Art—and Boulderdash." *New York Times Magazine,* February 1, 1970, pp. 16–17, 22–30.

Bourdon, David. "What on Earth!" *Life* 66 (April 25, 1969): 80–86. A report on Cornell's *Earth Art* exhibition.

———. *Designing the Earth: The Human Impulse to Shape Nature.* New York: Harry N. Abrams, 1995.

Burnham, Jack. *Great Western Salt Works.* New York: George Braziller, 1974.

Butterfield, Jan. *The Art of Light and Space.* New York: Abbeville Press, 1993.

Cameron, Dan. *The Savage Garden: Landscape as Metaphor in Recent American Installations,* exhibition catalog. Madrid: Sala de Exposiciones de la Fundación Caja de Pensiones, 1990.

Campbell, J., and J. Cruikshank. *Artists and Architects Collaborate: Designing the Wiesner Building.* Cambridge, Mass.: MIT Committee on the Visual Arts, 1985.

Castle, Ted. "Art in Its Place." *Geo* 4 (September 1982): 64–75, 112.

Celant, Germano. *Arte Povera.* New York: Praeger Publishers, 1969.

Cembalest, Robin. "The Ecological Art Explosion." *Artnews* 90 (Summer 1991): 96–105.

Clay, Grady. "Earthworks Move Upstage." *Landscape Architecture* 70 (January 1980): 55–57. Report on Seattle earthworks project.

Crawford, Donald. "Nature and Art: Some Dialectical Relationships." *Journal of Aesthetics and Art Criticism* 42 (Fall 1983): 49–58.

Cruikshank, Jeffrey, and Pam Korza. *Going Public: A Field Guide to Developments in Art in Public Places.* Amherst: Arts Extension Service, Division of Continuing Education, University of Massachusetts, 1988.

Davies, Hugh, and Onorato, Ronald. *Sittings,* exhibition catalog. La Jolla, Calif.: La Jolla Museum of Contemporary Art, 1986. Includes the work of Alice Aycock, Richard Fleischner, Mary Miss, and George Trakas.

Différentes Natures: Visions de l'art contemporain, exhibition catalog. Paris: Etablissement Public pour l'Aménagement de la Région de La Défense, 1993.

"Discussions with Heizer, Oppenheim, Smithson." *Avalanche,* no. 1 (Fall 1970): 48–71.

Doss, Erika. *Spirit Poles and Flying Pigs: Public Art and Cultural Democracy in American Communities.* Washington, D.C.: Smithsonian Institution Press, 1995.

Earth Art, exhibition catalog. Ithaca: Andrew Dickson White Museum, Cornell University, 1970. Includes essays by William C. Lipke and Willoughby Sharp.

"Earth Movers." *Time* 92 (October 11, 1968): 84. Review of Dwan Gallery *Earthworks* exhibition.

Earthworks: Land Reclamation as Sculpture, exhibition catalog. Seattle: Seattle Art Museum, 1979. A project of the King County Arts Commission; essay by Robert Morris.

Feinberg, Jean, and C. Greentree. "Art Between Classes." *Landscape Architecture* 77 (March–April 1987): 82–87. A report on the environmental sculpture on the campus at the University of California, San Diego.

Foote, Nancy. "The Anti-Photographers." *Artforum* 15 (September 1976): 46–54.

———. "Monument-Sculpture-Earthwork." *Artforum* 18 (October 1979): 32–37. Report on the Seattle earthworks project.

Forgey, Ben. "Art Out of Nature Which Is about Nothing but Nature: Work of Michael Singer." *Smithsonian* 8 (January 1978): 62–64.

———. "You Can Range-Ride or Rope a Steer in This Work of Art." *Smithsonian* 14 (December 1983): 134–43. Report on Alan Wood's *Ranch* project.

Friedman, Bruce Jay. "Dirty Pictures." *Esquire* 75 (May 1971): 42, 112–17.

Friedman, Martin, et al. *Sculpture Inside Outside,* exhibition catalog. Minneapolis: Walker Art Center, 1988.

———. *Visions of America: Landscape as Metaphor in the Late Twentieth Century,* exhibition catalog. Denver: Denver Art Museum; Columbus, Ohio: Columbus Museum of Art; New York: Harry N. Abrams, 1994.

Fuller, Patricia. *Five Artists at NOAA: A Casebook on Art in Public Places.* Seattle: Real Comet Press, 1985.

Gabriel, Bertram. "Works of Earth." *Horizon* 25 (January–February 1982): 42–48.

Garraud, Colette. *L'Idée de nature dans l'art contemporain.* Paris: Flammarion, 1993.

Gilbert-Rolfe, Jeremy. "Sculpture as Everything Else: Twenty Years or So of the Question of Landscape." *Arts Magazine* 62 (January 1988): 71–75.

Glueck, Grace. "Art in Public Places Stirs Widening Debate." *New York Times,* May 23, 1982, section 2, pp. 1, 30.

———. "Serving the Environment." *New York Times,* June 27, 1982, section 2, pp. 25–26. Recent public environmental artworks.

Gottschalk, Earl C., Jr. "Earth-shaking News from the Art World: Sculpturing the Land." *Wall Street Journal,* September 10, 1976, pp. 1, 19.

Harris, Stacy Paleologos, ed. *Insights/ On Sites: Perspectives on Art in Public Places.* Washington, D.C.: Partners for Livable Places, 1984. Includes essays by Richard Andrews, Cesar Pelli and Nancy Rosen, Anita Contini, Kathy Halbreich, and Mary Miss.

Heiss, Alanna. *Dennis Oppenheim: Selected Works 1967–90,* exhibition catalog. New York: Institute for Contemporary Art, P.S. 1 Museum; Harry N. Abrams, 1992.

Herd, Stan. *Crop Art and Other Earthworks.* New York: Harry N. Abrams, 1994.

Herrera, Hayden. "City Earthwork." *Art in America* 64 (September 1976): 100–101. Suzanne Harris's *Locus Up One.*

Hickey, Dave. "Earthscapes, Landworks and Oz." *Art in America* 59 (September–October 1971): 40–49.

Hobbs, Robert, ed. "Earthworks: Past and Present," special issue. *Art Journal* 42 (Fall 1982): 191–233. Includes nine essays.

Howett, Catherine. "New Directions in Environmental Art." *Landscape Architecture* 67 (January 1977): 38–46.

Johnson, Jory. *Modern Landscape Architecture: Redefining the Garden.* New York: Abbeville Press, 1991.

Johnson, Linda L. *A Dialogue with Nature: Nine Contemporary Sculptors,* exhibition catalog. Washington, D.C.: Phillips Collection, 1992. Includes Patrick Dougherty, Jim Sanborn, and Meg Webster.

Junker, Howard. "The New Sculpture: Getting Down to the Nitty Gritty." *Saturday Evening Post* 241 (November 2, 1968): 42–47.

Kardon, Janet. "Janet Kardon Interviews Some Modern Maze-Makers." *Art International* 20 (April–May 1976): 64–68.

Kepes, Gyorgy, ed. *Arts of the Environment.* New York: George Braziller, 1972.

Kern, Hermann. "Labyrinths: Tradition and Contemporary Works." *Artforum* 19 (May 1981): 60–68.

Kingsley, April. "Six Women at Work in the Landscape." *Arts Magazine* 52 (April 1978): 108–12.

Kluesing, Cherie. "Site Artists: The Role of Outsiders in Landscape Design." *Landscape Architecture* 78 (April–May 1988): 120, 104–6.

Krauss, Rosalind. *Passages in Modern Sculpture.* London: Thames and Hudson; New York: Viking, 1977.

———. "Sculpture in the Expanded Field." *October,* no. 8 (Spring 1979): 31–44.

"Landscape Sculpture: The New Leap," special issue. *Landscape Architecture* 61 (July 1971): 296–343. Includes editorial by Grady Clay, essays by Richard Koshalek, James Wines.

Larson, Kay. "New Landscapes in Art." *New York Times Magazine,* May 13, 1979, pp. 20–23, 28–38.

———. "The Expulsion from the Garden: Environmental Sculpture at the Winter Olympics." *Artforum* 19 (April 1980): 36–45.

Leider, Philip. "How I Spent My Summer Vacation, or, Art and Politics in Nevada, Berkeley, San Francisco and Utah." *Artforum* 9 (September 1970): 40–49.

Lippard, Lucy R. "Complexes: Architectural Sculpture in Nature." *Art in America* 67 (January–February 1979): 86–97.

———. "Gardens: Some Metaphors for a Public Art." *Art in America* 69 (November 1981): 136–50.

———. *Overlay: Contemporary Art and the Art of Prehistory.* New York: Pantheon Books, 1983.

Masheck, Joseph. "The Panama Canal and Some Other Works of Work." *Artforum* 9 (May 1971): 38–42.

Matilsky, Barbara C. *Fragile Ecologies: Contemporary Artists' Interpretations and Solutions,* exhibition catalog. New York: Rizzoli International, 1992.

McFadden, Sarah. "Report from Lake Placid. The Big Secret: Art at the Olympics." *Art in America* 68 (April 1980): 53–63.

Müller, Gregoire. *The New Avant-Garde: Issues for the Art of the Seventies.* New York: Praeger Publishers, 1972. Photographs by Gianfranco Gorgoni.

Noah, Barbara. "Cost-Effective Earth Art." *Art in America* 68 (January 1980): 12–15. Report on the Seattle earthworks project.

Oakes, Baile. *Sculpting with the Environment: A Natural Dialogue.* New York: Van Nostrand Reinhold, 1995.

Onorato, Ronald J. "The Modern Maze." *Art International* 20 (April–May 1976): 21–25.

Pepper, Beverly, with Jan Butterfield. "Beverly Pepper: A Space Has Many Aspects." *Arts Magazine* 50 (September 1975): 91–94. Interview.

Reutersward, Patrik. "The Quarries of William Bennett." *Konsthistorisk tidskrift* 51 (Stockholm, 1982): 143–46.

Richardson, Trevor. *Meg Webster: Sculpture Projects,* exhibition catalog. Greensboro: Weatherspoon Art Gallery, University of North Carolina at Greensboro, 1992.

Rosenberg, Harold. *The De-definition of Art: Action Art to Pop to Earthworks.* New York: Horizon Press, 1972.

———. *Art on the Edge: Creators and Situations.* New York: Macmillan Publishing, 1975.

Schwendenwien, Jude. "Breaking Ground: Art in the Environment." *Sculpture* 10 (September–October 1991): 40–45.

Senie, Harriet. *Contemporary Public Sculpture: Tradition, Transformation, and Controversy.* New York: Oxford University Press, 1992.

Sonfist, Alan, ed. *Art on the Land: A Critical Anthology of Environmental Art.* New York: E. P. Dutton, 1983.

Tiberghien, Gilles A. *Land Art.* New York: Princeton Architectural Press, 1995.

Tillim, Sidney. "Earthworks and the New Picturesque." *Artforum* 7 (December 1968): 42–45.

Tomkins, Calvin. *The Scene: Reports on Post-Modern Art.* New York: Viking Press, 1976.

———. "The Art World: Like Water in a Glass." *New Yorker* 59 (March 21, 1983): 92–97. Report on recent public environmental artworks.

Urban Encounters: Art, Architecture, Audience, exhibition catalog. Philadelphia: Institute of Contemporary Art. University of Pennsylvania, 1980. Essays by Janet Kardon, Lawrence Alloway, Ian L. McHarg, and Nancy Foote.

Wagenknecht-Harte, Kay. *Site + Sculpture: The Collaborative Design Process.* New York: Van Nostrand Reinhold, 1989.

Weilacher, Udo. *Between Landscape Architecture and Land Art.* Basel, Switzerland, and Boston: Birkhauser, 1996.

Werkner, Patrick. *Land Art USA: Von den Ur-sprungen zu den Grossraumprojekten in der Wuste*. Munich: Prestel, 1992.

Siah Armajani

Kardon, Janet. *Siah Armajani*, exhibition catalog. Philadelphia: Institute of Contemporary Art, University of Pennsylvania, 1985.

Phillips, Patricia. "Siah Armajani's Constitution." *Artforum* 24 (December 1985): 70–75.

Princenthal, Nancy. "Master Builder." *Art in America* 74 (March 1986): 126–33.

Shermeta, Margo. "An American Dictionary in the Vernacular." *Arts Magazine* 61 (January 1987): 38–41.

Herbert Bayer

Bayer, Herbert. *Herbert Bayer: Painter, Designer, Architect*. New York: Reinhold Publishing, 1967.

Herbert Bayer: A Total Concept, exhibition catalog. Denver: Denver Art Museum, 1973.

Herbert Bayer: From Type to Landscape. Designs, Projects and Proposals, 1923–73, exhibition catalog. Hanover, N.H.: Dartmouth College Museum and Galleries, 1977. Text by Jan van der Marck.

Constantin Brancusi

Bach, Friedrich Teja, et al. *Constantin Brancusi, 1876–1957*, exhibition catalog. Philadelphia: Philadelphia Museum of Art; Cambridge, Mass.: MIT Press, 1995.

Brezianu, Barbu. *Brancusi in Romania*. Bucharest: Editura Academiei Republicii Socialiste Romania, 1976.

Geist, Sidney. *Brancusi: The Kiss*. New York: Harper and Row, 1978.

———. *Brancusi: A Study of the Sculpture*, rev. ed. New York: Hacker Art Books, 1983.

Hulten, Pontus, Natalia Domitresco, and Alexandre Istrati. *Brancusi*. New York: Harry N. Abrams, 1987.

Jianou, Ionel, and Constantin Noica. *Introduction à la sculpture de Brancusi*. Paris: Arted, 1976. Chapter 5: "L'Ensemble monumental de Targu-Jiu," pp. 53–71.

Miller, Sanda. "Brancusi's 'Column of the Infinite,'" *Burlington Magazine* 122 (July 1980): 470–80.

Nauman, Francis. "From Origin to Influence and Beyond: Brancusi's 'Column Without End.'" *Arts Magazine* 59 (May 1985): 112–18.

Noguchi, Isamu. "Noguchi on Brancusi." *Craft Horizons* 36 (August 1976): 26–29.

Shanes, Eric. *Constantin Brancusi*. New York: Abbeville Press, 1989. See especially chapter 6, "The Avenue of Heroes."

Tucker, William. "Brancusi at Tirgu-Jiu." *Studio International* 184 (October 1972): 117–21.

———. *Early Modern Sculpture*. New York: Oxford University Press, 1974. Chapter 7: "Brancusi at Tirgu Jiu," pp. 129–43.

Varia, Radu. *Brancusi*. New York: Rizzoli, 1986. See especially chapter 15, "The Monumental Ensemble of Targu-Jiu."

Scott Burton

Princenthal, Nancy. "Social Seating." *Art in America* 75 (June 1987): 130–37.

Richardson, Brenda. *Scott Burton*, exhibition catalog. Baltimore: Baltimore Museum of Art, 1986.

Scott Burton, exhibition catalog. London: Tate Gallery, 1985. Text by Richard Francis.

Christo

Bourdon, David. *Christo*. New York: Harry N. Abrams, 1972.

Christo: The Pont-Neuf Wrapped, Paris, 1975–85. New York: Harry N. Abrams, 1990.

Christo: The Reichstag and Urban Projects. Munich: Prestel, 1993.

Christo: Surrounded Islands. New York: Harry N. Abrams, 1985. Introduction by Werner Spies.

Christo: *Valley Curtain*. New York: Harry N. Abrams, 1973. Photographs by Harry Shunk.

Christo's Running Fence. New York: Harry N. Abrams, 1978. Photographs by Gianfranco Gorgoni, preface by Calvin Tomkins, captions by David Bourdon.

Fineberg, Jonathan. "Theater of the Real: Thoughts on Christo." *Art in America* 67 (December 1979): 92–99.

Frankenstein, Alfred. "Christo's 'Fence,' Beauty or Betrayal?" *Art in America* 64 (November–December 1976): 58–61.

Ratcliff, Carter. "Unwrapping Christo." *Saturday Review* 7 (December 1980): 18–22.

Spies, Werner, and Volz, Wolfgang, photo-graphs. *The Running Fence Project: Christo*. New York: Harry N. Abrams, 1977.

Tomkins, Calvin. "Onward and Upward with the Arts: Running Fence." *New Yorker* 53 (March 28, 1977): 43–46.

Vaizey, Marina. *Christo*. New York: Rizzoli, 1990.

Walter De Maria

Adrian, Dennis. "Walter De Maria: Word and Thing." *Artforum* 5 (January 1967): 28–29.

Beardsley, John. "Art and Authoritarianism: Walter De Maria's Lightning Field." *October*, no. 16 (Spring 1981): 35–38.

Bourdon, David. "Walter De Maria: The Singular Experience." *Art International* 12 (December 20, 1968): 39–43, 72.

De Maria, Walter. "The Lightning Field." *Artforum* 18 (April 1980): 51–59.

"High Priest of Danger." *Time* 93 (May 2, 1969): 54.

Leder, Dennis. "Walter De Maria: Mounds, Mines, Markers." *America* 142 (March 15, 1980): 219–20.

Walter De Maria, exhibition catalog. Stuttgart: Staatsgalerie, 1987.

Walter De Maria: 5, die Funf Kontinente Skulptur, exhibition catalog. Stuttgart: Hatje, 1991.

Wortz, Melinda. "Walter De Maria's 'Lightning Field.'" *Arts Magazine* 54 (May 1980): 170–73.

Ian Hamilton Finlay

Abrioux, Yves. *Ian Hamilton Finlay: A Visual Primer*. Edinburgh: Reaktion Books, 1985.

Bann, Stephen. "A Description of Stonypath." *Journal of Garden History* 1 (April–June 1981): 113–44.

Brown, David. "Stonypath: An Inland Garden." *Studio International* 193 (January–February 1977): 34–37.

Gintz, Claude. "Neoclassical Rearmament." *Art in America* 75 (February 1987): 110–17.

Hawkins, Ann W. "Stonypath." *Garden Design* 4 (Autumn 1985): 32–39.

McIntosh, Christopher. "A Garden of Many Dimensions: Stonypath, Lanarks." *Country Life* 162 (October 6, 1977): 928–30.

Nature Over Again after Poussin: Some Discovered Landscapes, exhibition catalog. Glasgow: Collins Exhibition Hall, University of Strathclyde, 1980. Essay by Stephen Bann; "Unconnected Sentences on Gardening" by Ian Hamilton Finlay.

Potter, Everett. "A Forgotten Art: A Conversation with Ian Hamilton Finlay at Stonypath, Scotland." *Arts Magazine* 62 (September 1987): 79–83.

Selected Ponds. Reno: West Coast Poetry Review, 1975. Photographs of Stonypath by Dave Paterson, essays by Stephen Bann and Bernard Lassus.

Harvey Fite

Brandau, Robert, and Eleanor Ward. "Stone upon Stone: The Craft of Dry Stone Masonry." *Historic Preservation* 27 (April–June 1975): 26–29.

Dalton, Deborah. "Still Life in a Quarry." *Landscape Architecture* 75 (May–June 1985): 66–69.

Kent, Norman. "A Sculptor's Quarry." *American Artist* 22 (January 1958): 25–31.

McFadden, Sarah. "Going Places, Part II: The Outside Story. Opus 40." *Art in America* 68 (Summer 1980): 52–54.

"Opus 40: Mysticism in Stone." *House and Garden Building Guide,* Fall–Winter 1976–77, pp. 110–11.

"The Quarrymaster of Saugerties." *Artnews* 76 (October 1977): 23–24, 26.

"Sculptor Nearing an End to a Massive 40-Year Task at an Abandoned Quarry." *New York Times,* August 3, 1968, p. 27.

Richard Fleischner

Davies, Hugh. "Richard Fleischner's Sculpture of the Past Decade." *Arts Magazine* 51 (April 1977): 118–23.

Davies, Hugh, and William H. Jordy, preface. *Richard Fleischner,* exhibition catalog. Amherst: University Gallery, University of Massachusetts, 1977.

Hannum, Eric. "Richard Fleischner's Education Courtyard, Dallas Museum of Art." *Landscape Architecture* 75 (July–August 1985): 78–79.

Onorato, Ronald J. "Reviews: Richard Fleischner." *Artforum* 16 (November 1977): 70–71. Cow Island project.

———. "Richard Fleischner's Baltimore Project." *Arts Magazine* 56 (October 1981): 64–67.

Richard Fleischner: Critical Distance, exhibition catalog. Des Moines: Des Moines Art Center, 1992.

Richard Fleischner: Projects, exhibition catalog. Providence, R.I.: David Winton Bell Gallery, List Art Center, Brown University, 1995.

Hamish Fulton

Auping, Michael. "Hamish Fulton: Moral Landscapes." *Art in America* 71 (February 1983): 87–93.

"Hamish Fulton." In *Landscape: Theory,* pp. 77–93. New York: Lustrum Press, 1980. Includes the text of an interview with Peter Turner.

Morgan, Robert C. "Hamish Fulton: The Residue of Vision/The Opening of Mind." *Arts Magazine* 60 (March 1986): 86–89.

Andy Goldsworthy

Goldsworthy, Andy. *Andy Goldsworthy: A Collaboration with Nature.* New York: Harry N. Abrams, 1990.

———. *Hand to Earth: Andy Goldsworthy Sculpture, 1976–1990.* New York: Harry N. Abrams, 1993.

———. *Stone.* New York: Harry N. Abrams, 1994.

———. *Wood.* New York: Harry N. Abrams, 1996.

George Hargreaves

Beardsley, John. "Poet of Landscape Process." *Landscape Architecture* 85 (December 1995): 46–51.

Hargreaves, George. "Post-Modernism Looks Beyond Itself." *Landscape Architecture* 73 (July–August 1983): 60–65.

Hargreaves: Landscape Works. Process Architecture 128, Tokyo: Process Architecture Co., 1996.

Rainey, Reuben M. "Environmental Ethics and Park Design: A Case Study of Byxbee Park." *Journal of Garden History* 14 (July–September 1994): 171–78.

Helen Mayer Harrison and Newton Harrison

Adcock, Craig. "Conversational Drift: Helen and Newton Harrison." *Art Journal* 51 (Summer 1992): 35–45.

Green Heart Vision, exhibition catalog. The Hague: Cultural Council of South Holland, 1995.

"Helen and Newton Harrison," special section. *Arts Magazine* 52 (February 1978): 126–33. Essays by Kim Levin, Peter Selz, and Kristine Stiles.

The Lagoon Cycle, exhibition catalog. Ithaca, N.Y.: Herbert F. Johnson Museum of Art, Cornell University, 1985.

The Serpentine Lattice, exhibition catalog. Portland, Ore.: Douglas F. Cooley Memorial Art Gallery, Reed College, 1993.

Michael Heizer

Bourdon, David. "Working with Earth, Michael Heizer Makes Art as Big as All Outdoors." *Smithsonian* 17 (April 1986): 68–77.

Davis, Douglas. "The Earth Mover." *Newsweek* 84 (November 18, 1974): 113.

Gruen, John. "Michael Heizer: You Might Say I'm in the Construction Business." *Artnews* 79 (December 1977): 96–99.

Heizer, Michael. "The Art of Michael Heizer." *Artforum* 8 (December 1969): 32–39.

Kertess, Klaus. "Earth Angles." *Artforum* 24 (February 1986): 76–79.

Massie, Sue. "Timeless Healing at Buffalo Rock." *Landscape Architecture* 75 (May–June 1985): 70–71.

McGill, Douglas. *Michael Heizer: Effigy Tumuli.* New York: Harry N. Abrams, 1990.

Michael Heizer, exhibition catalog. Essen: Museum Folkwang: Otterlo: Rijksmuseum Kröller-Müller, 1979.

Michael Heizer/Actual Size, exhibition catalog. Detroit Institute of Arts, 1971.

Michael Heizer: Double Negative. Los Angeles: Museum of Contemporary Art; New York: Rizzoli, 1991.

Michael Heizer: Sculpture in Reverse. Los Angeles: Museum of Contemporary Art, 1984.

Thorson, Alice. "A Paragon of Art in the 80s." *Artnews* 85 (January 1986): 11–12.

Waldman, Diane. "Holes Without History." *Artnews* 70 (May 1971): 44–48, 66–68.

Yau, John. "Sculpture as Archaeology." *Vogue* 171 (August 1981): 290–93, 347.

Nancy Holt

Castle, Ted. "Nancy Holt: Siteseer." *Art in America* 70 (March 1982): 84–91.

Forgey, Benjamin. "A Park Grows in Rosslyn." *Washington Post,* September 17, 1983, pp. C1, C2.

———. "Park for Art's Sake." *Washington Post,* July 7, 1984, pp. D1, D7.

Holt, Nancy. "Sun Tunnels." *Artforum* 15 (April 1977): 32–37.

———. "Stone Enclosure: Rock Rings." *Arts Magazine* 53 (June 1979): 152–55.

LeVeque, Terry Ryan. "Nancy Holt's Dark Star Park, Rosslyn, Virginia." *Landscape Architecture* 75 (July–August 1985): 80–82.

———. "Nancy Holt's Sky Mound." *Landscape Architecture* 78 (April–May 1988): 82–86.

Marter, Joan. "Nancy Holt's Dark Star Park." *Arts Magazine* 59 (October 1984): 137–39.

McGill, Douglas C. "Jersey Landfill to Become an Artwork." *New York Times,* September 3, 1986, pp. C1, C19.

Rosenberg, Avis Lang, and Keziere, Robert. "Stone Enclosure: Rock Rings." *Vanguard* 8 (February 1979): 22–27.

Sargeant, Georgia. "Dark Star Park." *International Sculpture* (January–February 1987): 34–35.

Yau, John. "Nancy Holt: Dark Star Park." *Artforum* 23 (April 1985): 97–98.

Robert Irwin

Esterow, Milton. "How Public Art Becomes a Political Hot Potato." *Artnews* 85 (January 1986): 75–79.

Irwin, Robert. *Being and Circumstance.* Larkspur Landing, Calif.: Lapis Press, in conjunction with the San Francisco Museum of Modern Art, 1985.

McEvilley, Thomas. "Robert Irwin." *Artforum* 22 (June 1984): 96. Review of *Nine Spaces/ Nine Trees.*

Robert Irwin, exhibition catalog. Los Angeles: Museum of Contemporary Art; New York: Rizzoli, 1993.

Weschler, Lawrence. "Lines of Inquiry." *Art in America* 70 (March 1982): 102–9.

———. *Seeing Is Forgetting the Name of the Thing One Sees.* Berkeley: University of California Press, 1982. Biography of the artist.

———. "Taking Art to Point Zero." *New Yorker* 58 (March 8 and March 15, 1982): 48–50+; 52–54+.

Wortz, Melinda. "Surrendering to Presence: Robert Irwin's Esthetic Integration." *Artforum* 20 (November 1981): 63–65.

Charles Jencks

Jencks, Charles. *What Is Post-Modernism?* 3d edition. London: Academy Editions; New York: St. Martin's Press, 1989.

———. *The Language of Post-Modern Architecture,* 6th edition. New York: Rizzoli, 1991.

———. *The Architecture of the Jumping Universe: A Polemic: How Complexity Science Is Changing Architecture and Culture.* London: Academy Editions; New York: St. Martin's Press, 1995.

Andrew Leicester

Doss, Erika. "Andrew Leicester's Cobumora." *Landscape Architecture* 76 (January–February 1986): 64–68.

———. "Andrew Leicester's Mining Memorials." *Arts Magazine* 61 (January 1987): 34–37.

Kudalis, Eric. "The Art of Place." *Architecture Minnesota* 12 (November–December 1986): 46–51.

Morganthau, Tom. "Get Rid of That Eyesore." *Newsweek* 110 (August 17, 1987): 23.

Rockcastle, Garth. "Art as Architecture: Leicester Sculpture." *Progressive Architecture* 65 (October 1984): 94–97.

Maya Lin

Buckley, Christopher. "The Wall." *Esquire* 104 (September 1985): 61+.

Danto, Arthur. "Art: The Vietnam Veterans Memorial." *Nation* 241 (August 31, 1985): 153.

Forgey, Benjamin. "Models of Simplicity." *Washington Post,* November 14, 1981, pp. C1, C4.

———. "A Solution with Pride, Harmony and Vision." *Washington Post,* February 9, 1983, pp. F1, F4.

Griswold, Charles L. "The Experience of the Vietnam Veterans Memorial." *Critical Inquiry* 12 (Summer 1986): 688–719.

Hess, Elizabeth. "A Tale of Two Memorials." *Art in America* 71 (April 1983): 120–27.

Hubbard, William. "A Meaning for Monuments." *Public Interest* 74 (Winter 1984): 17–30.

Maya Lin: Public/Private, exhibition catalog. Columbus: Wexner Center for the Arts, The Ohio State University, 1994.

McCombs, Phil. "The Memorial's Moment of Truce." *Washington Post,* February 9, 1983, pp. F1, F6.

Sorkin, Michael. "What Happens When a Woman Designs a War Monument?" *Vogue* 173 (May 1983): 120, 122.

Richard Long

Compton, Michael. *Some Notes on the Work of Richard Long.* London: British Council, 1976. Published on the occasion of Long's exhibition at the Thirty-seventh Venice Biennale.

Field, Simon. "Touching the Earth: Simon Field Examines the Work of Richard Long." *Art and Artists* 8 (April 1973): 14–19.

Foote, Nancy. "Long Walks." *Artforum* 18 (Summer 1980): 42–47.

Fuchs, R. H. "Memories of Passing: A Note on Richard Long." *Studio International* 187 (April 1974): 172–73.

———. *Richard Long,* exhibition catalog. New York: Solomon R. Guggenheim Museum, 1986.

Johnston, Jill. "Walking into Art." *Art in America* 75 (April 1987): 160–69, 235.

"Nineteen Stills from the Work of Richard Long." *Studio International* 179 (March 1970): 106–11.

Ana Mendieta

Clearwater, Bonnie, ed. *Ana Mendieta: A Book of Works.* Miami Beach: Grassfield Press, 1993.

Jacob, Mary Jane. *Ana Mendieta: The "Silueta" Series, 1973–1980,* exhibition catalog. New York: Galerie Lelong, 1991.

Perreault, John, and Petra Barreras del Rio. *Ana Mendieta: A Retrospective,* exhibition catalog. New York: New Museum of Contemporary Art, 1987.

Robert Morris

Grand Rapids Project: Robert Morris. Grand Rapids, Mich.: Grand Rapids Art Museum, 1975.

Morris, Robert. "Aligned with Nazca." *Artforum* 14 (October 1975): 26–39.

————. "The Present Tense of Space." *Art in America* 66 (January–February 1978): 70–81.

————. "Notes on Art as/and Land Reclamation." *October,* no. 12 (Spring 1980), pp. 87–102.

Robert Morris/Projects, exhibition catalog. Philadelphia: Institute of Contemporary Art, University of Pennsylvania, 1974.

Robert Morris: Selected Works, 1970–1981, exhibition catalog. Houston: Contemporary Arts Museum, 1981.

Robert Morris's Observatory in Oostelijk Flevoland. Amsterdam: Stedelijk Museum, 1977.

David Nash

Adams, Hugh. "The Woodman." *Art and Artists* 13 (April 1979): 44–47.

Beal, Graham. *David Nash: Voyages and Vessels,* exhibition catalog. Omaha: Joslyn Art Museum, 1994.

Hughes, Robert. "From Sticks to Cenotaphs." *Time* 115 (February 11, 1980): 65.

McPherson, Alan. "Interview with David Nash." *Artscribe,* no. 12 (June 1978): 30–34.

Nash, David. *Wood Primer.* San Francisco: Bedford Press, 1987.

Sixty Seasons: David Nash, exhibition catalog. Glasgow: Third Eye Centre, 1983. Essay by Hugh Adams.

Waldman, Diane. *British Art Now: An American Perspective,* exhibition catalog, pp. 80–99. New York: Solomon R. Guggenheim Museum, 1980.

Wood Quarry: David Nash, Otterlo 1982, exhibition catalog. Otterlo, The Netherlands: Rijksmuseum Kröller-Müller, 1982.

Isamu Noguchi

Altshuler, Bruce. *Isamu Noguchi.* New York: Abbeville Press, 1994.

Altshuler, Bruce, and Diane Apostolos-Cappadona, eds. *Isamu Noguchi: Essays and Conversations* (New York: Harry N. Abrams, 1994).

Ashton, Dore. *Noguchi East and West.* New York: Alfred A. Knopf, 1992.

Friedman, Martin. *Noguchi's Imaginary Landscapes,* exhibition catalog. Minneapolis: Walker Art Center, 1978. Environmental and stage designs.

Grove, Nancy, and Diane Botnick. *The Sculpture of Isamu Noguchi, 1924–79.* New York: Garland Publishing, 1980. Catalogue raisonné.

————. "Isamu Noguchi: Shaper of Space." *Arts Magazine* 59 (December 1984): 111–16.

Noguchi, Isamu. *The Isamu Noguchi Garden Museum.* New York: Harry N. Abrams, 1987.

Noguchi, Isamu, and R. Buckminster Fuller, foreword. *A Sculptor's World.* New York: Harper and Row, 1968. Autobiography.

Noguchi, Isamu, and Thomas Armstrong, foreword. *Isamu Noguchi: The Sculpture of Spaces,* exhibition catalog. New York: Whitney Museum of American Art, 1980. Environmental projects and theater sets.

James Pierce

Beardsley, John. "James Pierce and the Picturesque Landscape." *Art International* 23 (November–December 1979): 6–15.

Pierce, James. "The Pratt Farm Turf Maze." *Art International* 20 (April–May 1976): 25–27.

————. *Pratt Farm: Garden of History,* exhibition catalog. Macon, Ga.: Mercer University, 1976.

Anne and Patrick Poirier

Freed, S. "Colossal Collaboration." *Landscape Architecture* 77 (January–February 1987): 23.

Gintz, Claude. "Ruins and Rebellion." *Art in America* 72 (April 1984): 148–51.

Sargeant, Georgia. "Promenade Classique." *International Sculpture* (January–February 1987): 22–25.

Thorson, Alice. "Readymade Ruins." *Artnews* 86 (February 1987): 32–33.

Martin Puryear

Benezra, Neal, and Robert Storr. *Martin Puryear,* exhibition catalog. Chicago: Art Institute of Chicago, 1991.

Brenson, Michael. "Maverick Sculptor Makes Good." *New York Times Magazine,* November 1, 1987, pp. 84–93.

Calo, Carole Gold. "Martin Puryear: Private Objects, Evocative Visions." *Arts Magazine* 62 (February 1988): 90–94.

Davies, Hugh M., and Helaine Posner. *Martin Puryear,* exhibition catalog. Amherst: University Gallery, University of Massachusetts, 1984.

Martin Puryear: Public and Personal, exhibition catalog. Chicago: Chicago Public Library Cultural Center, 1987. Essays by Patricia Fuller and Judith Russi Kirshner.

Morgan, Ann Lee. "Martin Puryear: Sculpture as Elemental Expression." *New Art Examiner* 14 (May 1987): 27–29.

Charles Ross

Ranney, Edward. "Excavating the Present." *Aperture,* no. 98 (Spring 1985): 42–47.

Ross, Charles. "Sunlight Convergence/Solar Burn." *Arts Magazine* 47 (December 1972–January 1973): 48–50.

————. *Sunlight Convergence/Solar Burn: The Equinoctial Year, September 23, 1971–September 22, 1972.* Salt Lake City: University of Utah Press and Art Department, 1976.

The Substance of Light: Sunlight Dispersion, The Solar Burns, Point Source/Star Space. Selected Works of Charles Ross, exhibition catalog. La Jolla, Calif.: La Jolla Museum of Contemporary Art, 1976.

Martha Schwartz

Meyer, Elizabeth K., and Heidi Landecker. *Martha Schwartz: Transfiguration of the Commonplace.* Washington, D.C.: Spacemaker Press, 1996.

Richard Serra

Bois, Yve-Alain. "The Meteorite in the Garden." *Art in America* 72 (Summer 1984): 108–13. A report on the installation of *Clara-Clara* in the Tuileries, Paris.

Krauss, Rosalind. *Richard Serra/Sculpture.* New York: Museum of Modern Art, 1986.

"Richard Serra," special section. *Arts Magazine* 55 (November 1980): 118–33. Includes interview with Douglas Crimp, essay by Donald Kuspit, journal by Robert Pincus-Witten.

Senie, Harriet. "The Right Stuff." *Artnews* 83 (March 1984): 50–59.

Serra, Richard, with Clara Weyergraf. *Richard Serra: Interviews, Etc., 1970–1980.* Yonkers, N.Y.: Hudson River Museum, 1980.

Storr, Robert. "'Tilted Arc': Enemy of the People?" *Art in America* 73 (September 1985): 90–97.

Charles Simonds

Abadie, Daniel. *Charles Simonds* (Art/Cahier 2). Paris: SMI, 1975.

Beardsley, John. "Charles Simonds: Extending the Metaphor." *Art International* 22 (February 1979): 14–19, 34.

———. "Hybrid Dreams." *Art in America* 83 (March 1995): 92–97.

Castle, Ted. "Charles Simonds: The New Adam." *Art in America* 71 (February 1983): 94–103.

Charles Simonds, exhibition catalog. Paris: Editions du Jeu de Paume, 1994.

Linker, Kate. "Charles Simonds' Emblematic Architecture." *Artforum* 17 (March 1979): 32–37.

Lippard, Lucy, and Charles Simonds. "Microcosm to Macrocosm/Fantasy World to Real World." *Artforum* 12 (February 1974): 36–39. Interview.

Molderings, Herbert. *Schwebende Städte und andere Architekturen* (Floating Cities and Other Architectures), exhibition catalog. Münster: Westfälischer Kunstverein, 1978.

Neff, John H. *Charles Simonds,* exhibition catalog. Chicago: Museum of Contemporary Art, 1981. Includes essays by Daniel Abadie and John Beardsley and "Three Peoples" by the artist.

Patton, Phil. "Charles Simonds' Lost Worlds." *Artnews* 82 (February 1983): 84–90.

Michael Singer

"Making Art of Trash." *Architectural Record* 12 (June 1994): 98–103.

Michael Singer: Artist-in-Residence, Recent Projects, exhibition catalog. Hanover, N.H.: Jaffe-Friede and Strauss Galleries, Hopkins Center, Dartmouth College, 1996.

Muschamp, Herbert. "When Art Becomes a Public Spectacle." *New York Times,* August 29, 1993, section 2, p. 1.

Sheffield, Margaret. "Natural Structures: Michael Singer's Sculpture and Drawings." *Artforum* 17 (February 1979): 48–51.

Waldman, Diane. *Michael Singer,* exhibition catalog. New York: Solomon R. Guggenheim Museum, 1984.

Robert Smithson

Alloway, Lawrence. "Robert Smithson's Development." *Artforum* 11 (November 1972): 52–61.

Bear, Liza, and Nancy Holt. "Robert Smithson's Amarillo Ramp." *Avalanche,* no. 8 (Summer–Fall 1973): 16–21.

Hobbs, Robert. *Robert Smithson: Sculpture.* Ithaca, N.Y.: Cornell University Press, 1981. Includes essays by Lawrence Alloway, John Coplans, and Lucy R. Lippard.

Holt, Nancy, ed. *The Writings of Robert Smithson.* New York: New York University Press, 1979. Anthology of the artist's writings, published and unpublished.

Horning, Ron. "In Time: Earthworks, Photodocuments, and Robert Smithson's Buried Shed." *Aperture,* no. 106 (Spring 1987): 74–77.

"Robert Smithson," special issue. *Arts Magazine* 52 (May 1978): 96–144. Includes fifteen essays on or tributes to Smithson.

Robert Smithson: Drawings, exhibition catalog. New York: New York Cultural Center, 1974. Essays by Suan Ginsburg and Joseph Masheck.

"Robert Smithson's Spiral Jetty," special section. *Arts Magazine* 56 (October 1981): 68–88. Includes essays by Elizabeth C. Childs and Donald B. Kuspit.

Shapiro, Gary. *Earthwards: Robert Smithson and Art after Babel.* Berkeley: University of California Press, 1995.

Sobieszek, Robert A. *Robert Smithson: Photo Works,* exhibition catalog. Los Angeles: Los Angeles County Museum of Art; Albuquerque: University of New Mexico Press, 1993.

Tsai, Eugenie. *Robert Smithson Unearthed: Drawings, Collages, Writings.* New York: Columbia University Press, 1991.

Ned Smyth

Ned Smyth: Three Installations, exhibition catalog. Coral Gables, Fla.: Lowe Art Museum, University of Miami, 1987.

Princenthal, Nancy. "On the Waterfront." *Art in America* 75 (April 1987): 201–11, 239.

Athena Tacha

Johnson, Ellen H. "Nature as Source in Athena Tacha's Art." *Artforum* 19 (January 1981): 58–62.

Marter, Joan. "Athena Tacha's Sculpture: Outdoor Sites Transformed." *International Sculpture* (July–August 1987): 12–15.

Tacha, Athena. "Rhythm as Form." *Landscape Architecture* 68 (May 1978): 196–205.

———. *Public Sculpture.* Cleveland: Athena Tacha, 1982. Includes essays by Theodore H. Wolff and Ellen H. Johnson.

———. "Blair Fountain, River Sculpture." *Landscape Architecture* 74 (March–April 1984): 72–74.

George Trakas

Davies, Hugh. *George Trakas: Log Mass—Mass Curve,* exhibition catalog. Amherst: University Gallery, University of Massachusetts, 1980.

George Trakas, exhibition catalog. Montreal: Montreal Museum of Fine Arts, 1979.

Linker, Kate. "George Trakas and the Syntax of Space." *Arts Magazine* 50 (January 1976): 92–94.

Tousley, Nancy. "Natural Hierarchy of Materials: An Interview with George Trakas." *Artscanada* 36 (August–September 1979): 24–26.

James Turrell

Adcock, Craig. *James Turrell,* exhibition catalog. Tucson: University of Arizona Museum of Art, 1986.

———. *James Turrell: The Art of Light and Space.* Berkeley: University of California Press, 1990.

Air Mass: James Turrell, exhibition catalog. London: South Bank Centre, 1993.

Failing, Patricia. "James Turrell's New Light on the Universe." *Artnews* 84 (April 1985): 71–78.

Gablik, Suzi. "Dream Space." *Art in America* 75 (March 1987): 132–33, 153.

Hapgood, Fred. "Roden's Eye." *Atlantic* 260 (August 1987): 46–52.

Hughes, Robert. "Poetry Out of Emptiness." *Time* 117 (January 5, 1981): 81.

James Turrell: Light and Space, exhibition catalog. New York: Whitney Museum of American Art, 1980. Introduction by Melinda Wortz.

Larson, Kay. "Dividing the Light from the Darkness." *Artforum* 19 (January 1981): 30–33.

Light Projections and Light Spaces, exhibition catalog. Amsterdam: Stedelijk Museum, 1976.

Marmer, Nancy. "James Turrell: The Art of Deception." *Art in America* 69 (May 1981): 90–99.

Occluded Front: James Turrell, exhibition catalog. Los Angeles: Museum of Contemporary Art and Lapis Press, 1985.

Tomkins, Calvin. "The Talk of the Town: Light." *New Yorker* 56 (December 15, 1980): 29–31.

Peter Walker

Jewell, Linda. *Peter Walker: Experiments in Gesture, Seriality, and Flatness,* exhibition catalog. New York: Rizzoli, 1990.

Peter Walker, William Johnson and Partners: Art and Nature. Process Architecture 118, Tokyo: Process Architecture Co., 1994.

Walker, Peter, and Leah Levy. *Peter Walker: Minimalist Gardens.* Washington, D.C.: Spacemaker Press, 1996.

Walker, Peter, and Melanie Simo. *Invisible Gardens: The Search for Modernism in the American Landscape.* Cambridge, Mass.: MIT Press, 1994.

Elyn Zimmerman

Elyn Zimmerman, exhibition catalog. Tampa: Contemporary Art Museum, University of South Florida, 1991.

Elyn Zimmerman. New York: Gagosian Gallery, 1996.

Feinberg, Jean. "Terrain: Elyn Zimmerman's Garden Courtyard." *Landscape Architecture* 78 (March 1988): 84–88.

Gopnik, Adam. "Elyn Zimmerman's Marabar." *Arts Magazine* 59 (October 1984): 78–79.

Sargeant, Georgia. "Marabar." *International Sculpture,* January–February 1987, pp. 26–29.

INDEX

Page numbers in *italic* refer to illustrations.

PHOTOGRAPHY CREDITS